The Higher Power of the Twelve-Step Program

Hindsfoot Foundation Series on
Spirituality and Theology

The Higher Power of the Twelve-Step Program

FOR BELIEVERS
& NON-BELIEVERS

Glenn F. Chesnut

Authors Choice Press

San Jose New York Lincoln Shanghai

The Higher Power of the Twelve-Step Program
FOR BELIEVERS & NON-BELIEVERS

Authors Choice Press
an imprint of iUniverse.com, Inc.

For information address:
iUniverse.com, Inc.
5220 S 16th, Ste. 200
Lincoln, NE 68512
www.iuniverse.com

ISBN: 0-595-19918-6

Printed in the United States of America

The author may be contacted through the Hindsfoot Foundation,
P.O. Box 4081, South Bend IN 46634

ACKNOWLEDGMENTS

The author also wishes to thank the following publishing houses for permission to quote excerpts:

From *Twenty-Four Hours a Day* by Richmond Walker © 1954, 1975, 1994 by Hazelden Foundation; from *The Golden Book of Resentments* by Ralph Pfau © 1955 by Hazelden Foundation; and from *The Little Red Book* © 1996 by Hazelden Foundation. Reprinted by permission of Hazelden Foundation, Center City, MN, for whose kindness I am extremely grateful. Telephone orders for books from Hazelden Publishing and Educational Services may be placed at (800) 328–9000.

From *Having Had a Spiritual Awakening*, © 1998 by Al-Anon Family Group Headquarters, Inc. Reprinted by permission of Al-Anon Family Group Headquarters, Inc.

From the translation of the Heart of Transcendent Wisdom Sutra in *Scriptures of the World's Religions* © 1998 by the McGraw-Hill Companies.

Old and New Testament quotations are in the author's own translation.

For the captain of the *Jack,*
nuclear fast attack sub SSN-605.

Contents

The Twelve Steps of Alcoholics Anonymous

1. We admitted we were powerless over alcohol*—that our lives had become unmanageable.
2. Came to believe that a Power greater than ourselves could restore us to sanity.
3. Made a decision to turn our will and our lives over to the care of God *as we understood Him.*
4. Made a searching and fearless moral inventory of ourselves.
5. Admitted to God, to ourselves, and to another human being the exact nature of our wrongs.
6. Were entirely ready to have God remove all these defects of character.
7. Humbly asked Him to remove our shortcomings.
8. Made a list of all persons we had harmed, and became willing to make amends to them all.
9. Made direct amends to such people wherever possible, except when to do so would injure them or others.
10. Continued to take personal inventory and when we were wrong promptly admitted it.
11. Sought through prayer and meditation to improve our conscious contact with God *as we understood Him,* praying only for knowledge of His will for us and the power to carry that out.
12. Having had a spiritual awakening as the result of these steps, we tried to carry this message to alcoholics,† and to practice these principles in all our affairs.

*Other twelve-step groups replace the word "alcohol" with the appropriate word or phrase: Narcotics Anonymous uses the phrase "our addiction," Overeaters Anonymous uses the word "food," Emotions Anonymous uses "our emotions," Gamblers Anonymous uses "gambling," and so on.

†Similarly, instead of "carry this message to alcoholics," other twelve-step groups make the appropriate modifications. For example, Narcotics Anonymous says "carry this message to addicts," Overeaters Anonymous says "carry this message to compulsive overeaters," Gamblers Anonymous says "carry this message to other gamblers," Al-Anon says "carry this message to others," and Emotions Anonymous says simply "carry this message."

Reprinted through the permission of A.A. World Services, Inc.

Chapter I

Discovering a Higher Power

First part originally given as a lecture to the
Northern Indiana Counselors Association,
October 21, 1999 at Quiet Care in South
Bend, Indiana.

In substance abuse treatment, in this part of northern Indiana, an attempt
is often made to involve the alcoholic or drug addict in one of the twelve-
step programs, either Alcoholics Anonymous or Narcotics Anonymous.
I'm going to talk mostly about A.A., because that's what I know most
about—also it's the original twelve-step program, with sixty-four years
experience behind it now. Now the first step, as we know, says: "We

admitted we were powerless over alcohol [or our addiction]—that our lives had become unmanageable."

It's hard enough to get some people even to that point! But then comes what for some people seems like an even bigger problem, steps two and three: "Came to believe that a Power greater than ourselves could restore us to sanity" and "made a decision to turn our will and our lives over to the care of God *as we understood Him*." The problem is this: at least 95% of alcoholics are totally hostile to organized religion in all its forms. Many of them are outright atheists: "There is no God, and the whole notion is a piece of absurd superstition, a crutch for the weak and ignorant." Others are agnostics: "Well, maybe there's a God, but I dunno. I've heard arguments both ways."

Of the few who are positively disposed towards religion, some of these think A.A. is a kind of revivalistic cult, and start trying to talk themselves into the kind of hyped-up emotions and emotionalistic conversion experiences they have seen on TV, when they tuned in to one of the more flamboyant televangelists. These people go to a few A.A. meetings, but then most of them disappear—back to drinking themselves to death—and never show up again.

I've done a study of A.A. in this area—South Bend, Mishawaka, Elkhart, and Goshen—going back to when the program was first started here in 1943. I've listened to the tape recordings (and sometimes found the writings) of the old timers, and talked to a lot of present-day A.A. members, and I've done a kind of phenomenological study of what actually happens when people start going to A.A. meetings, and eventually find a Higher Power which makes sense to them, and to whose care they can abandon themselves wholeheartedly. I've written up part of this in a history of the beginnings of A.A. in this region, called *The Factory Owner and the Convict*.[1]

Now in looking at the way people came into the program during that period of almost sixty years, and actually developed a workable understanding of a higher power, I noticed some important things which I would like to sum up under twelve basic headings.

1. You cannot learn it by going to church or synagogue or mosque

My first observation is that no one—absolutely no one—learns to work the twelve-step program well, who has not cut the umbilical cord connecting them with their childhood religious beliefs. As an adult, you cannot *truly* go back to your childhood religious beliefs.

Some people, when they begin the twelve-step program, make the mistake of trying to get a better grasp of the spiritual dimension of the program by going to church services or synagogue services, or reading the bible, or something like that. At best, this is totally ineffectual but comparatively harmless. But a lot of people who try it this way end up going back out and going back to their addiction. The sermons and the worship services and the traditional language simply throw them back into their childhood religious beliefs, which contain major errors and misunderstandings. The emotions they start to feel, and the attitudes which they once again take up, put them into intolerable emotional states or drive them into unconsciously self-destructive behavioral patterns once again, and they finally go out and get drunk again (or whatever their addiction is) to relieve the pressure.

In fact, many of the people who make this particular mistake are just trying to avoid working the twelve steps, because the churches and synagogues and mosques won't *force them* to do that. The twelve-step program is the greatest outpouring of real spirituality in today's world, where people make more progress, and far faster than anywhere else, in genuinely learning how to live the spiritual life. If you can't recognize real spirituality when you see it right in front of your face in the twelve-step program, you'll certainly never recognize it anyplace else.

I'm talking about just *the first year* in A.A., because, interestingly enough, if we check back again after three years, and look at the survivors who have now been clean and sober for those three years, we will discover that perhaps as many as two-thirds of them are attending some kind of religious services on a regular basis by this point. But it is not always the religious denomination in which they were brought up as children—sometimes it's something wildly different—and even if it is the religion of their childhood, they now see it through different eyes and hear it through different ears. And the most devout will insist the most strongly that no one else in the A.A. program needs to hold the beliefs or practices of their particular religious group.

You learn the A.A. spiritual program by going to A.A. meetings and actually doing what the people there tell you they do. A.A. people never talk about "getting the program" or "understanding the program"—they talk about *working the program.* You learn A.A. spirituality by hanging around with A.A. people as much as you can—closed meetings, open meetings, going out for coffee after meetings, spending time with your sponsor just chatting about things, picnics, dances, service projects—so hanging around a church or synagogue or mosque during that first year is just fooling around and wasting time.

You learn A.A. spirituality at a deep level only by working through all the twelve steps. If there is anyone here today who is not a believer, you will get absolutely nothing from my talk which will turn you into a believer. The Higher Power of the twelve-step program is encountered only when you actually work the program, with complete honesty and total commitment, over an extended period of time. *You have to work a lot of the program without understanding what you are doing while you are doing it.* It is only after actually working the first eleven steps that we come to the twelfth step: "Having had a spiritual awakening as the result of these steps."

It's another one of those great A.A. paradoxes: You have to practice the program until you can practically do it in your sleep. And then is when you wake up! Then is when it begins to dawn on you why you had to do some of those things that you did without really understanding what you were doing. And then you're so grateful that you did it.

So how can we talk about it at all? As I said before, I can give an account of what many people in the A.A. program actually experienced in their early days in the program, and what they said were valuable starting points *for them.*

2. It does not matter what name you put on this Higher Power

When Moses heard the voice from the Burning Bush and asked this higher power what his name was, he answered only "I am what I am." Names do not matter. In the philosophical theology of Judaism, Christianity, and Islam all three, this higher power is a transcendent ground, from which all other being emerges into existence.[2] When this universe exploded into being in the Big Bang, ten or twelve billion years ago, this was what it came *out of.* This transcendent ground of being is above all human language and most this-worldly physical laws and rules— probably even all of them. No names are truly accurate, so any name which at least points in the right direction *for me* is as adequate as we are going to get.

When people in the program in this area use the word "God" while speaking at meetings, they frequently begin with the phrase "my higher power whom I choose to call God." They want to make it clear to the newcomers (and to everyone else) that if you don't want to use the G-word, you can use anything you want to. Often when they use the word "he" in referring to their higher power, they will check themselves and say, "or she, or it, or whatever you prefer." Everyone knows that you will make meaningful contact with this higher power only by using language that you yourself are comfortable with, and that for this reason, no one has the right to dictate to anyone else about what kind of language the other person is going to use.

So I can use names like God or Father or Great Spirit, but only if I *want* to. One person in the South Bend program calls his higher power Grandfather. One regular weekly meeting prays at the end to "our Father and Mother." A surprising number of people conceptualize their higher power as a kind of Good Boss, and begin their day every morning by saying something like, "O.K., boss, what kind of job have you got for me to do today?"

Nick Kowalski, one of the South Bend old-timers, spoke of this higher power as the Force of Creation itself.[3] Some of the Al-Anons around here think of the Universe itself as their higher power—but a universe which is filled with life, creativity, guidance, help, and love. Sue C., a skilled craftswoman, wrote one prayer in which she spoke of the higher power as the weaver of the world, the spinner of every thread:[4]

> I am but a small stitch
> in my higher power's majestic tapesty,
> but I am a perfect thread, carefully placed,
> to complete the beauty of the great picture.
> I feel the presence of a universal power
> and know that with each breath I take,
> I am guided to a greater harmony and peace.
>
> I surrender my will,
> trusting that all I need will be provided to me.
> What I must know, I will be taught;
> no problem will appear without a solution.
> I need only trust in his goodness,
> and give freely of the love I am given,
> sharing the lessons I am taught.

I do not question the perfection of the universal design,
nor do I question my placement in
the continuous flow of events
that make up the colors and textures of life.

But you have to work all this out for yourself. Lori C., who's in both A.A. and N.A., remembers her sponsor taking her over to the window—it was early evening, during the winter—and saying to her: "Make the sun rise."

Lori said, "Huh?"

Her sponsor said, "Make leaves grow on that tree."

Lori said, "Huh?"

Her sponsor said, "So you're willing to admit that there is something in this universe more powerful than you are?" That's all a beginner has to recognize.

3. God as the Good Itself, or the voice of deep conscience

The ancient pagan Greek philosopher Plato said that the highest power was the Good Itself, that transcendent principle by whose light we could tell the difference between good and bad, right and wrong, appropriate and inapppropriate. The first-century Jewish philosopher Philo borrowed this kind of Platonic language to interpret the Torah. The spirit of the Ten Commandments—don't lie, don't steal, don't commit murder—was the spirit of a universal code of good action. On the Christian side, St. Augustine likewise said that God was the *bonum ipsum* (the Good Itself). And he also said that God was *verum ipsum* (Truth Itself), which is why people can't get this program until they get honest with themselves.[5]

So some atheists and agnostics, when they first enter the A.A. program, turn the word God into an acronym: G.O.D. is short for Good

Orderly Direction. This is not a personal God of any sort, but it is something that they can make sense of. Most substance abusers, when they first enter the twelve-step program, have personal lives that have disintegrated into total chaos. At one level, they can see and understand this. And so the people in the program tell them: "Can you see the difference between putting a little bit of Good Orderly Direction into your life, instead of trying to live life in the totally chaotic, disorganized fashion you are attempting now? Well, just let that be your higher power for now." There are many old-timers who began in just that way, and over the months and years that followed, they found that, little by little, G.O.D. turned into God, into an actual transcendent personal being who could not only give meaning to their lives, but also act in their lives.

A month and a half ago, a newcomer said, "Well, I don't know whether I believe in this God thing or not, but for now, I'm just trying to live by my conscience." And the old-timers nodded, and made it clear that they thought that was a quite excellent position for him to take at this point.

Or as an experienced Al-Anon said, when this story was repeated to her, "Oh yeah, when the shame is removed, this is an excellent starting point." What she meant was, that if the word conscience referred to the kind of Freudian superego that just produces neurotic guilt-complexes, or introjected parental admonitions (you know, "Mommy says always do this," and "Daddy says never do that"), or *any* of the old shame-based injunctions on which she used to live her life, then trying to "follow your conscience" would only make you sicker. But if you referred instead to what I call *deep conscience*—our fundamental internal sense of whether we are acting with love, or instead acting with cruelty or the desire to control or get revenge or to show off what good people we are—then this will put us on the right path.

The Al-Anon said, "After all, what I myself mean by the voice of God is what I hear my conscience telling me, and what I hear in meetings. God talks to me through my conscience, and through the words of the other people at the meeting."[6] And an A.A. old-timer nodded his head in agreement.

In medieval theology, some theologians argued that all human beings had within them what they called the *scintilla*, a little spark of knowledge about who God was and the difference between right and wrong—not enough in itself to save the person by itself, but if you could take that little spark and blow on it and feed it with the proper fuel, it could flare up into a glowing beacon clearly displaying God and his moral principles to us.[7]

4. The hint of the infinite in the world of nature

In the Hebrew bible we are told that the seraphim continually fly about the divine throne, singing the hymn, "Holy, holy, holy, Lord of hosts, all the earth is full of his glory." In later Jewish thought, the word glory (*kabod*) is replaced by the word *shekinah* or "dwelling place." The visible universe is the palace God lives in, and his invisible presence can somehow be discerned in and through what we can see.[8]

One A.A. old-timer, a retired nuclear submarine commander, had been in an alcohol treatment center for several weeks when he walked outside and looked up into the sky, and suddenly realized the breath-taking magnificence of a flock of wild geese flying overhead. This was part of the spiritual breakthrough which he experienced after he finally began not only to look at himself honestly, but also *to look outside himself* wholeheartedly. One woman old-timer begins her day every morning by taking an insulated container of coffee with her and driving in her car to a nearby riverbank. She looks at the flowing water, and the ducks swimming and cavorting, and without conscious words or thoughts, gets in tune with her higher power. There are at least two old-timers in A.A. in this area who explain that going fishing every weekend is their basic mode of meditation. They do not consciously think about God *per se*, but merely let themselves relax into the flow of casting the line, and admiring the beauty of the lake. And gradually, everything else in their lives goes into perspective.

5. The world as mirror of God in the negative sense

But we must be careful. As the psychiatrist M. Scott Peck pointed out in his book, *The Road Less Traveled*, he had discovered that all his patients had a concept of God, whether they realized it consciously or not.[9] He would get them talking about what they thought "the world was like," or what "life was like." One man might say, "The world is a jungle. You've got to get there first and fight with everything you have to get *your* piece." A woman might say, "First you get old, then you die. I've been running on the same treadmill for years, and what do I have to show for it?"

Someone who believes that the world is a merciless jungle, or that life is a meaningless treadmill leading to oblivion, will necessarily—in their hearts—conjure up an image of God to match. "God is cruel," "God is unfair," "God is hateful," "God's done nothing but shit on me." To which the old-timers in A.A. and Al-Anon say to the newcomer: "Then why'd he work so hard to bring you here where you're gonna get a chance to save your life?"

But this is sometimes a place where good psychotherapy and counseling can be of special help to people working twelve-step programs. People can be locked into destructive images of the world around them which will prevent them from ever linking up with any kind of positive view of a higher power, and it sometimes takes a highly skilled professional to lead that person towards some healing of their inner rage and bitterness and fear.

In my observation, quite a few of the A.A. old-timers who have impressive amounts of serenity and faith in a higher power, have also made good use of psychotherapy during their early years in the program. A.A. doesn't pretend to be able to do that, and never has.

6. God in the mirror of the soul

As a person actually honestly works the twelve steps over a period of time, that person will undergo a radical personal transformation. It will show up in the person's inner attitudes, which in turn will change the person's emotional affect. And that in turn will alter the way the person interacts with other people.

It is the other people who usually notice it first. After a few months in the program, an alcoholic runs into someone he knew before, and spends some time with that other person. At the end, the other person says something like, "You know, you seem like a totally different person now. I really like the way you are now!" Then the recovering alcoholic starts to notice that when he experiences things which used to make him angry, he reacts with just momentary minor irritation, and sometimes even fails to notice it at all. Situations which used to totally throw him for a loop, he now sails through with only minor discomfort.

It finally begins to dawn on him that he is experiencing within himself such attributes as compassion, patience, unselfish giving of himself, and forgiveness. But these are the very attributes which the old-timers tell him are the characteristics of the higher power.

St. Thomas Aquinas called this the analogy of being. We learn what God's characteristics are by looking at what God creates. We say that God is compassionate and forgiving, because when we ourselves turn our lives and wills over to his care, he creates compassion and a forgiving nature in us.[10]

And newcomers look at other people who came into the program around the same time they did, and they can see even more clearly the enormous transformation that starts occurring in some of these other newcomers. One evening, one of the other newcomers will walk into the meeting, and this person will be actually relaxed, and smiling at people, and full of a new self-confidence. Some power changed that person, in a truly dramatic way. "Oh," the observer says, "that is the actual effect of this higher power on people's lives. But…what an extraordinary kind of higher power this must be!" And now the observer knows something real about who and what this higher power actually is.

We talked before about the medieval doctrine of the *scintilla*, the little spark within the human soul, which already in some sense knows who God is. And this is linked with the traditional theological doctrine that the human soul is the image of God, the *imago Dei*, a little mirror which can reflect the light of God's love.[11] So in one method of meditation and contemplation, as we pray we enter into the utmost depths of our own souls—and some people in the program, at least, say that they can "feel" the flow of God's love and the illumination of his healing light in action down there within their own souls. So this is another way that some people in the program begin to flesh out their understanding of who and what this higher power actually is.

We cannot draw a picture on a piece of paper of what God in himself actually looks like, or carve his image in a stone statue. But when I believe that I truly know another human being deeply, is it just that I can recognize a photograph of that person? Of course not. To truly know *who another human being really is*, I must learn to know that person's moral character: What are the values by which that person actually lives his or her life? Can I count on him or her? And if so, in what kinds of situations?

In the twelve-step program, when we slowly begin to discover who this higher power is, that is what we actually learn. Not a philosophical or theological theory or ecclesiastical doctrine or dogma. We learn God's moral character (Hebrews 1:3, the *charactêr tês hypostaseôs autou*), and in that fashion—which is actually far deeper and more profound than any other way of "knowing someone"—we come to know who God really is.[12]

7. Other people as messengers, and the spirit of the tables

When some people first enter the A.A. program, they choose what they call "the spirit of the tables" as their higher power. By that they mean what a person feels, experiences, and hears while attending a good twelve-step meeting. You can go to some A.A. meetings and quickly realize, that if these people were still drinking, and were all put into the same bar, there would be blood on the barroom floor in very short order. Something about the atmosphere of an A.A. meeting makes even the worst barroom brawler start behaving differently—there is a power or force of some kind there. Taking the spirit of the tables as your higher power is one of the commonest and most effective ways through which atheists and agnostics can start to work the program at the beginning.[13]

The Greek word for faith, *pistis*, fundamentally means *trust*. When people first begin the twelve-step program, none of them really fundamentally trust God all that much, as they will acknowledge once they start to get honest with themselves. With the atheists and agnostics it's obvious, but the ones who claim they are believers have just as much problem. They just don't really trust God.

But those who make it in the program discover one or more recovering alcoholics who are already in the program, whom they *can* trust. The first kind of proto-faith which newcomers to the program develop is not a faith in God *per se*, but a trust in the people who are talking about God.

And remember, in Christianity, when people first begin, they are told that if they cannot trust God whom they cannot see, they should put their faith in God's messenger Jesus (e.g. John 12:45 and 6:46). To be Jewish, you have to trust that Moses was God's messenger, and Muslims have to trust Mohammed—I mean, you didn't work all those great truths about God out by yourself, did you? Or you have to *start* by trusting Buddha, or *somebody*, until you learn more for yourself.

Remember again, *real* knowledge of the higher power comes only in the twelfth step, after the person has genuinely worked the other eleven steps very thoroughly, and in order. This normally takes at least two or three years at minimum. So at the beginning of the A.A. program, whether the person believes in God or not is not relevant—the only thing that is important is that they devise some method for starting their journey through the steps, which they themselves can accept and live with.

So taking the spirit of the tables, or the A.A. program itself, as your higher power, is a beginner's starting point which has repeatedly been shown to work quite excellently. A beginner who has no faith in God, but feels somehow that he *can* trust one or more of the old-timers around the table, can handle things for a long time that way, as long as this trust can supply the impetus to actually start working the steps.

Psychotherapists and counselors all know that trust is one of the most important factors in producing real healing. A patient will attend counseling sessions for weeks, and suddenly develop enough trust to start talking about some deep, hidden secret that he has never before revealed to the counselor. The counselor feels very good about this, because now the two of them can start working at the real healing process. As has been noted from the beginning, a recovering alcoholic in the A.A. program can often achieve a level of trust from a newcomer with such incredible speed that it's breathtaking.

As psychotherapists, you can use this productively. If you can get your substance abusers into A.A. or N.A., and they start talking honestly and openly for the first time in A.A. or N.A. meetings, you will find that they will now have the trust and courage to start telling *you* truthfully some of the things you need to know in order to help them more fully.

8. Learning to see God in the fabric of our daily lives

Many people who have trouble with the idea of God, believed as children in a kind of magical God who operated like a sort of brain-damaged genie in a bottle. If you stroked the bottle in exactly the right way, and muttered the correct magical phrases (with lots of thee's and thou's), and used exactly the right name to address the genie, then he would magically give you everything that you asked for. A lot of people who call themselves atheists are people who believed that as a child, or thought they were supposed to believe that. Now that they are adults, they find the whole idea ridiculous.

Nevertheless, during their first year or two in the A.A. program, some beginners waste a lot of time trying to find that sort of dungeons-and-dragons and magical sorcerers kind of higher power. They come to meetings and talk about how "I prayed for such-and-such, and the very next day...." The old-timers try to caution them. "God always answers prayers," they may say. "Sometimes he says yes, and sometimes he says no. And sometimes he says 'wait,' and that can be the most uncomfortable answer of all." Or the old-timers will caution the newcomers to end their prayers with the words "thy will be done." Because A.A. is not a magical way for me to get whatever I want whenever I want it—real life just doesn't work that way.

But the old-timers will say other things too: "It's all right to pray to God and ask him for things, as long as you don't get upset if he says no." "God never closes one door on you without opening another one—into something even better." "Sometimes God knows that the only way I will learn such-and-such is to suffer some real pain." "God will never lay any burden on you which is too heavy for you to carry—or if he does, he will help you carry it." And one of the old-timers will sometimes say, "God has given me gifts so wonderful and marvellous that I would never even have dreamed of praying for them." And the other old-timers will nod their heads in solemn, grateful agreement.

So newcomers slowly come to see God's hand in the fabric of their everyday lives. There are a number of standard categories for fitting these events into:[14] A totally unexpected, delightful thing happens, for which I immediately express a prayer of heartfelt gratitude; or a painful sequence of events occurs, which finally drives me into learning something about myself and God, which then makes my life far richer and fuller. Perhaps something seems like a stone wall across my path. No matter how hard I try, I cannot get past this obstacle. As one old-timer (a very wise woman) once put it, "How do I know the will of God? When I hit a stone wall, turn left." God—for whatever reason—doesn't want me to go down that particular path. I may some day realize why, but then again, I may never truly know what reason he had for turning my life into a different path at that point. Perhaps God makes sure that I don't have the money for lobster and steak dinners. I finally realize that he is trying to teach me that I can enjoy hamburgers and macaroni and cheese too, and learn how to practice gratitude in any conceivable situation.

A man in the program slipped on his stairs and broke his back. The doctors told him that if the bone had broken one millimeter further, he would have been paralyzed from the armpits down. He immediately started thanking God in his heart and felt only the most profound gratitude. He hardly ever noticed the pain at all, convalesced quickly, and within three months was as good as new. He talked at meetings about the most important thing he had learned, which was when he was first brought into the emergency room, in extreme agony: "The only thing that really matters," he said, "is me and God. In the final analysis, that's all there really will be. Material things, people fussing around, foolish pride and egotism—none of these things really matter at all."

9. The pragmatic test

An engineer has a theory about how to build bridges, and builds one on the basis of that theory. Every time a really heavy vehicle drives across it, and every time the waters rise and the current becomes swift, the bridge collapses. Then he devises a different theory about how to build bridges, and builds one according to this new theory. This time the bridge holds rock solid, no matter what happens.

So is this second theory still "just a theory"? Is it the engineer falling into autosuggestion and wishful thinking and self-delusion? No, we say now that the second method of building bridges has been field-tested, and that its superiority has been conclusively shown in actual field conditions.

A.A. members who tried to live their lives without any kind of realistic God or higher power, and then started experimenting with "this higher power idea" in their daily lives, found that, under actual field-testing, their lives worked better in an uncountable variety of ways when they turned their wills and lives over to the care of a loving and compassionate and all-powerful higher power. As one old-timer put it, "I don't *believe* there is a God. I *know* there is a God. Otherwise, I wouldn't be here, where I am, right now."

This pragmatic test[15] is the hardest to defend when you are giving a lecture in front of an audience of atheists and agnostics—unbelievers will quickly start running you around in logical circles which you will never get out of—so I don't even try to defend it rationally and logically. But the pragmatic test is what actually turns nonbelievers into believers during the first two or three years of the A.A. program. It is more powerful than any other demonstration of the existence of God.

10. The discovery of a personal God

It's not that hard sometimes to convince a nonbeliever that there might be some impersonal universal absolute: some transcendent ground out of which this universe exploded in the big bang, some impersonal principle of good orderly direction, or some moral ground of behavior revealed in the deep conscience. But beyond that, the nonbeliever argues, isn't it all really self-hypnosis, autosuggestion, wishful thinking, and a kind of contorted set of devices for accounting for anything at all that happens, while still arguing that this too was the deliberate, purposeful act of a personal God?

You can get into a similar set of arguments when you get a group of scientists debating whether a computer could ever be built which would actually be able to think. Would it be possible to construct an artificial intelligence which would nevertheless react like a genuinely personal being, instead of just blindly and mechanically? A man named Alan M. Turing wrote an important article on this topic back in 1950 in the philosophy journal *Mind*, where he proposed what is now called the Turing test.[16] Now no one is suggesting that a computer of this sort would think exactly the same way human beings do. But if we ask what we really mean by a personal being, we mean something which would be recognized as such by another personal being. So you put a human being at one computer terminal, connected to another computer in another room. In that other room, there will be either another human being, or a computer program cleverly designed to produce the same kind of responses a human being would. Turing argues that, if you could devise a kind of computer and computer programming which could consistently convince a human questioner that it was another human being, then at the only level that truly matters and ultimately makes sense, you would have to admit that you had produced a computer which could actually think.

What is the only adequate judge of whether something else can think like a personal being? You and me, at the level of our own gut-level intuition of what's going on. Because we ourselves are personal beings by definition—that's the only meaningful way to define what a personal being would be, something that thinks a little bit like us—and "it takes one to know one"!

No one pretends that God thinks exactly like a human being does. But people who have been in the twelve-step program for two or three years, and have worked all the steps honestly and thoroughly, find again and again that they can find no other way to interpret what they have actually experienced, than to acknowledge that there not only is a higher power, but that he is a highly personal being, with a mind and personality of his own. It is interesting here, in that the A.A. people regularly discover, as a first step in that direction, that this higher power has what can only be described as a highly developed sense of humor. They suddenly realize that this higher power had just played a little joke on them, and is now laughing heartily at their reaction, and then they start laughing too, and realize for the first time that there is indeed a God, and that he is a God of joy and merriment.

11. The extraordinary works of God

Bill W., the founder of A.A., had an extraordinary experience where he was lying on his hospital bed, and suddenly saw the entire room lit up with a divine light, and felt himself transported into an entirely new dimension. But he never talked about this experience, really, until A.A. had been founded and had been in operation successfully for many years.[17] He realized that this sort of experience was not common, and was not necessary, and was not to be expected.

Some people in the A.A. program have in fact experienced quite amazing things: One old-timer, Brooklyn Bob, tells how he was struggling to get the program without success. He went to meeting after meeting, but simply could not stop drinking. He finally walked out into the middle of a field, fell to his knees, and cried out, "God, please, all I want is some peace of mind." Immediately, he reports, it was like a wave of incredible warmth swept over his entire body, and although he still had struggles past that point, he had crossed that necessary divide which separates those who are finally getting the program from those who are struggling to no avail.

An extremely rationalistic college professor reported seeing angels repeatedly—angels like the ones in C. S. Lewis' *Perelandra* trilogy—during his early days in the program. A psychiatric nurse found herself repeatedly entering the heavenly realm of the Uncreated Light, the goal of the Hesychastic monks at Mt. Athos in Greece. A salesman named Chuck was driving to call on a new client in another city, and almost going crazy trying to figure out what that man might say to this or that, and exactly how he would frame his response. He had been in the A.A. program for a short while, but now he felt himself falling back into his old craziness again, as bad as ever. He cried out to God, "Please, please help me return to some-place sane." Then he heard the *bath qol*, the Heavenly Voice, speaking inside his head, clearly and distinctly saying the simple words, "You're already there." And instantly, he says, his anxiety disappeared, and he drove the rest of the way without worrying or thinking at all about what he was going to say. He introduced himself to the potential client, just talked simply and naturally, and found himself with a client for life as a result.

Chic L., from over in Goshen, Indiana, tells how he finally decided, one day, that he had to do something about his drinking, and headed home to get on the phone and see if he could find out anything from anybody about this A.A. business. He was suddenly totally desperate, he relates. Just as he was walking in his front door, a car drove up and parked in front of his house, and a man he knew only after a fashion got out and walked up to him and said, "You know, we don't know each other all that well, but you see, I'm an alcoholic, and I'm in the A.A. program, and something or other somehow prompted me to come pay a call on you and try to talk to you a little about our program—I don't actually know if you would be interested in it or not."

Most people who get sober in A.A. have NOT had an experiences of this sort. But on the other hand, no one in A.A. shows the least bit of surprise when stories like this are told. They aren't common, they certainly aren't necessary, but they do happen all the time, and people in A.A. simply take for granted that God can and does do things like this whenever he thinks it is the best way.

Experiences like this also do NOT give you any special lock on attaining long-term serenity and sobriety. They apparently get the person over one hump, and one hump only, in a spiritual path that will contain many other periods of really tough slogging. So this is nothing at all like the claims made in some revivalistic versions of Protestantism, where it sometimes seems as though we are being told that if you have a single instantaneous conversion experience of the right sort, you will automatically be able, smoothly and effortlessly, to start living a good life with no real struggles or problems at all.

I should also say that many varieties of organized religion seem to engage in a lot of manipulative techniques for getting people to mood alter temporarily. They use emotional manipulation to artificially create certain emotions. It may be hooting and hollering and people shouting out "praise Jesus" to create a kind of semi-hysterical state of almost manic enthusiasm. Or it may be done by using soft music and incense and stained glass windows to create what these groups call "a worshipful experience."

There really are people, called religion-oholics, who become addicted to this kind of artificial mood-altering. This method of mood-altering is not all that powerful, however, so as they build up a tolerance, they are frequently forced to develop additional addictions. Compulsive overeating is quite common—when you enter a religious establishment of this sort, a quick glance at the vast numbers of terribly overweight people in the congregation will warn you immediately that this is not a truly spiritual place at all, but an inwardly miserable and frightened collection of religious addicts. Secret drinking and secret sexual addictions are also quite common: in recent years, some of the television evangelists got caught in this, but it was in fact not actually unexpected behavior, if you learn the difference between real spirituality and, on the other side, the misuse of religion to produce artificial mood-altering.[18]

The twelve-step program is not designed to change our emotions directly by artificial mood-altering. The twelve-step program is instead designed to slowly but surely change our basic *attitudes*. Attitudes are not emotions; they are part of the cognitive framework of our minds. However, when you truly change the underlying attitudes, the emotions which the person feels in various situations will automatically change.

12. Practicing the presence of God

Those old-timers who have the greatest serenity make a big point of continually practicing the presence of God during the course of every day. They develop a kind of God-consciousness which permeates in one way or another all of their waking thoughts.

They begin every morning by simply saying, "God, please keep me sober today." Then they purposefully commit themselves to turning their lives and wills over to the care of God for the next twenty-four hours. Some recite the third-step and seventh-step prayers every morning:[19]

> God, I offer myself to Thee—to build with me and to do with me as Thou wilt. Relieve me of the bondage of self, that I may better do Thy will. Take away my difficulties, that victory over them may bear witness to those I would help of Thy Power, Thy Love, and Thy Way of life. May I do Thy will always!

> My Creator, I am now willing that you should have all of me, good and bad. I pray that you now remove from me

every single defect of character which stands in the way of
my usefulness to you and my fellows. Grant me strength,
as I go out from here, to do your bidding. Amen.

But the precise wording here is not important. It is the spirit of these two
prayers, and the basic intent. The simplest prayer is nearly always the
best.

Note that in the seventh-step prayer in particular, I turn the bad in
me over to God's all-accepting love just as much as the good. And I let
God be the judge as to whether or not something which I think is a
serious character defect actually hinders my usefulness to him in his
plan for my life. Sometimes we fall into the error of setting superhuman
and totally unrealistic and hyperperfectionistic standards for our own
behavior, and refuse to allow ourselves to be simply ordinary fallible
human beings. Our Creator knows better, and loves and cherishes our
eccentricities and inherent limitations and peculiarities, and has no
desire whatever to change us one bit, as long as we are not doing grave
harm to ourselves or to others.

When God wanted creatures who acted like angels all the time, he simply created actual angels. When he wanted some comic relief in his universe, he created monkeys whom he intended to act just like monkeys
actually do. In the same way, he created human beings to be just what we
are. Sometimes we're even funnier to watch than the monkeys, but that's
exactly what the Creator wanted. And that's the spirit—an attitude of real,
honest humility—with which we want to begin our days.

The old-timers tell us that they end every day by simply saying, "God,
thank you for keeping me sober today." Some of the most spiritual of the
old-timers tell us that they also go through the day saying "thank you" over
and over again, keeping themselves in a continual attitude of gratitude. I
wake up in the morning and feel the comforting warm of the covers, and
utter a "thank you" for having a warm place to sleep for the previous night.

When I bite into a bologna sandwich or some tuna fish salad for lunch, I appreciate the taste and the way it relieves my hunger, and I silently utter a little "thank you" inside my head. When I get in my car to go to work, I can feel bitter or resentful or unhappy because it's an old, beat-up car, or I can instead say to God, "thank you," when the engine turns over and starts. Or if I don't have a car, I can say "thank you" when I climb onto my bicycle to go to work, or if I don't have a bicycle, I can say "thank you" because my legs are still working and I can walk to work. And if I'm ill and my legs don't work and I don't even have a job at all, I can say "thank you" because I'm still breathing.

When I see a beautiful bed of flowers, or the reds and golds of the fall leaves, I say "thank you." When it snows, I say "thank you" and learn to appreciate the way the sun glistens off the white, blowing flakes. When it rains and thunders, I remember that, to the ancient Israelites, the thunder symbolized the rumbling wheels of God's war chariots, and the lightning represented the flaming blades of the swords of fire which God's war angels wielded in battle—this was the totally awe-inspiring magnificence of the Lord of Hosts (Yahweh of the Warrior Bands) riding forth to battle on the clouds of heaven. From the stars of heaven to the lowliest caterpillar crawling along a twig, all is beauty, all is magnificence, all is grandeur—and my proper human response is to say "thank you."

The human mind cannot simultaneously be in a state of true gratitude, and also be craving the madness of alcohol or drugs, or stuffing yourself with food until you are sick and torpid, or craving any other of the unhealthy things which we allow to become destructive compulsions. True gratitude and an overpowering sick compulsion cannot coexist simultaneously in the same human mind.

I practice the presence of God by repeatedly, consciously, reminding myself to make the motivation of my daily tasks a motivation which is in line with God's spirit and way of life: love, service, patience, and joy.

I practice the presence of God by noticing when I am starting to grow resentful, or am getting too angry, or begin to feel sorry for myself, or start falling into too much anxiety, worry, and fear. I consciously and deliberately turn the matter over to God, and then simply stop thinking about it. If I am too upset, I take time to be quiet and let God's peace and calm enter my soul, and then simply ask myself, "What is the next right thing?" Then I just go do the next right thing, and stop worrying and fretting.

I make sure that I take time off repeatedly throughout the day—even two or three minutes is enough—to be quiet and feel God's love, and get myself re-centered. This is a time to feel gratitude, to turn everything over to God once more, and to enjoy my own inner peace. This is a time to totally relax, quit my nonstop thinking-thinking-thinking, and just enjoy and appreciate being in the Here and Now.

My true goals will usually be quite simple: Getting through the day without taking the first drink means experiencing a true miracle for an alcoholic. Getting through the day without hitting anyone or screaming in blind rage at anyone is a miraculous display of God's power for the truly emotionally upset. Making it through some situations without getting myself killed or seriously injured for life is an adequate accomplishment for many a person who is self-destructively violence-prone—my object is to *survive*, not to be "right," or to avoid being "humiliated" or being "disrespected." Getting up out of bed and putting my clothes on is a major step for the severely depressed, and getting to the end of the day without trying to commit suicide may require an impressive display of God's grace and power in my life if my depression has driven me to total despair. Behaving honorably and honestly and responsibly in a very bad situation can require as great a heroism as any human being ever displayed. Remaining reasonably tolerant and practicing detachment in the face of extraordinary provocation is one of the true victories of the spirit.

I call on God for help whenever I need it. Practicing the presence of God means *remembering to do this* at whatever point in the day I actually need this help. And I discover that I do not always feel immediate relief from my inner turmoil (although people who have been in the program for long enough frequently do feel the burden lifted from them instantly), but somehow I do then find the inner power to actually get through what has to be done. Before, I always failed in these situations, but now that I ask God for help whenever I need it, through the course of every day I find myself succeeding in handling problems which I could never deal with when I was trying to do it all on my own.

You see, alcoholics and drug addicts and food-stuffers and over-controlling Al-Anons come into the twelve-step program wanting *immediate emotional relief.* That was the whole idea that motivated their old behaviors. The twelve-step program teaches us however that what we really need is the power to stop acting destructively. As I learn how to do this, the emotional relief will always ultimately follow, but (particularly for newcomers to the program) not always instantly. *If I learn to shape my attitudes and my actions in the right way, then the emotional relief*—the satisfaction, the serenity, the burst of gratitude, the delights of truly living and feeling— *will in fact follow*, eventually and in its time, if not with the magical instant rush of an artificial narcotics fix.

Our check-list for spiritual growth: resentment, self-pity, and fear

The twelve-step program provides an automatic check-list for spiritual growth, a method for continually testing whether we are working the program well or poorly. We learn to start looking for the three internal warning signs: resentment, self-pity, and fear.[20]

Am I dealing with my present situation with the appropriate sort of attitude? If I am feeling too much resentment, self-pity, or fear (including all the various kinds of worry, anxiety, panic, and so on), then my attitude must be wrong. Or I can ask other kinds of questions using this same method: Is one particular method of prayer or meditation right for me? If practicing it regularly helps reduce my resentment, self-pity, and fear, then I must be doing something right. And vice versa, if it's not really helping at all, then it doesn't matter who wrote that particular prayer, or which religious group devised that particular method of meditation, it's not the right one *for me*. I can also ask questions about my actions using this same check-list. So for example, what about the way I'm acting right now? Is it good or bad, saintly or sinful, appropriate or inappropriate? If my resentment, self-pity, or fear just keep on mounting higher and higher, then I'm clearly not acting the way I should, *in some way*. Remember that guilt and shame are modes of fear. So maybe I need to change the way I'm acting (and I need to quit trying to defend it), or maybe I need to change my attitude, or learn how to pray about it differently, or *something*.

This is why the twelve-step program cannot be grasped instantly. Each person has to do his or her own experiments. Each person has to figure out where the problem really lies, for himself or herself. It could be what the person is actually doing, it could be the inner attitude which accompanies those actions, it could be a failure to work out the best way of praying and meditating. It could also be something else entirely—inappropriate toxic shame or guilt, a compulsive and self-destructive hyperperfectionism, poor impulse control, or a childish unwillingness to delay gratification.

It takes weeks, months, *years* to work these things out thoroughly. But even small steps forward significantly reduce the amount of resentment, self-pity, and fear which so overwhelmed the substance abuser's mind when he first started the program. So those who throw themselves into the program with wholehearted commitment actually begin to experience the positive fruits of their efforts very quickly. With some it comes almost immediately, with others it starts to appear in a few weeks. After three or four months, everyone who is working the program will be able to point towards significant personal transformation in some areas of their lives, which they can see and feel.

Serenity and God's love

Serenity is not an emotional state *per se* at all. Serenity means freedom from obsessive resentment, self-pity, and fear—freedom from being at the total mercy of painful, hellish emotions which we can neither manage nor control, but which do manage and control our lives, and turn them into a living hell.[21] For those who have never truly tasted real serenity at all, it is an experience so extraordinary that all words fail for expressing it. Everyone who genuinely attempts to work the steps will obtain at least brief tastes of real serenity during their early period in the program—and once having tasted it, will want nothing but more, and more, and more. This is the real driving force, the real motive force, behind the total zeal with which so many alcoholics work the A.A. program. This is the Pearl of Great Price, for which the merchant in the ancient tale sold all that he had, just so that he could lovingly hold this one pearl in his hand and enjoy its unbelievable beauty.[22]

In some kinds of organized religion, God is portrayed as a being whose love we have to earn. We are told that we have to achieve this or that before God will love us. We are given long lists of rules, and told that God will cast us off, and hate us, and punish us with unbelievable cruelty and sadism if we violate even a single one of these complex and totally arbitrary rules. Or we are taught that God requires us to maintain a perfectionistic life in which we never ever get angry, never ever feel doubt in him, never ever behave selfishly in the tiniest little way, always make A's in all our classes, always make the football team or the cheerleading squad, never get tired and totally exhausted, never need sleep or rest or just being by ourselves. If I am doing a task which I really dislike doing, and my mind wanders for even a moment, or I invent ways to delay getting started right away, I condemn myself—for I feel sure that this kind of God would condemn me for that. If I make an honest mistake, I beat myself up psychologically, because I know this kind of God would tolerate no mistakes ever at all. I must drive myself unmercifully like an old dray horse and earn this God's love by being absolutely perfect in every way.

Those who live by the twelve steps tell us that the truth of the matter is that this higher power is all-loving and all-accepting. We do not have to do or accomplish anything to "earn" this higher power's love. Now there are some people, who regard themselves as very religious, who believe that if we ever told anyone this fundamental truth, everyone would just go around acting with the grossest immorality, and the entire planet earth would immediately go to hell in a handbasket. But *in fact* in the twelve step program, this is not at all what actually happens. In the twelve step program, people discover that when we fall into excessive anger and violence, and stealing and cruelty, and gross dishonesty and out-of-control personal selfishness, we in fact turn our own lives into a living hell.

Pain is the great motivator. When we hurt enough inside our minds, then and only then will we seriously start trying to work on our spiritual problems and change our lives to make them better. And that's true for everybody in the world—not just for people in the twelve-step program.

So we ask God for help in amending our lives—not because we want to "earn" God's love (we already have that totally)—but because we are so miserable, and we know that he has all power and that he is good, and that he will in fact help us. At one level, we could be tempted to say that the reason people in twelve step programs try to live better lives is a totally selfish one—it is for me, not to earn or keep God's love, that I want this. But the appropriate term for this approach is not selfishness; the ancient Greek philosopher Aristotle called this a eudaimonistic ethic,[23] and the Roman Catholic church has traditionally proclaimed this eudaimonistic approach to be the correct one. In the Old Testament, it says openly and nakedly that those who follow the Torah (God's Way of Life) will receive rewards in all areas of their lives, and that *this is the clear and obvious reason for doing that.*

So the twelve-step program proclaims a higher power who welcomes us with an all-accepting love, just as we are, but the program also says that if we ourselves—for our own personal satisfaction and quality of life—wish to learn how to live a life of faith, service, unselfishness, courage, honesty, and integrity, that this great higher power will cheerfully send us his free grace, and re-mold us and re-shape us and empower us by his divine strength so that we can live this better way.

We must always remember *the order of loving.* As it says in 1 John 4:10 and 19, "In this is love, not that we loved God but that he loved us.... We love *because he first loved us.*" In the order of loving, God's all-accepting love for us has to come first, because we human beings cannot learn to love truly, in a manner which is tolerant, accepting, and capable of giving in a genuinely unselfish manner, until we learn how to attune ourselves within the flow of the all-powerful creative love of the universal spirit, in which we live and move and have our being.

In a good twelve-step group meeting, I can actually feel this divine spirit of love reflected in the way the group reacts to me, and embodied in the way the members of the group live and act. They genuinely care about me, they accept me just the way I am, and they will help me if I myself honestly want it. If I choose to turn my back on them and walk away, they will be saddened, but they will not cease to care what happens to me, nor will they refuse to welcome me back again. No matter how far I have gone away, when I return to live once more within God's spiritual presence, God says to me only "Welcome home." And if I am wounded, and genuinely cry out for help, he moves to heal my wounds insofar as it is actually still possible, and taking however much time it actually requires to heal that particular kind of injury.

Getting rid of the gimme God and the getcha God

When we were children, some of us had religious beliefs where we believed in a gimme God. If I pray the right prayers with exactly the right ritual phrases, and believe all the right things, all I have to do is pray to God and he will magically give me everything I selfishly want. There is in reality no gimme God. Learning this is part of growing up and becoming an adult.

When we were children, some of us had religious beliefs where we believed in a getcha God. God was like some minor near eastern potentate, a nasty old tyrant sitting on a throne and constantly inventing hundreds of rules that we had to follow. Oh, he was a foul-tempered and unbelievably touchy old tyrant! You look the wrong way, do the slightest thing at which an old fuss-budget might take offense, and he exploded in an out-of-control temper tantrum. The only time a smile ever appeared on his face was when he caught you breaking one of these thousands of petty rules. Then he would smirk maliciously as his thugs dragged you off to the torture chambers underneath his palace.[24]

There is in reality no getcha God. There are only horrifyingly nasty adults who try to terrorize helpless little children and force them to follow the adults' own neurotic control wishes, by claiming that their depraved desires have the sanction of God himself. This is blasphemy, and there is many a poor neurotic who needs some very good psychotherapy to get out of this shame-based set of attitudes and on the road to real mental health.

But the higher power who emerges as people work the twelve steps is neither of these. He is not a magical gimme God, but he will help us become better people, and shower us with a multitude of gifts which he knows are actually good for us. He is not a nasty getcha God, but a compassionate and forgiving and tolerant power who has no patience with complex rules and laws. And above all, he is a joyous, laughing God, who teaches us how to learn and grow and enjoy life to its fullest, by learning to laugh at ourselves, and not take ourselves so very seriously all the time.

The power to *lieben und arbeiten,* to love and work

Ever since Freud's time, psychotherapists have realized that our psychological problems are, for the most part, created by our illusions and delusions about the world and reality. Mental health, Freud said, was measured by our ability to *lieben und arbeiten*—to love and to work productively in our daily lives. Falling prey to illusions and delusions would always end up blocking our ability to *lieben und arbeiten* to the fullest.

So I will conclude by posing a little puzzle for any unbelievers in this audience. If belief in a loving, compassionate, all-powerful higher power is indeed an illusion or a delusion—then why in fact do those who actually work the twelve-step program discover an incredible ability to both *lieben und arbeiten*, an inner power which continues to grow without bounds the more years they spend in the program? At the Michiana Regional A.A. Conference this past month, one of the speakers was a 96-year-old man who had been in the program since 1945. He was a black man, who played a heroic role in helping to integrate the South Bend A.A. program back at the beginning, and there he was, 54 years in the program, coming back to South Bend to speak with spirit and power to the huge crowd, still going strong. I wish everyone here could have seen this man at first hand, to see what is really meant by the power to *lieben und arbeiten*.

A real higher power—merely illusion? merely delusion? The people who stay clean and sober long enough don't think so. What do drugs and alcohol give you? A world of illusion, delusion, fantasy, and running away from reality. Is the idea of a real higher power no more than just another illusion or delusion or fantasy? It will keep you from dying in your own vomit or being locked up in an insane asylum, and it will truly give you— *if you work it*—the power to truly *lieben und arbeiten*, to love and work and enjoy life in all its fullness. What other choice would any sane person make?

Chapter II

Beginner's Blocks

We've described twelve of the common ways that newcomers to the twelve-step program in this part of the country actually go about discovering a higher power. It's also worthwhile talking about some of the blockages that beginners often have to overcome in order to find a power greater than themselves. These six "beginner's blocks" will literally kill us if we do not figure out how to get past them.

1. The belief that I am
too strong, too smart

Myths and legends

In spite of the fact that they are obviously killing themselves by their own behavior—in spite of the fact that their lives have turned into a total shambles at the really important level, and that they cannot even stand their own thoughts any longer—newcomers to the twelve-step program all too often scoff at any notion of dependence on a higher power. They say inside their heads, "I am too cool, too modern and up-to-date, too macho, too smart, too worldly-wise, too scientific (or what have you) to believe in that kind of ignorant, superstitious nonsense." They say, "That might work for other people, who are not as smart as I am, but you see, I am different from all these other people around the table—*I'm a special case.*"

If you start asking them what they mean, a lot of them will start talking about their religious experience as small children. A prominent and successful lawyer in Elkhart, Indiana, told how his Sunday School teacher had talked about Jesus ascending into heaven after his resurrection from the dead. He started asking one of his aunts how this could possibly be. "How could a man just rise up in the air without a propeller or rocket? And where would he go after he rose high enough? The earth's atmosphere would run out, and there he would be in empty space, doing what? Rotating in orbit around the earth?" And his aunt couldn't answer these questions, and the little boy at that point wrote off all religion, down in his heart, as superstitious and unscientific nonsense.

Bushes in the desert that start burning but magically don't burn up, people walking on water, or parting the Red Sea down the middle so they can walk through on dry land. You're standing in your chariot just before a battle, and your chariot-driver suddenly changes into the blue-skinned god Krishna. A little Japanese boy or girl asks, "Where did Buddha *actually* go when he entered Nirvana?"—and try explaining that one to a small, literalistically minded child!

And the rules of organized religion can seem rigid and foolish to many people. This Protestant group tells women that if they cut their hair or wear makeup they will go to hell, while this Muslim leader tells women that no, the crucial issue is that if women let any of the hair on their head show in public at all, they will be nothing but prostitutes and will be sent into the eternal flames. This Jewish congregation says that eating a pork chop will damn you, while this Hindu community lets sacred cows roam freely through the streets of their modern city and is convinced that harming one of these cows would be a horrendous sin. Even if you yourself believe that one of these groups is in fact right, the beliefs of all the other groups will still seem misguided or even bizarre.

In the Big Book, Bill W. talked about his own profound scepticism during the dark period before his friend Ebby came to visit.[1] In Bill W.'s case, his cynicism and doubt revolved around the kind of Christianity taught in the little New England Protestant churches where he had been brought up as a child (pp. 10–11):

> When they talked of a God personal to me, who was love, superhuman strength and direction, I became irritated and my mind snapped shut against such a theory.
>
> To Christ I conceded the certainty of a great man, not too closely followed by those who claimed Him. His moral teaching—most excellent. For myself, I had adopted those parts which seemed convenient and not too difficult; the rest I disregarded.
>
> The wars which had been fought, the burnings and chicanery that religious dispute had facilitated, made me sick. I honestly doubted whether, on balance, the religions of mankind had done any good. Judging from what I had

seen in Europe and since, the power of God in human affairs was negligible, the Brotherhood of Man a grim jest. If there was a Devil, he seemed the Boss Universal, and he certainly had me.

But then came the startling revelation (p. 12) which Bill's friend Ebby brought with him, which broke through that crippling blockage:

> My friend suggested what then seemed a novel idea. He said, "*Why don't you choose you own conception of God?*"
>
> That statement hit me hard. It melted the icy intellectual mountain in whose shadow I had lived and shivered many years. I stood in the sunlight at last.
>
> *It was only a matter of being willing to believe in a Power greater than myself. Nothing more was required of me to make my beginning.* I saw that growth could start from that point. Upon a foundation of complete willingness I might build what I saw in my friend. Would I have it? Of course I would!
>
> Thus was I convinced that God is concerned with us humans when we want Him enough. At long last I saw, I felt, I believed. Scales of pride and prejudice fell from my eyes. A new world came into view.

Some people from Christian or Jewish backgrounds who come into the twelve-step program are biblical literalists who believe that every word of the Bible is infallibly true, exactly as written. Other people from the same background believe that the Bible is filled with numerous myths and legends passed down from olden times, telling tall tales about things which could not possibly have happened in the real world.

So what do we actually do in the twelve-step program? We sit around the same tables, and avoid controversial statements about this kind of thing, and love and support one another regardless of the other person's attitude towards doctrines and dogmas of that sort.

It's important to remember that even if I myself believe that a good many religious beliefs are ignorant and superstitious, this does not mean there is no God. It was not that long ago, here in this country, when there were people who believed that a black cat could be used by a witch as a familiar, which would help her fly through the air on a broomstick on nights when the moon was full. I don't think there's anybody left who actually believes that tale, but it can be scientifically demonstrated that cats and broomsticks do in fact exist. So if I am forced to admit that cats and broomsticks actually exist, I will also have to admit that a real God could also exist, even if some people have had some very strange beliefs about him.

The twelve steps actually work—alcoholics who join A.A., for example, are actually able to stop drinking—and the steps make it clear that a higher power of some sort must be involved in this process. What I have to do is start working the steps, and then—based on my own personal experience and what I see occurring in the lives of other people in the program—I have to start developing my own uniquely personal conception of this compassionate and healing force which I will find leading me to a fuller vision of what is holy, good, and beautiful in this universe in which we live. That is what we are talking about when we say that the twelve-step program deals with *spirituality, not religion.* Religion is a set of very detailed formal doctrines and dogmas which forms a communal rule for an organized religious institution. Everybody who joins that group is expected to believe exactly the same thing. Spirituality on the other hand is the private inner journey of my own soul toward my own inner vision of the holy, the good, and the beautiful.

At an A.A. meeting several years ago an American Indian from Mississippi talked about how he looked up in the sky once, and realized that there were not two suns shining up in the heavens—a Catholic sun and a Protestant sun—but only a single sun whose light shone on all of us human beings. We could take that further. There are not six suns or eight suns—a Buddhist sun and a Hindu sun and a Muslim sun and a Navajo sun and a scientific sun (which shines by internal thermonuclear reactions, converting hydrogen into helium and so on like a nuclear bomb)—but only the one sun, which all human beings can use to find their path again when they have gotten lost in the woods. And there is likewise only one higher power which is the actual source of the sunlight of the spirit, whose kindly light can lead us out of the inner darkness of the soul. The only important thing is to turn the eyes of your spirit towards that source of light and grace, and then honestly describe to yourself what you yourself see.

The spirituality of the foxhole

In time of war, you might see three American soldiers huddled in a fox-hole, while enemy fire rains down upon them, and all three of the soldiers praying. One is a Catholic, let us say, and has his rosary beads out praying to the Blessed Virgin Mary. One is a Protestant, perhaps, and is reciting the Twenty-Third Psalm over and over, while visualizing the picture of Jesus which hung in his Sunday School room as a child. And maybe the third soldier is a Jew, and he is reciting Hebrew prayers to the Holy One, Blessed be He, which he had to memorize for his Bar Mitzvah years earlier. And in that situation, when death is raining down on your head, they respect one another's prayers. The shrapnel from that enemy shell is not going to care what words you are using to pray to the only power which could conceivably make a difference.

Alcoholics Anonymous was started by two men, Bill W. and Dr. Bob, who had been raised as New England Congregationalists, with the help of high church Anglo-Catholic Episcopalians like Father Sam Shoemaker. Bill W. and Dr. Bob worked out a good deal of the practical aspects of their program in conjunction with an Irish-American Roman Catholic nun named Sister Ignatia, who belonged to the Sisters of Charity of Saint

Augustine, and had already been working with alcoholics at St. Thomas hospital in Akron, Ohio.[2]

Sister Ignatia would lead alcoholics who had just come into the program into the little chapel at St. Thomas hospital, and have them get down on their knees with her while they all prayed together—and she did it with the Protestants just like she did with the Roman Catholics. Now this was long before the Second Vatican Council, when many Protestants feared Catholics down to their core, and when Roman Catholic bishops routinely ordered their people never to pray with Protestants on any kind of occasion. And yet important Protestant pastors and Roman Catholic clergy quickly began writing letters of testimonial praising the new A.A. program. The kind of doom which awaited an alcoholic was so horrifying and heart-rending to behold, that everyone with any sense realized that this called for the spirituality of the foxhole. A bottle of bourbon to an alcoholic was just like a mortar shell exploding over a hastily dug foxhole—the whiskey didn't care what words you used to make your prayer—so you just had to pray, because the only thing that seemed to save lives was if you *did* pray.

When the first Jewish alcoholic was brought in, Sister Ignatia compromised by making him get down on his knees *outside* the chapel while they prayed together. Bill W. was delighted when the first Buddhist religious leaders read a copy of the Big Book, and immediately declared that there was no problem they could see at all in adapting this program to a Buddhist society, because it saved Asians from a horrifying death in the same way that it saved Americans. In modern England, Christians and Muslims meet in the same A.A. meetings and likewise find that, when looking death in the face, quibbles about doctrines and beliefs will simply get you killed.

So the way past this first blockage that newcomers often collide with, is to make it clear to them that they are free to discard any traditional religious belief that they believe to be wrong or misguided—as long as they come up with *something* for a higher power which will have a power of grace sufficient to pull them back out of the path to destruction.

The spirituality of the knight and the samurai

Some people get stymied by one version of this particular block, when they start saying things like "religion is a crutch and I don't need a crutch," and "religion is just for weaklings." It would be more embarrassment and humiliation than they could stand, to get down on their knees and pray. What if one of their tough friends actually *saw* them doing that!

It is truly amazing how an alcoholic who disgraces himself by urinating in his pants, insulting other people in gross fashion, and passing out in public places, suddenly gets up on his high horse and says, "Well, I couldn't possibly do such-and-such. Why, that would be *humiliating*!" Narcotics addicts, sexual addicts, and gambling addicts humiliate themselves on a regular basis. Compulsive overeaters dread the comments and jokes that other people make about their weight. Recovering members of Al-Anon can tell you, from their memories of their pre-program days, that someone who is married to an alcoholic or narcotics addict knows how to raise personal public humiliation to an art form.

In the middle ages in western Europe, a knight in shining armor would enter a church daily and kneel in total humility before the altar. Was he a weakling and a coward? In medieval Japan, a samurai warrior would engage in special Zen meditative exercises in order to perfect the inner harmony of his being. Were samurai warriors wimps and sissies? Homer made it clear that the great Greek hero Odysseus was able to accomplish his mighty feats because he had earned the love and gracious help of the goddess Athena, and that he would have totally failed, regardless of his cleverness and physical strength, had it not been for the power of the Grey-eyed Goddess.

The idea that spirituality is weakness is the biggest piece of hokum in the world, heard mainly from the mouths of angry and resentful losers, and this has been true in all parts of the world for all of human history. So start hanging with the winners, and quit hanging with the losers.

2. Too frightened of God to enter his presence

There are many people in the twelve-step program who will tell you that their biggest blockage at the beginning was their belief that they had done things *so bad* that God would never hear their prayers or help them.

Now there are all sorts of people who come into the program, and some of them have not in fact ever done anything that was horrifically evil. Probably most of the people in the program were at least "cash register honest," or at least most of the time. It is not unusual to find newcomers to the program who were able to keep up an external façade, where many regarded them as hard workers, as successful in their field of endeavor, and as responsible folk who kept food on their families' tables. And this is not just in Al-Anon, where most members made a full-time profession of keeping up a phony façade to cover their inner sickness of heart, but in A.A. and all the other twelve-step programs as well. And yet even these outwardly righteous ones invariably had their secrets—things which they had done, so disgusting in their own eyes, that their fifth step was the first time they ever admitted these things to another living human being.

But there are also those who did great evils indeed. Anyone who goes to enough twelve-step meetings and conferences will hear about every kind of human behavior under the sun. Nick K., a famous A.A. old-timer in South Bend, Indiana, had murdered a stranger in a house of prostitution and been sent to the penitentiary for his crime. But in 1944 he found Alcoholics Anonymous there in the prison, and was eventually paroled. He was one of the people who reached out to a professional burglar who came into the program thirty years later, in 1974—a man who had built his old life around stealing and theft and gross dishonesty. This burglar in turn transformed his life and now, twenty-five years later, is one of the good old-timers himself. A well-known Al-Anon speaker from Arkansas tells how she once grew so angry that she held her husband down in the bath tub and drowned him—although fortunately, in this case, she then came to her senses and dragged him back out and gave him artificial respiration until he started breathing again. One can meet women (and men) who once worked as prostitutes; men (and women) who once were accustomed to savagely beat their spouses or their children on a regular basis. There is the man who would insert his male member into an empty light socket when he was masturbating, and then turn the current on; and the nun who used a razor blade to cut crosses on her thighs while she masturbated, until she finally found a twelve-step program which concentrated on sexual addictions.[3]

God's unconditional acceptance

What is the point here? There are many people in the twelve-step program who have done things like these, who today do NOT do those things—who are moreover filled with extraordinary honesty, profound compassion, and deep serenity, and are able to reach out to newcomers and love them until they learn how to love themselves. No one has the power to undergo such a total personal transformation without the aid of God's grace, and no one can reach out to other human beings and teach them how to love unless that person is being used by God as a channel of his grace. That is the proof that they have been forgiven by God.

The real higher power opens his arms, to everyone who enters the twelve-step program and begins to try to work it honestly, with an unconditional acceptance. All you need to do is to start going to twelve-step meetings, and you can see with your own eyes the reality of forgiveness, the visible power of grace, and thousands of living examples of new life.

There's a metaphor Martin Luther loved to use, of the higher power as the good physician.[4] How strange it would be if I got sick and went to a doctor, and the doctor took out his stethoscope and checked my heart, and looked me over, and then jumped back and said, "Ew, you're sick! You've got a *disease*! I don't treat sick people. Get out of my office, and don't come back until you're completely well." How strange it would be if I went to a psychotherapist, and he listened to me talk for a while, and then he suddenly jumped up and said, "Ew, you're insane! You're totally neurotic! I don't treat crazy people. Get out of my office, and don't come back until you're totally sane." Why would a situation like this be so completely bizarre? Because physicians and psychotherapists are supposed to be healers. You go to healers *because* you're sick, and the sicker you are, the more fun you are for them to work on, because you're more challenging!

The higher power of the twelve-step program is the universal force of Healing itself. It is *assumed* that there are really bad things wrong with you, at some level or another. No one ever walks into their first twelve-step meeting because their lives were going so perfectly, and they'd never done anything wrong in their lives, but they just thought it would be a fun way to spend an evening. You pray to the higher power who is the universal force of healing because, by golly, that is *for sure* what *you* need! My own doctor has sometimes scolded me and said, "Why didn't you come in with this a whole lot sooner?" The experience of people in the twelve-step program is that God doesn't even do that—he simply reaches out to help us the minute we sincerely ask.

The friends of God

An unreasonable fear of God sometimes comes out in another form: When we pray to him, we think we have to talk to him in thee's and thou's and archaic, formalistic language from three centuries ago. Or we have to use special phrases, or talk in a "churchy" tone of voice. But the great religious leader Moses used to talk to God every day, we are told, "as a man talks with his friend" (Exod. 33:11). And this is what we are trying to bring about in the twelve-step program: to become the friends of God. (A lot of us used to work hard at being his bitterest enemies, so this is quite a switch-around in the way we now live our lives.)

What the higher power of the twelve-step program wants from us is not a lot of phony-baloney religious-sounding language, but a little bit of ordinary honesty. People who come into the twelve-step program don't know much about honesty—this is foreign territory to them—so they have to start learning how to speak honestly, and simply tell the truth. If I'm angry at God, then I need to come out and say, in a single, plain, simple English sentence: "I'm angry at you because…." If I'm afraid, then I need to tell God this in plain Anglo-Saxon terms: "I'm frightened to death because I think such-and-such is going to happen to me." If I lack faith, then I need to simply pray, "God please give me more faith."

I once asked a man named Tex from Chicago how you found the higher power of the twelve-step program. He had forty-four years in the A.A. program at that time. He looked at me and said, "I just tell people to remember two things. He's not you. And he's not stupid. Once people get that straight, they can always work it out O.K." God is not stupid. I should assume that he is *at least* as bright as I am! He already knows every thought I think, and certainly knows the kind of words I ordinarily use to express my feelings to my friends—or this is what traditional religion has always said—so do I seriously think he is so stupid that I can get down on my knees for two minutes and fool him into thinking that I am really Miss Goody Two-Shoes or Mr. Television Evangelist, or an eastern guru who just loves to sit on a bed of nails in his saffron-colored robes?

As long as I am afraid to let God see who I actually am, I can never obtain any deep consciousness of his presence, because I am always putting up a phony front that gets in the way. It's my own eyes which I blindfold when I do that, not his.

There are a lot of things about the twelve-step program that do not make any rational sense. The third step talks about finding God "as we understood Him," but I don't think I myself understand God. I don't personally understand why God does all sorts of things. When somebody first comes into the program, he can ask, "Why would God love somebody like me?" But it's a pointless question, because nobody's actually expected to *understand* why he does; the only thing that's important is just to realize that it has been proven concretely in the twelve-step program, over and over again, that God really does love and accept people like us. As it says in Hebrews 4:16, "Let us therefore boldly approach the throne of grace, so that we may receive mercy and find grace to help in time of need." Amen.

3. Over-intellectualization

A lot of people have trouble when they first get into a twelve-step program because they think they have to come up with an intellectual theory about who or what this higher power is—an intellectualization which they can put into words, and use to explain what they are doing when they pray. There was a psychotherapist who joined Overeaters Anonymous when he developed diabetes, but still could not control his urge to eat sweets. He read dozens of scholarly books about various world religions, and spent weeks trying to figure out exactly the right words for describing the higher power. His sponsor let him flail around, but did keep on insisting that he pray every day. When the program began to click in and start working, the psychotherapist told his sponsor with amazement: "You know, the words don't really matter!" He never worried about the issue again, and in fact, soon started referring to his higher power as "God," which is what most people in the twelve-step program do, because it's a simple, one-syllable word that takes less time to say, and does the job quite well. Of course, if you prefer to keep on referring to your higher power as "the transcendent Beyond which breaks the chains of karmic enslavement"—or whatever else you want—that's perfectly O.K. too. It has to be something you yourself are really comfortable with.

But it's a useless waste of time to try to devise a tight intellectual theory about who and what God is. You see, all the higher religions of the world use different terms for referring to this highest power which is the ultimate ground of all being—God, Allah, Zeus, Being-Itself, the One, the Atman, the Tao—but all are agreed that this ground of being is so radically different from anything in the physical world around us which we can perceive through our five senses and describe by our science, that we cannot on principle describe this transcendent ground comprehensively in any kind of human words and human theories. Most of our human attempts to describe God are only symbols and metaphors and analogies, not literal descriptions.

St. Thomas Aquinas, for example, the great Roman Catholic philosophical theologian of the thirteenth century, did say that we could make one literal statement about God: God was Being-Itself, the act or energy through which Being came out of nonbeing. But beyond that, St. Thomas said, we had to talk in analogies and metaphors, or use the *via negationis*, where we were in fact only saying what God was NOT: When we say that God is infinite, for example, we are not actually saying what God is, but simply that he is NOT finite. When we say that God is eternal and incorporeal, all we are actually saying is that God is NOT some kind of physical object in the realm of ordinary space and chronological time, like a tree or a big rock or an especially large star.[5]

Or let's take something more modern. Modern physics can describe the inner workings of the atom, and the history of the universe all the way back to the Big Bang, when this present universe first exploded into existence ten or twelve billion years ago. But what caused the Big Bang? What already existed, that the Big Bang could explode out of? There must have been some kind of preexistent ground of being which existed before the Big Bang. Whatever this preexistent ground of being is, it cannot follow the ordinary laws of physics. For example, it cannot obey the normal laws of thermodynamics, because it has to be immune to the law of entropy. No modern physicist has yet worked out a way to account for the existence of our present universe without violating the law of entropy. What this means is, that in effect, this ground of being has literally infinite power. But by that very fact, it cannot be described by the ordinary laws of physics.

Our human minds can ask all kinds of additional intellectual questions: "But if this ground created the Big Bang and the universe which emerged from it, then what created that ground?" The problem is that, for that ground to have been able to do what it obviously did, it must be something which has always existed, and never had a beginning in time. So the answer is that nothing created it, it has simply always been there. So again and again we are driven back to the same point: that highest power from which all else has come into existence cannot be adequately described in any detail in ordinary human language, because—by its very nature—it has to be something which breaks all the normal rules.

The control issue

Why do so many beginners in the twelve-step program nevertheless try so hard to figure out some kind of intellectualizing theory of God? One of the three or four most basic existential anxieties is anxiety over *not being in control*. Control neuroses are at the heart of countless human miseries which are trucked into psychotherapists' offices. If I can come up with a theory of God, an intellectual concept of God, then I subconsciously believe that I will be back in control of things. If I can work out the theory in enough detail, then I will be able to start manipulating God and getting him to do just what I want him to do. Or at least, I will be able to figure out exactly what God is going to do in advance.

It is perfectly normal to have an enormous fear of the unknown. But one of the great A.A. old-timers named Goshen Bill once told a story about a man who had just come into the program. Now the sponsor who was working with him had quite a few years of sobriety, and told the newcomer that it was praying that had kept him sober. But the newcomer thought of himself as an atheist. He not only didn't believe God existed, he didn't have the slightest idea who or what he could pray to. So he kept on going back out and getting drunk, over and over again. Finally, in desperation, the newcomer got down on his knees and then pointed to his sponsor and looked up to heaven and cried out, "Whoever it is helping this other man, help me!" And from that day on, Goshen Bill said, the new man was able to stay sober too.[6]

In the New Testament, the example given of the faith that saves, in more than one place, was a man who was not a Christian himself at all—the man Abraham, who was a nomad living in a tent and shepherding a flock of sheep and goats in what is present-day Iraq, ranging from Ur down near the border with Kuwait, to Haran up in the western mountains, almost four thousand years ago. One day the higher power told Abraham, "leave here, and head west." Abraham did not have the foggiest idea where he was going to end up, or what was going to happen there, but he had enough faith to pack up his tent and set out. And that simple act of faith ended up saving his soul. The faith that saves is a homeless nomad trudging along through the trackless desert, keeping the faith one day at a time, and not demanding to know the far-off future.[7]

So we fear the unknown, we fear not being in control, and we try to compensate neurotically by attempting to devise intellectual theories about God. "I can't pray to something I don't even understand," the newcomer says. But that's nonsense. Of course you can. And if you want to save your life, you will have to pray every day, all the rest of your life, to a higher power whom you will never, ever truly understand—except to understand that this higher power loves you, accepts you just as you are, and will save you from your own self-destructiveness if you simply ask for help, and genuinely mean it.

I come into the twelve-step program claiming that I myself am too intelligent to accept this superstitious nonsense about a higher power, and I stand up defiantly and say, "I'm not going to pray to anything like that unless you can prove to me by some elaborate intellectual theory that a being like that actually exists." But this is all phony-baloney. In reality, I'm scared to death of anything new and unknown, scared to death of anything where I'm not totally in control, and most of all, totally unwilling to accept help from anything or anybody else. All the intellectual clap-trap, and me puffing my chest out and trying to talk all the time about how much more intelligent I am than other people is obvious nonsense from the start—if I were that smart, why have I been driven into the twelve-step program in the first place? Why have I messed up my life in every conceivable way, why am I at my wit's end, why am I collapsing inside in total despair, if I'm so smart and in such total control?

Beginning over again like a little baby

Raymond I., who now owns a little clothing store, has been in the A.A. program since 1974. He often talks about how he protested about this higher power idea to his sponsor Bill Hoover. Bill told him, "Raymond, you're nothing but a little baby." Raymond, who had a fiery temper, exploded at this idea. But Bill kept on talking, and he said, "Raymond, *spiritually* you're nothing but a little baby. You've got to start at the beginning, and you've got to start by figuring out how to take your first step." And when little babies learn to walk, they have to hang onto things like chairs and coffee tables when they first start, and they fall down a lot. But if they keep on trying, they eventually start toddling all around, and then they learn how to run, and the next thing you know they're out playing chase with the family dog, and playing baseball, and that kind of thing.

It's the same thing with a little baby learning how to talk. At first, he tries his best, all he can do is go "Goo goo" and "bah bah." Then he starts saying things like "Me go with you store?" You sing to the child, "Twinkle, twinkle, little star," and the little child asks, "What's a star?" You have to explain it to the child. You have to point at things and explain what words like red, and yellow, and blue refer to.[8]

Same thing with a newcomer to the twelve-step program. "What do you mean by faith? What do you mean by grace? What do you mean by higher power?" Somebody who's been around for long enough to know more about what the words mean has to point at things, and say the words, and do it over and over again, until something clicks.[9]

> "You came dragging into your first meeting here, hands shaking so hard you couldn't hold the coffee cup to your lips, and somebody put her arms around you. She held that coffee cup to your lips so you could drink. And when that meeting was over, they asked you to come back, and told you that your life was going to start getting better now, that you had come to the right place. That's what we mean by love, and that's what we mean by grace."

And maybe the first time they explain it to you, you still can't understand what those words mean. And maybe even the 314th time. But then, the 315th time, something clicks, and you start to understand a little bit what is meant by the words "love" and "grace." And when you start understanding what those words mean, you'll start understanding a little better what the words "higher power" mean.

But a baby doesn't learn to walk overnight; a baby doesn't learn to talk overnight. A baby learns to walk by trying to walk; a baby learns to talk by trying to talk. If a baby had to have a scientific theory of the laws of motion, or an intellectual theory of language and meaning, before it could learn how to walk and talk, there would never be any baby in this world who ever learned how to walk and talk. You learn by doing it. You learn how to pray to a higher power by praying to a higher power.

Psychologizing

One way of trying to over-intellectualize the twelve-step program is trying to psychologize everything. Treatment centers and psychotherapists can be very helpful to newcomers to the twelve-step program, but I have also seen too many people trying to turn everything into a psychological theory or a set of psychological gimmicks. It's all well and good to talk about "triggers" and "relapse prevention techniques" and "coming in contact with my inner child" and all that sort of thing. But people who try to turn the program into nothing but a set of psychological gimmicks and methods for autohypnotic suggestion, never end up making it. Alcoholics who try this, gimmick themselves back into another drunk; narcotics addicts who try this, autohypnotize themselves back into another visit to the dope dealer, and so on. Overeaters and compulsive spenders and gambling addicts who need the twelve-step program will find that all the psychological analysis and insights in the world will not keep them away from the next binge on chocolate ice cream, the plastic credit card, or the betting window at the race track.

This is just another way of trying to play control games. If I can turn everything into a psychological theory about my own inner neurotic compulsions, then I can put myself back in control, and can start manipulating things once again, and by golly, I'll be able to save myself without having to take that higher power business seriously. But the Big Book says, ominously, that the program will not work until I *abandon myself* to God unconditionally, until I *surrender myself* to God unconditionally, until I genuinely ask for help from a power I will never be able to manipulate or control.[10] So, ultimately, if I'm the kind of person who needs the twelve-step program, I will never be able to save myself from my own self-destructive obsessions and compulsions by just figuring out the right psychological theory or gimmick.

4. Blaming God and hating God

With some people coming into the twelve-step program who claim that they're atheists, or don't believe in God, the real problem is that they blame God for their own misfortunes, and actually hate God. It's not really an *intellectual problem* that arises because they are so "much more intelligent than these other people in the program." They may like to talk that way, but that's not what's really blocking them off from God, down in the bottom of their hearts. Genuinely bad things have happened to them, their lives have been miserable, and *they blame God for that*.

Blaming God for things I actually brought on myself

For some of us—not all of us, but some of us—the best remedy may be to start practicing a little bit of simple self-honesty. Am I blaming God for things I actually brought on myself?

In the Big Book, on p. 65, there is a sample fourth step written by an alcoholic who was feeling terribly sorry for himself. His boss was threatening to fire him, his wife was treating him badly, and there was a nosy old gossip named Mrs. Jones who he was afraid was going to tell his wife he was having an affair with another woman. We hope that this drunk finally realized that if he just stopped showing up drunk at work, padding his expense account, and running around with that other woman, most of his problems would automatically disappear. God didn't do that to him. He brought it on himself.

If I'm in trouble with the law because I got caught drunk driving, did God hold a gun to my head and make me drink that liquor? Did God then force me to get in my car and drive? Or say I'm a newcomer to Al-Anon who blames God because I'm married to a man who gets drunk and screams at me, and I'm afraid he's going to start hitting me next. Did I really *not know* that he drank a lot, and that he had a temper, when I married him? "Oh, but it wasn't that bad at first." Do I really want to pretend that I *knew nothing* about his personality and tendencies before I married him? If it was a mistake, was it God or me who made that very bad mistake?

Cargo cults

On some jungle islands in the tropics, back around the middle of the previous century, what were called cargo cults sometimes developed. Some of the savages who lived on that island would see cargo planes flying through the sky over the island, and they knew that those airplanes had all sorts of good things inside: beads, mirrors, transistor radios, bolts of colored cloth. So someone would get the bright idea of luring one of those airplanes to land on their island. The natives would clear off a patch of jungle to make a landing strip, and then build a full-sized model of an airplane out of sticks and leaves to act like a kind of duck decoy. When an airplane would fly overhead, the natives would whoop and holler and chant magic phrases, because if they could just figure out the right way of praying, that airplane would swoop in and land on their little jungle island, and they'd get all those goodies in the airplane, and they'd never have to work again.

Does this sound ignorant and naive? When it's people on a jungle island, it's easy to sneer. But a lot of people who come into the twelve-step program are angry at God because they tried doing things that weren't any different at the basic level, and God never came swooping in and gave them the goodies they wanted. A man, let's call him Tim, owned a major construction company, and then drank himself out of business. He never got the twelve-step program because every time he would get sober for a few months, he would invest what little money he had scraped together into some hair-brained get-rich-quick scheme, pray to God as though he were some sort of magical genie in a bottle, and then lose all that money too (because he invested in really stupid things, and then refused to actually put any real work into it). And then he'd blame God.

The twelve-step program is not some magical cargo cult which will guarantee—if you just chant the right magical phrases—that you will make a million dollars without working for it, stay out of jail even though you're breaking the law, be magically reunited with the spouse whom you treated so shoddily, and be able to cure fallen arches, balding hair, and ingrown toenails. If you are an alcoholic, the twelve-step program will enable you to stop drinking, and start learning how to enjoy and appreciate life more. It will stop a compulsive overeater from eating himself to death, a compulsive spender from continuing to destroy himself financially, and a sexual addict from continuing to endanger his health and his good standing in the community. It will allow an Al-Anon to learn how to detach constructively from the person who is drinking and drugging, and start building up a real inner sense of personal self-esteem.

Being traumatized by earlier life experiences

But there are also people who come into the twelve-step program, to whom truly horrifying things have happened—things where they were genuinely totally innocent victims. And a lot of these people hate God, or certainly don't trust him.

There's one famous psychiatrist who talks about this: a man named Viktor Frankl, who survived the Nazi death camps, and who had to learn for himself how to deal with horror beyond imagining. He developed a kind of psychotherapy called logotherapy. The Greek word *logos* can be translated in some contexts as "meaning," and Frankl realized that survivors of this sort of unbelievable nightmare had to find some kind of meaning or purpose to life again if they were ever to be able to get past their traumas.[11]

But we don't need to talk psychological theories. In the twelve-step program, what we do is go to people who actually experienced whatever it is we're trying to deal with, and ask them what worked. So let's the take the case of a young woman—let's call her Annette to preserve her anonymity. She has a good job now as a licensed mortician, working at a funeral parlor in a city in the Midwest, and taking a real sense of pride and accomplishment at being able to give a small amount of comfort to grieving relatives by preparing the bodies of automobile accident victims and so on, so that there can be an open casket at the funeral. From the time she was six years old, her drug-addict father was raping her, and beating her savagely because her tiny body was too small for his penis. The only thing that kept her from being beaten to death was his suicide when she was ten years old.

She says that when she came into the twelve-step program, already an alcoholic and addict at the age of eighteen, her attitude towards a higher power was one of total hostility. "*How dare* there be a God, sitting up there with all that power, sitting in judgment on me, who allowed my six-year-old body to be tortured!" So how did she handle that? Her words were simple: "I decided I wanted to live. And that has made all the difference—that is what allowed me to commit."

A professional baseball player who was an alcoholic, staggered drunk one day into the path of a rapidly moving car. His body got hung on the front bumper, and the car dragged him for three hundred yards before the driver could stop. His entire buttocks were scraped off on the pavement. He still remembers lying in the hospital, where the doctors had given him up for dead—and even if he miraculously lived, he would certainly never walk again. And then, he says, "I decided—and I remember lying there, and just suddenly deciding—I want to live." He went into A.A., and although he has to use a cane, he walks anywhere he wants to now, and can ride a bike, and is married, and has a good life for himself.

Listen to the people who've been there. If you've had to deal with some kind of truly traumatic event, where you were an innocent victim of something unbelievably horrifying, I can't give you any kind of smug rationalization. I can't give you any kind of intellectualization for explaining that all away. But I can tell you that there is a gut level decision that you are going to have make: I want to live. And once you've made this decision, you're going to have to turn to that higher power in order to actually carry that out.

Or listen to a woman who was snatched up from the parking lot at a mall, and raped and beaten savagely by a maniac. She was injured so badly that she is confined to a wheelchair now, and will never walk again. Someone asked her if she held anger at the man who had done that to her. "No," she said. "He destroyed my legs, I'm not going to let him destroy my life."

Acceptance and gratitude

For beginners, one of the hardest passages in the Big Book to hear and make yourself read, is the little section on page 449 in the third edition:

> And acceptance is the answer to *all* my problems today. When I am disturbed, it is because I find some person, place, thing, or situation—some fact of my life—unacceptable to me, and I can find no serenity until I accept that person, place, thing, or situation as being exactly the way it is supposed to be at this moment. Nothing, absolutely nothing happens in God's world by mistake. Until I could accept my alcoholism, I could not stay sober; unless I accept life completely on life's terms, I cannot be happy. I need to concentrate not so much on what needs to be changed in the world as on what needs to be changed in me and in my attitudes.

"Nothing, absolutely nothing happens in God's world by mistake." Or as Ralph P. (Father John Doe) put it in his Golden Books, I must face the fact that God either willed it to be so, or allowed it to be so. And sometimes, later on down the line, I get a little glimmer of why he may have allowed things to happen that way. But a lot of the time, I (as a frail human being with a brain that's not much bigger than a cantaloupe or a muskmelon) will never know how the universe looks from God's perspective, or why God did this particular thing or that particular thing.

The way I learn how to be serene, and enjoy life pretty well most of the time, is to work on my serenity and satisfaction and gratitude—you know, work for what you actually want. If it's happiness I want, then knowing the reason why doesn't necessarily make anybody happier. I teach college, and in my experience, *in fact* explaining to a student exactly why he flunked your course never makes that student suddenly start smiling and being happy. Knowing the reason why is not always that great, in real life, if it's genuine happiness I want. And on the other hand, the twelve-step program demonstrates over and over again that human beings can learn to feel serenity, and can learn to start feeling some satisfaction and gratitude about their lives, without ever knowing the reason why for anything at all. Knowing the reason why is grossly overrated as a solution to life's problems.

If what you really want is serenity and a sense of basic satisfaction with your life, then acceptance is the first thing you actually have to work on. And that will be easier if you start working on gratitude also. Good sponsors often make their pigeons write out a gratitude list, and read through it every morning when they first get up. If I focus on what's wrong with my life, and the bad things that have happened to me, in actual practice my life will just get worse, and even worse things will happen to me. If I start paying serious attention to what is good in my life, and the good things that invariably happen to me every single day of my life, I will discover. to my surprise that I will be able to put a life together for myself that's pretty good—astonishingly good in fact. And once that happens, I won't be blaming God and hating God anymore.[12]

5. The Dark Night of the Soul

In the traditional language of the spiritual life, some of the spiritual masters have talked about what they call the Dark Night of the Soul. When I pass through this, I feel completely cut off from any kind of contact with a higher power, and my heart is filled with tormenting resentment, grief, self-pity, worry, anxiety, and feelings of futility and despair. In order to grow in the spiritual life, and make deeper and fuller contact with my higher power, it will be necessary for me to pass through this Dark Night of the Soul, maybe more than once. This is the place where many people lose it when they are trying to work the twelve-step program.[13]

Some of it is ordinary grief. To the alcoholic, the bottle was his best friend, and losing someone whom you regard as your best friend will produce a period of grief. To the sexual addict, the trance-like period when you are acting out is the beloved friend who washes all your anxieties away. The plastic credit card is the compulsive spender's best buddy. A man who is a compulsive gambler will push the most beautiful and loving woman in the world out of the way to get at a pair of dice—that's his lover and his girlfriend. To many Al-Anons, losing themselves in caretaking was freedom from themselves, and it bought them temporary reprieve from their own inner hell. Anybody who comes into the twelve-step program is going to go through a period of ordinary grief, because they're going to have to lose something they thought of as a friend. But the thing about ordinary grief is that it is self-limiting: the human mind, the human body, processes the grief and then finishes grieving and moves on.

Quit worrying about God not magically removing that period of grief and mourning, and do your grief-work. It doesn't mean that God has abandoned you, or doesn't love you. You can be there for someone, but you can't work through the grief for someone else.

Pathological perfectionism

I can sometimes bring the Dark Night of the Soul on myself by perfectionism, or what the old Catholic spiritual masters used to call scrupulosity.[14] A scruple in old English was a tiny weight used by druggists which was roughly ten thousandths of an ounce—something so small as to be almost invisible. I fall into perfectionism, or scrupulosity, when I set impossibly high standards for my own behavior. I do a tolerably good job at something, and then my mind goes into overtime, and I start imagining ways that I could have done it even better. Anybody can do this, but intelligent people can really do a hatchet job on themselves this way. Then I guilt-trip myself.

There is no human being living who cannot imagine—if he puts his mind to it—more than he could ever actually perform. I get hypercritical, and I point out mistakes here and mistakes there, until that's all I can see. And then, since even the smallest mistake means that *I'm no good at all* (because this is part of the neurotic self-torture game I'm playing on myself), my imagination tells me that God must be condemning me too, and there's no point in praying, because why would a perfect God listen to a miserable failure like me?

Now when I was a child, there may have been so-called religious people who played that game on me. That's an even nastier version of that game, where someone takes his own perfectionism and scrupulosity, which is making his own life miserable, and dumps it on some innocent child. But the point is, it was not the real God who was dumping that stuff on me. And I'm the one who's dumping that stuff on me NOW, and if I'm the one who's doing it to me NOW, I can learn to quit doing it NOW. It is not God who is shutting his love and grace off from my soul, it is me who is refusing to turn to God because I'd rather play sick, neurotic, self-torture games, and—in a bizarre little neurotic twist—blame it all on him.

Aridity

Sometimes the Dark Night of the Soul produces periods of what traditionally was called aridity. The word arid means dry, and I feel as though I am lost in a spiritual desert. St. Teresa of Avila, and many others of the great spiritual teachers of the past talked about the problem of aridity. The biggest problem in aridity is that I do not feel as though I can pray. I try to say the words, and it feels as though my tongue is sticking to the bottom of my mouth. Or I say the words, and they sound empty and hollow: "I don't really mean these words in my heart," I say to myself, "so it's all hypocrisy, and it's no good saying these words, and I don't feel God hearing them."

What do the great spiritual masters of the past say? John Wesley, St. Teresa of Avila, and so on? *Pray anyway.* There may be so much mental static in my head that I can't feel God's response, but that doesn't mean God can't hear me. If I pray a prayer I don't mean, because *some little part of me* still wishes *I did mean it,* God will give me credit anyway for having meant it. God is strange that way: he gives me credit for having the gumption to pray to him in this situation, because it means that there is some small fragment of my will that still sincerely wants him and needs him. And that's all God needs, a little toehold in my heart someplace, even if it's just a little one, and he'll be able to start to work helping me.

Some of the current television evangelists give us the misleading impression that when God genuinely works in my soul, I will feel some overwhelming sense of emotional power sweep through me—you know, maybe even visions or a heavenly voice speaking inside my head, or suddenly seeing burning bushes flaming in front of my eyes, or angels climbing up and down ladders from heaven. The real higher power is the one who invented the concept of anonymity, and he in fact loves to work most of the time in secrecy and quietness. Pray the prayer, and keep praying the prayer, and trust that it is being answered even as I pray it.

If I get an infection, say a bad sore throat, and a doctor prescribes an antibiotic for me, do I feel a drug rush when I swallow one of those tablets? Do I instantly feel an overpowering sense of health sweeping over my body? No, but I'll feel a little bit better the next day, maybe, if I keep on taking those pills every four hours as prescribed, and a little better yet the next day, and eventually my sore throat will have been healed.

People who come into twelve-step programs want instant gratification. I'm feeling frustrated by something—toss down a pint of whisky and make it go away instantly. I'm feeling blue—sniff or swallow or smoke a chemical that will instantly dissolve all my woes in a rush of drug-induced euphoria. I'm feeling worried and overwhelmed—wolf down a dozen doughnuts and it'll all go away on the spot. I'm feeling like a failure—start caretaking some hopeless drunk (or complaining about what a jerk he is) and I'll instantly feel like a superior person. People who come into twelve-step programs are looking for instant gratification, instant mood-altering, and the cheap shot.[15]

In the twelve-step program, on the other hand, the way I tell whether I'm praying effectively is to look at a little bit longer term results. If I am an alcoholic, but I pray, and I get through one period of twenty-four hours without drinking, then God has obviously been helping me, no matter how lousy I feel. If I am filled with rage, but I keep on praying, and my rage eventually goes away—even if it takes two or three days—and I get through that without hurting myself or anyone else, then God has obviously been helping me. After I've done this for a few weeks or months, and other people start commenting on how I've changed—and how much better they like the new me—then this is proof that God has been working a powerful transformation in my life.

The twelve-step program is an action program. What I actually end up doing is a whole lot more important that what I'm feeling. Ultimately, my moods will alter, and my emotions will dramatically change. *When you change the motion, eventually you will change the emotion.* When I actually live the right way and do the right things for a long enough period of time, I will find myself feeling in a good mood more and more of the time.

I will also find myself redefining what a good mood is. Feeling satisfied because, in a nasty situation, I nevertheless acted responsibly and did the right thing, is a very good mood to be in. Learning how to be truly happy with what I do have, rather than making myself sick with lust for what I don't have, is a very nice mood to be in. Feeling secure in the knowledge that there is a God who loves me, and program people who love me, no matter what, is the best mood in the world to be in.

Resentment

On page 64 of the Big Book, it says that resentment kills more alcoholics than anything else. When I fall into aridity, and feel as though I cannot pray, nine times out of ten, it is because my mind is so obsessed with some resentment. I'm so busy being angry, or sitting on the pity pot, that I can't feel God's presence, or his response to me. So what do I do? I must pray anyway. And what's the real problem that's gumming up the works? My resentment. So instead of praying to God to magically make the world run my way, what I need to be praying for is for him to use the power of his grace to remove the soul-sickness of my resentment. I will never obtain serenity, or any feeling of closeness to God, until I realize that the real problem is not changing the world, it is changing the way I think and feel and act.

6. Inability to commit yourself

Remember Annette's words, describing the decision that turned her life around: "I decided I wanted to live. And that has made all the difference—that is what allowed me to commit."

Many people who come into a twelve-step program *actually want to die*. Everyone I've ever talked to had already figured out a specific method for committing suicide. What they have already been doing to themselves was just a kind of slow suicide anyway, and *they didn't care*. "Sure I'm drinking myself to death, so what? I don't care. Go away and leave me alone." In his *Inferno*, Dante said that the sign posted over the gates of hell reads simply, "Abandon all hope, you who enter here." Total hopelessness—about God, and human beings, and the universe—is the very definition of hell. There's an old twelve-step saying: "Religion is for people who're afraid of going to hell; twelve-step spirituality is for those who've been there."

The higher power who will use his power to heal and remake our lives is the force of the three great virtues: faith, hope, and love. When you walk into a twelve-step meeting, *you can feel the love.* That is the spirit of the higher power flowing through these people's hearts. When you listen to the members talk about where they once were, and how very different it is now, *you can see the proof of hope with your own eyes.*

Hope and love: all that is lacking is faith, and faith in this sense does not mean believing in a bunch of religious doctrines, or intellectual theories. *Faith means a willingness to actually commit yourself.* Annette said it all: "I decided I wanted to live…that is what allowed me to commit." Because I remember Annette's early days in the program. She was afraid to go back to school. She was afraid to go on and do specialized work in mortuary science. She had uncomfortable experiences with men and with employers. She got mad at me once, and threw a *Twenty-Four Hour* book at me, and hit me square in the chest.

But she committed herself to the program, and she did not back down on that commitment, and slowly it all changed. The bad stuff at the beginning? That was then, this is now, and today she's comfortable with herself and with her life, and gets pleasure out of being able to help other people who are going through one of life's most unpleasant experiences, and making a positive difference in other people's lives. And who knows? Would she have been tough enough to do what she does now, and does so well, if she had not experienced all that she experienced? But who knows the answer to that one, and what would it matter anyway? People who're enjoying their lives don't worry about the answer to that kind of question—it's irrelevant.

The third step says we "made a decision to turn our will and our lives over to the care of God *as we understood Him*" (which was usually not much at all). This is sometimes called the act of surrender, but that doesn't mean just giving up on life, and saying, "It's impossible, I can't do anything, so who gives a damn anyway." Surrender means turning myself over to God unconditionally. Surrender means I stop fighting God. Surrender means I make a commitment to this higher power, and the program which will lead me into closer and closer contact with him, and this commitment has to be a continuing commitment, through thick and thin. Surrender means that I stop trying to figure things out, and simply abandon myself totally to the power of God's healing grace. I will begin to understand what that actually means only as I myself go about actually doing it.

It does not matter much what religious tradition you look at, the willingness to make a total commitment is what counts. The pagan Greek philosopher Socrates was condemned to death by the people of ancient Athens, where they called the high god Zeus, and as he prepared to drink the poison hemlock, he said, "I've been a soldier in the army. When your commander says hold that position, he doesn't mean hold it unless it starts to get dangerous or unpleasant. He simply means stands there and fight the good fight to the end. God has commanded me to preach about goodness and virtue to the people of Athens, and I will not abandon the position to which he has assigned me. I will obey God rather than man." And he drank the poison, and lay down, and died.[16]

Jesus in the Garden of Gethsemane prayed to God, "Let this cup pass from me," and sweat ran off him like clots of blood. But each time he prayed, he concluded with the words, "Not my will but yours be done."[17] In the Koran, Mohammed, another fighter, said simply, "There is no God but God." In the Big Book it says the same thing (page 59), "There is One who has all power—that One is God. May you find Him now!" That's my prayer for you, call him whatever you want to, may you find him now.

There is no real knowledge of God without commitment to God. Quit shilly-shallying around and trying to do it all backwards. You can't figure it all out intellectually, and work out a complicated theological or philosophical theory, and then decide whether you want to commit yourself to this theoretical God. *You have to commit yourself first.*

Joshua put it point-blank to the Israelites, "If you are unwilling to serve the Lord…choose this day whom you will serve" (Josh. 24:15). Because in the real world, we will always serve somebody or something: We will sacrifice anything else for alcohol, or drugs, or a degrading sexual addiction, or a piece of chocolate cake even though we're dying of diabetes, or the delusion that we can fix somebody else's life through the power of our love. Or if we're smart, we will put God before everything else, and paradoxically gain everything else we really needed.

"There is One who has all power—that One is God. May you find Him now!" Commit yourself unconditionally to that higher power, carry through unflinchingly on your commitment, and all the questions you ever really needed answered will receive their answers. Just say to yourself, and mean it, "I want to live." Stick to that, and I guarantee you that life abundant will be given you, beyond your wildest dreams and imaginations, because the real God is not only the force of faith and hope, but also the force of love: the power of infinite, cosmic love, reflected in every flower, every star, every sunrise, and reigning in power from the furthest depths of infinite space to the bottommost recesses of your own heart. See and behold the overwhelming beauty that lies before you, touch and be saved, hear and be healed!

Chapter III

Spiritual Awakening and the Power of Grace

Experiencing the Spiritual Dimension

The twelfth step says, "having had a spiritual awakening as the result of these steps." Some people in A.A. have had sudden, overpowering emotional experiences, of a very extraordinary sort. A travelling salesman woke up from a drunk in a motel room, in total despair. Helplessly he fell to his knees and cried out, "Oh God, please help me. I can't go on like this." Suddenly the horror lifted, and he found himself to his surprise calling the A.A. telephone number.

A young gourmet chef turned major Detroit drug dealer walked into his first A.A. meeting and saw an old man "who just glowed," he said. He seemed surrounded all around with an aura or halo of something almost like light. The old man, who had had Dr. Bob himself as his own sponsor, took the young man under his wing, and led him into sobriety.

The old Golden Key group which used to meet in South Bend on Thursday nights often talked about the nature of spiritual awakening. A man named Kenny who was at that meeting one night had had an experience of this sudden, instantly transforming kind. Kenny said, "I had my spiritual experience in jail. It was a kind of vision—the words 'a new way of life'—that was what did it."

But the people in A.A. who have had that kind of strange experience are in a small minority, and even those who have had an experience of that sort would say only that it got them over one crucial hump, and that as they continued to work at making progress in the program and growing in serenity, that they had many other difficult humps to get over along the way. The other difficult periods they had to slog through the hard way.

There is one kind of Protestant evangelical preaching which can lead a person to believe that a "real" conversion experience brings a person *instantly* from being lost in his sins to a continuous saintlike state of total peace, calm, faith, and joy. In A.A., that just doesn't happen. No one gets ten years of sobriety in ten minutes. Truly deep serenity comes only after slowly making progress in the program over a much longer span of time.

The appendix at the end of the A.A. Big Book says that "most of our experiences are what the psychologist William James calls the 'educational variety' because they develop slowly over a period of time."[1] There are a lot of people in the A.A. program in the upper Midwest who describe their own spiritual experience as being of the "educational variety." They will often say things like "I didn't see any burning bush or anything like that."

But there are also people who object to the phrase "educational variety," I think because the word education suggests to them that the A.A. program is something that you can memorize and learn in the way you study a textbook in a class in high school or college. Curt the fireman, for example, says that his experience was of having a series of *insights* over the months and years: a sudden insight into what this word really meant, or a sudden insight into how you actually worked that particular part of the program in your everyday life.

In the old Golden Key group, Chris the tree-trimmer said something similar one night:

> I don't like calling it the educational variety. The program has been a series of spiritual experiences for me, that were what I call moments of clarity. Like, "why was *I* spared when *he* died from alcoholism?" So I prefer to call these spiritual experiences moments of clarity. They say "expect miracles"—now I *depend* on miracles!—and it works. "Doors open"—boy, they do now, *and I step through*.

Rob G., a man from Michigan who had been an orderly in an insane asylum until he retired, was another member of the Golden Key group who preferred a different way of saying it:

> Spiritual experience: To me that means I hear something for 4,285 times, and then I hear it the 4,286th time and suddenly it makes sense.

St. Augustine, at the end of his *Confessions*, said that his own major spiritual breakthroughs had come when he suddenly *remembered* something that he *already knew*, or had *already experienced*.[2] But he had put the wrong name or the wrong interpretation on the experience, or he had forgotten that he had had such things happen and how often they had happened, or he had pushed it aside because "he didn't think it made sense" or "it couldn't possibly be real" or "it wasn't a scientific, rational way of looking at the world." Or he had turned and run away from the experience because it made him so uncomfortable, or told him something about himself and the world that he didn't want to look at.

But as he made more and more progress in his own spiritual life, Augustine said, he discovered that God had been there all along, taking care of him and reaching out to him, even back in his early years when he had denied that God existed and had prided himself on being a total sceptic about religion and spirituality. And so many recovering alcoholics also eventually come to realize how God had saved their lives on so many occasions back when they were still drinking, even in unbelievably dangerous situations where by all rights they should have gotten themselves killed, and how God had led them and prodded them into the A.A. program even while they were screaming to everybody that they were atheists and didn't *believe* in God.

But eventually they woke up, and that's what spiritual awakening really means: we get a series of wake-up calls, and slowly, little by little, we begin opening our eyes to one aspect of the spiritual life, and then another. Sometimes we have to have the spiritual equivalent of God shouting in our ear and finally beating us over the head with a two-by-four, before we open our eyes and begin to notice.

A psychotherapist came into the O.A. program after his doctor told him that he had Type II diabetes, and he discovered that he could not stop binging on sweets like candy and doughnuts and cheesecake, even though he knew rationally that this was going to kill him, and in a very slow, painful way: going blind, having to have a leg amputated, going into kidney failure, having a stroke and being put into a nursing home, and so on. He had been brought up in a Jewish family, but now he was an intellectual and a sceptic, totally hostile to any full-fledged notion of God. He tried Zen Buddhist meditation and other esoteric forms of prayer, searching for unusual spiritual states or awarenesses, while he kept on going on eating binges every few days. Finally his sponsor said to him one afternoon:

> You're looking in all these strange, exotic places for terribly subtle things. When God really wants to speak to you, he shouts at you as loud as he can. God speaks to you through the other people around you and through the events going on in your life. What he is now shouting at you at the top of his lungs is: "If you don't change your fundamental attitude towards me and towards life in the universe I run, you are going to die miserably. And this time, I'm going to let you die. And your blood will be on your own head."
>
> You've read the Hebrew scriptures. When the God who commanded Joshua to fight the battle of Jericho, and David to fight the Philistines, says something like this to you, does he mean business? You bet your boots he means business!

I don't think anyone starts to work the twelve-step program seriously until they wake up to the fact that it is for them a matter of life and death.

Spiritual Awakening No. 1
Waking up to the fact that I am caught in a spiritual life
or death situation, and maybe even a literal life or death
situation.

The death rate among alcoholics who do not make it into the A.A. program is at least 40%, and many of those who do not die escape this only by being locked up for the rest of their lives, or by having family who act as their total caretakers. Al-Anon people talk about how often they seriously considered suicide, and all know of people who were beaten to death or shot or stabbed to death by their alcoholic or drug-addict spouses. Sexual addicts die from sexually-transmitted diseases like AIDS or are beaten to death in back alleys. Chronic overeaters die from heart attacks or strokes, or eventually suffocate from the weight of their own body mass pressing on their chests, while anorexics literally starve themselves to death.

But it is the death of the spirit which weighs most heavily on people who need the twelve-step program. They become locked into a living hell of loneliness and isolation, bitterness and rage, the injured sense of being wronged, anxiety and desperation, despair and the numbing of all feelings. There is an old A.A. saying: *Religion is for people who are scared of going to hell, twelve-step spirituality is for people who have already been there.* As an old-timer from Ft. Wayne, Indiana, once put it, "I've been to the pit and seen the varmint." Only those who have actually been there understand that *this kind of language is no exaggeration.*

The spirituality of the twelve-step program is very different from the spirituality of the medieval monasteries and convents, and the teaching heard in most churches, synagogues, mosques, and Buddhist or Hindu religious centers. What makes the twelve-step program different is that it is such a *tightly focused spirituality.* It takes one central problem and brings together a group of people, all of whom share that one central problem. The life or death of their spirits, and perhaps even the life or death of their bodies, depends upon whether they can work together to find some solution to that one central problem.

Alcoholics Anonymous, the original twelve-step group, was from the beginning determined never to water their program down by trying to include people who suffered from any problem other than alcoholism. This was because they found from the beginning—partially from their experience with the Oxford Group—that if you destroyed the central focus by trying to deal with any and all sorts of spiritual problems, that this kind of spirituality didn't work at all any more.

Having this central focus gives a spiritual group of this sort a great advantage: a totally objective criterion for determining whether I am really working the spiritual program at all. We remember one of the old A.A. mottos: *Any day I don't drink is a good day.* If I am an alcoholic, then no matter how well I can delude myself into *thinking* I am working the program, if I'm still going out there and drinking, I'm only kidding myself.

But on the other side, if I'm feeling low and depressed and think that I'm screwing the program up, and that I don't understand anything, and that I'm just a failure at working the program—but day after day, twenty-four hours at a time, I'm keeping the plug in the jug—then these thoughts aren't real either. Any day I don't drink is a good day. If I'm not drinking, then I'm doing *something* right in my spiritual life—and something that is very, very hard to do—much harder by far than the little stuff I'm so worried about right now, which in fact I'll also eventually learn to handle, in due time.

The biggest danger in any spiritual program is self-delusion. I learn how to say the right words; on many occasions I learn how to make it *look like* I am doing the right thing. But in fact I'm just kidding myself: I'm not really going at it wholeheartedly, in complete surrender and totally single-minded commitment, at the levels that really matter.

Keeping everyone's eyes on this central focus—the problem of alcohol in the case of the alcoholic—also enables the members of the group to separate the wheat from the chaff, the essential from the inessential, in all the other areas of the spiritual life. The early A.A. program discovered some surprising things this way: that a lot of the different kinds of doctrines and dogmas that most religions stressed so strongly didn't in fact seem to matter at all, but that there were certain central spiritual attitudes and certain basic kinds of actions which had to be taken with a total seriousness and single-minded intensity that made a good many ordinary religious folk look like mere amateurs by comparison.

Spiritual Awakening No. 2
Waking up to the fact that I am a spiritual being, but with only a weak human spirit. I am not superhuman, I am not all-powerful, and I am not a god.

In the A.A. program, the first step says "We admitted we were powerless over alcohol—that our lives had become unmanageable." The hardest thing for an alcoholic to do was to admit his powerlessness, over *anything at all*. At the spiritual level, one of the principal symptoms of the disease was the alcoholic's belief that he not only could, but had to, manage and control *everything* in his life. He had to do everything by sheer will-power, by iron self-control, by outwitting everybody else, by being more aggressive, or by being more cleverly manipulative. Since he was, like God, the "judge of all men" who ruthlessly condemned everybody who didn't meet his own high standards, he believed that he had to make himself meet those same impossibly perfectionistic standards by sheer will-power. Since no human being alive has that much power, the alcoholic eventually finds himself plunged into either gross hypocrisy and denial, or (if he's more honest with himself) shame and hopeless depression.

People who enter the twelve-step program have to have a painful wake-up call here. Yes indeed, I myself am a spiritual being, but I am only an ordinary fallible human spirit with strictly limited power. Trying to pretend that I myself am superhuman—that is, that I myself am God, or that I *have to be* my own God because that's all there is, *me*—is the basic underlying thread which runs through most of my other spiritual delusions. Waking up to the fact that I am not God is a truly profound spiritual awakening to somebody who's been snoozing away on that one for most of his life.

These first two acts of spiritual awakening are quite profound realizations, but people need to wake up to some other things too, in order to get properly launched into working the twelve-step program. The second step in the twelve-step program, for example, says: "Came to believe that a Power greater than ourselves could restore us to sanity."

Spiritual Awakening No. 3
Waking up to the fact that there is some spiritual power outside myself which I can draw on to stop being over-powered by my own self-destructive urges.

The Big Book stated frankly that the removal of this overwhelming compulsion required a miracle: a miracle which our higher power had to work for us every day, one day at a time. The only thing which could have the power to block the alcoholic's uncontrollable desire to drink was something which had a kind of energy which we could not explain by ordinary scientific principles or rational analysis: a great universal force which operated in a way which was obviously real, but also uncanny and fundamentally mysterious in the way it worked.

The second step also talks about sanity and insanity. In order to work the steps, we not only have to realize our total powerlessness over the compulsion which is destroying us, we also have to grasp—a tiny partial recognition anyway—that our behavior in this area is totally insane.[3] The way we give in to our compulsion to self-destruct is weird and outlandish in a grotesque and horrifyingly irrational way. There has to be something uncanny about the higher power which can save us, *because there is something uncanny about the force which is destroying us.*

An Irishman who owned a major advertising company talked once about his horror, towards the end of his drinking career, when he faced his first drink of the day. He didn't want the drink, he didn't want what the alcohol would do to him, he didn't want how it would make him feel—but some bizarre inner compulsion made him reach out and pour a drink from the bottle into a glass. It wasn't until his third glass or so of whiskey, he said, that he could pour another drink without the horror.

A compulsive overeater who was trying to work the O.A. program went to a Christmas party where he worked. The woman at the food table said to him, "Be sure and grab a piece of that cheesecake before it's all gone." The next thing he knew he had piled a piece on his plate, on top of his mashed potatoes, and found himself gobbling it down. He didn't like that kind of cheesecake, he didn't like the way it tasted, it was all mixed up with his mashed potatoes, he didn't like the way it was making him feel, but he couldn't stop himself. He began to feel a little sick and headachy almost immediately, and then, to his even greater horror, he went back and got another piece of the cloyingly sweet cheesecake and ate that too. Then he felt physically ill and like he had a hangover for hours afterwards.

The compulsion that is destroying us makes no sense in any normal kind of sense. The only way to combat an uncanny and totally nonrational destructive power is by calling on a kind of higher power which is also—though in a good way, instead of an evil way—uncanny and unexplainable in the way it works. When we're dealing with this kind of insane compulsion, the human reason is out of its depth through and through.

Now one of the biggest problems here is that the insanity which is driving us into destroying ourselves—and not even caring about the fact that we are obviously destroying ourselves—seeps through and permeates all our other thoughts as well. Only when I'm a newcomer to the program, I can't see that yet. "Maybe the way I'm destroying myself with alcohol (or whatever) is insane," I say, "but all my other thinking is totally logical, and I'm an extremely intelligent person, who knows a whole lot more and is much smarter than all these other people around me."

No, the problem is that when I'm trying to figure out what's possible and what's impossible, what's real fact and what's just fancy theories, what's genuinely logical and rational and what's superstitious nonsense or just plain stupid, *the insanity which is making me destroy myself with alcohol* (or whatever) *is also creeping in and corrupting my thinking here too.* Over and over I need to remind myself of one of the classic sayings of the A.A. old-timers: My best thinking got me here. That means, no matter how hard I think, even my very best thinking will never get me out of my mess. My best thinking got me here. That means I'm going to have to do some things which don't make sense to me, and I'm going to have to honestly try some things which I am convinced would never work.

Spiritual Awakening No. 4
Waking up to the fact that the higher power can never be
fully comprehensible to me, so I must always do some things
on faith. I do not know all the answers, and never will.

One important type of spirituality in early Christianity claimed that the ultimate mystical vision of God was a truly keen awareness of the totally incomprehensible nature of the ultimate ground of this universe. St. Gregory of Nyssa in the fourth century was one of the major early teachers who spoke that way. He said that this mystical vision felt a little like staring over the edge of a cliff, and seeing that the abyss which lay beneath was literally bottomless. And yet it was O.K. to look at it, and I didn't fall plunging into it. Something held me up even though I could see nothing there. And that was enormously comforting, because then I started to understand that it did no harm to my spirit when I didn't know all the answers, and that there was a *something* which held my spirit up even when I seemed to have no control at all over my surroundings.[4]

The word mystical in Greek (*mystikos*) basically meant "secret." What this fourth kind of spiritual awakening is giving us is a handy little secret about the universe that most of the world doesn't know. The world is full of people who think they know all the answers to everything. Waking up to the fact that I do not know all the answers, and never will, is a great spiritual awakening indeed for people who are stuck tight on a path that leads to certain doom.

Realizing that I am simply going to have to take certain things on faith is part of this great spiritual awakening. Nobody's asking any newcomer to the program to take anything on totally blind faith—this is not what's being asked. We get back to the criterion provided by the central focus of a twelve-step group. If I'm an alcoholic going to A.A. meetings, then all these people at the meetings who've been sober for years *must know something I don't know.* And so maybe I'd better at least experiment and try a few of the beliefs and behaviors which they say helped them so much.

So what happens? I try a few of these things and discover to my surprise that they actually do work. I can't argue with that, because now I can see it genuinely working in my own life. The genuine spirit of modern science is NOT deciding in advance, on grand theoretical grounds, what will and will not work. The genuine spirit of modern science is to try something and see what in fact actually happens: this is called "the experimental method."

And so I slowly start waking up to the fact that I don't know all the answers now, and it starts looking more and more like I never will know all the answers. The more I try to explain and make sense out of who and what this higher power is, the more *incomprehensible* the whole thing becomes. I try to ask old-timers in the program who or what this higher power actually is, and the longer they've been in the program, the less they seem to be able to say in answer to my question.

The reason I have mentioned St. Gregory of Nyssa and other spiritual teachers in his tradition, is to point out that the word "incomprehensible" is a good technical theological term. When something is incomprehensible to me, sometimes it means that the person talking to me is simply totally muddled and confused and stupid. When something is incomprehensible to me, there are other times when it's me who's too stupid to understand it. But when we use the word "incomprehensible" as a technical theological term for talking about God, what we mean is that God is infinite and my human mind is finite, so I have no internal way of *grasping* what that kind of infinite entity would be. Parts of the world around me may be reasonably comprehensible to me, but whatever we want to call God—the ground of being, or the creator of this universe, or the guiding spirit of nature—this higher power involves something which is intrinsically *beyond* all these comfortable and comprehensible parts of the world around me that I can analyze and categorize and bend to the framework of my own mind and will.[5]

Realizing that the higher power will never be fully comprehensible to me is a great spiritual awakening indeed. This is not just a realization that can be put in good, traditional technical theological terminology—waking up to *the fundamental incomprehensibility of the ground of being* has always been regarded in much of the Christian spiritual tradition as the primary knowledge which is truly attained only by the greatest saints. And this is equally true in many of the religions of Asia: in some varieties of Buddhism and Hinduism, this is what they call salvation itself.[6]

At this point, most newcomers to the twelve-step program are going to be saying to themselves, "This sounds like nothing but a totally bleak and cynical scepticism about *everything*. How could this kind of completely negative attitude possibly *save* anybody?" But the old-timers aren't reacting like that at all: instead, they're just nodding their heads, and saying, "Yep, incomprehensible to *me*. But what's your problem?" What these old-timers discovered was that finally waking up to this fact was, oddly enough, a *comforting* realization. Truly acknowledging this fact brings about an almost instant inner calm and serenity. The old-timers tried to sum up part of what they had experienced in a simple little piece of advice: Let go and let God.

Spiritual Awakening No. 5
Waking up to the fact that, when things are beyond my own power to sort out or control, it's perfectly safe to let go and let God.

When people first come into the twelve-step program the thing they find hardest to do is to simply let go and allow themselves to be vulnerable. "I can't be safe," they say to themselves, "unless *I'm* in control." In fact, if it's being safe that's all-important to you, what could be safer than to place yourself totally into the hands of an all-powerful, all-loving, all-forgiving, all-helping God?

But how do people in fact first arrive at this great spiritual awakening? We're never willing to try this at first until we're caught in a situation that seems totally impossible and hopeless. We flail and struggle and analyze and plot and scheme and attack and plead, and everything just gets worse and worse. We claw and scrabble and try to hang on, but we just keep slipping. Many a person in A.A. has made the comment, "I've never let go of anything that didn't have claw marks on it." So finally, as an act of pure desperation, I decide to follow the suggestion: *Let go and let God.*

As one experienced Al-Anon put it,[7] "I don't know why people always put surrendering in such a negative way. *When I'm fighting a war I'm losing, surrendering means I get to live instead of having to die.*"

And what happens? If I really do it, I feel a whole lot calmer right away. Most of the time, the problem then ends up resolving itself in a way that is much better than I could have managed. "Gee," I say to myself, "is it possible that God can actually run the universe better than I can?" Then I laugh at myself for saying that, because of course he can. Even in the worst possible cases, when I finally let go and let God, I will be able to walk away feeling *satisfied*—both satisfied with myself and satisfied with the outcome—at the most basic level. The inner torment will have ceased. My own spirit will no longer be tortured night and day, and I will rediscover a realm of calm and peace.

At one level, we could describe this fifth kind of spiritual awakening as learning how to have faith. That's another technical theological term. In the New Testament, the word for faith (*pistis*) does not mean believing in all sorts of complicated theological doctrines and dogmas: It does NOT mean believing in the doctrine of the Trinity or the Virgin Birth or the literal infallibility of the scriptures, or any of those things like that. The New Testament word for faith (*pistis*) simply means *trust*. In order to let go and let God, I have to trust this higher power just a little bit. In the New Testament, one of the most important examples which is given of the kind of faith which saves, is the faith of Abraham (who, interestingly, wasn't even a Christian). Abraham was a nomad, living in the deserts of Iraq, when God told him, "Go west." Abraham was not told what would happen as he went westwards, or where exactly he was eventually supposed to end up, and he wasn't told anything at all at this point about what he was supposed to do after he got there. But he simply began trudging westwards into the trackless desert, simply acting on trust.[8]

So the faith that saves is a kind of trust which gives us enough courage to venture out into the totally unknown. It sets us on a journey in which we frequently have no clear grasp of anything except the next step along the path. But faith in a good higher power *does* enable us to know what the next step is supposed to be.

Many a person in A.A. remembers coming in as a newcomer and having one of the old-timers snarl at him, *"Don't think, don't drink, go to meetings, do the next right thing."* And they say that the point when life started getting better was when they started trying to follow this advice.

So again, what actually happens? I'm frantic because I've got ten dozen things to do, all of which seem like they've got to be figured out and solved immediately. I'm getting so angry and irritable that I'm snapping at everybody who comes near me, or I'm falling into a blind panic and goofing up even simple things, or I'm starting to fall into global despair and terminal depression. The fundamental feeling is one of simply being *totally overwhelmed* by it all. Then I hear a whisper inside my mind, and this is when the really bad danger comes. The little voice whispers: "You need a drink," or "Eating a dozen doughnuts in one sitting would make you feel better," or "Why don't you take your credit cards and go shopping?" Wrong, wrong, wrong!!!

The twelve-step program tells me that what I need to do right now is find a place where I can calm down and relax a bit, and just remember that there is a higher power who rules this universe. Get into the Here-and-Now for a moment.[9] I need to tell all the committees which are meeting in my mind to go out and take a break too. And I need to let myself just relax and be where I am, in the Here-and-Now, not trying to figure out anything at all. I can say a short prayer of praise or gratitude to God if I want to, like "Thank you for the tree outside my window," or "God is all-great and all-powerful," but as long as I have some belief in a higher power, I actually don't have to *consciously* think about my higher power at all for this to work.

Then when I've gotten calmed down enough, I simply ask myself, "So what's the next right thing to do?" And at that point, newcomers to the program discover, to their enormous surprise, that they intuitively know what would be the next right thing to do. *Do the next right thing.* Son of a gun! Somehow or other, we actually know, just intuitively, what that should be.

Doing the next right thing is usually pretty simple: something like "wash the dishes," or "go have lunch," or "since you can't do anything about it tonight anyway, go to sleep and deal with it tomorrow." Sometimes doing the next right thing means: call my sponsor, or go to a meeting, or pray about it even if I don't think it will work. But I *will* know what it is that I should do.

What is especially interesting here is that there has to be a link somehow between something in my own spirit and something in the Universal Spirit, where if I just learn how to calm down and relax a little bit more, I find that I can receive an amazing amount of *guidance* (an idea that A.A. took over from the Oxford Group).[10] It is a kind of *spiritual* guidance that nevertheless tells me how to act in a totally *practical* and *common sense* way.

Some of the medieval theologians talked about what they called the *scintilla*, a little spark within the human spirit, which enabled me to know at least who God was basically, and the fundamental difference between right and wrong. The little spark wasn't big enough to enable me to save myself without the aid of God's grace and the help of God's messengers, but I could learn how to fan this little spark up until it grew into a much bigger blaze. It was the connecting point, the *Anknüpfungspunkt*, between God's grace and my soul. The *Twenty-Four Hours a Day* book talks about this divine spark in the readings for April 30 and March 4.[11]

So if I've having great difficulty making a certain decision, it often helps to go down into my own heart and consult with this little spark of what I myself call "deep conscience." I need to ask questions like, "Are there actually any deep moral issues involved here at all?" Some decisions don't involve any great moral issue really. But I also need to ask questions like, "Am I tempted one direction by the desire to hurt or harm another human being? To get even with them, or show them, or make it clear to them exactly what I think of them?" "Am I being driven one direction by pure, undiluted personal selfishness, where I really don't give a darn about the effect of my action on anybody else?"[12] And in fact, we DO KNOW at this fundamental level when our motives are bad—IF we take the time to stop and honestly ask ourselves.

Spiritual Awakening No. 6
Waking up to the fact that, by some inner spiritual capacity, as long as I remember that there is a higher power who governs this universe, I DO KNOW the difference between right and wrong well enough to make simple decisions about my own actions.

This particular act of spiritual awakening starts to make my life much calmer right away. I find myself handling all kinds of situations fairly smoothly, when before they used to drive me totally crazy. Other people may still cause me trouble, but now *I'm no longer continually bringing non-stop trouble on my own head by my own actions*. The twelve-step program teaches me a much nicer and better way to live, and this is something which I can evaluate firsthand for myself. I don't have to take anyone else's word for it in the long run.

The Two Red Flags of Spiritual Danger: Resentment and Fear

The twelve-step program is different from most other spiritual disciplines because it has such a tightly focused spirituality. If I am an alcoholic, then I have a totally objective criterion for measuring how well I am working my spiritual program: If I can stay sober today, then for today I've worked my spiritual program right, down at the basic and most important level. I have followed the life-saving principle: *First Things First.* If I am an alcoholic, but have nevertheless stayed sober today, then I know that God has been with me today, and that I stand as one approved.

But there is a second level of objective evaluation in the twelve-step program. If my spirit is being tortured by resentment or fear, these are the two major red flags of warning.[13] At some level or other, I am not working my spiritual program as well as I could. As long as I remain totally honest with myself, these two warning flags are also quite objective. I cannot delude myself into thinking that I am a marvellously spiritual person, when all I am doing is muttering fine words and going through the external motions. And I can also use these two red flags to evaluate other spiritual ideas. No matter how many theologians in fancy robes insist that I must pray using certain particular words, or that I must follow certain particular religious rules, if these words and rules in fact do not help in bringing me out of my resentment and fear, then *they are not right for me.*

It is resentment and fear which we will use as our guidelines to writing our fourth steps, when we make "a searching and fearless moral inventory of ourselves." But long before we get to the point of putting pen to paper and starting the actual writing, we need to learn that when a particular resentment or fear reaches too high a level, or sticks in our minds too long, that something is not working right in our spiritual programs.

I may have to do a lot of experimenting to discover what exactly is not working right, and to find out what I need to do to heal or repair it.

Trying a lot of experiments is necessary because different individuals are different enough from one another to make ironclad general rules practically useless. That was the most important thing the early A.A.'s learned from reading William James' book, *The Varieties of Religious Experience*. James, the greatest American psychologist of his time, pointed out that there had to be numerous different varieties of religious systems because different human beings had such different basic psychologies.[14] What would heal one person might make another person even worse.

So each individual who enters the twelve-step program has to make a whole series of experiments. That is why *it takes time* to get a feel for how to work the program, and *it takes time* to discover what works for me. It also *takes time* to heal a wounded spirit in the same way that it takes days, and sometimes even weeks and months, to heal a bodily injury. Even the best medical doctors sometimes have to experiment to see what medication or treatment will actually heal a particular patient's illness.

Resentment and fear are so deadly because they make my own inner life completely miserable. If I don't do something about this, then sooner or later the misery will become so great that I will be driven back to the bottle, or whatever escape mechanism it was that always destroyed me in the past. Resentment and fear also block me from being fully aware of the continual loving presence of my higher power, which means that I am cut off from the source of grace that keeps me from turning back once again down the road to doom.

Spiritual Awakening No. 7
Waking up to the fact that resentment and fear poison my
spirit and block my mind from the fullest conscious
awareness of my higher power.

Now resentment can take a whole bunch of different forms, so I need to become aware of how to recognize it when it begins to take over my thoughts. Some of the forms it takes are: Overpowering anger or rage that just continues to build up inside. Bitterness. Wanting to get revenge, to get even, to "show them." I find myself giving someone the cold shoulder, where whenever the other person tries to talk with me in a friendly way, I deliberately remain cold and distant. Self-pity is just a kind of cowardly form of resentment: I sit and brood on "how badly so-and-so treated me." A certain amount of what we call ordinary, low-level chronic depression is this kind of self-pity, produced because the depressed person cannot make himself let go of the resentment. Being judgmental towards other people all the time is also a form of resentment. It can take the form of furious tirades within my own mind against what I have labelled as the sins of the wrongdoer. This kind of judgmentalism is also strongly linked to a lot of ordinary, low-level chronic depression.[15]

When the typical newcomer to the twelve-step program falls into a destructive resentment against someone, he is apt to start arguing with the old-timers, "But you don't understand, I was right and he was wrong!" And the old-timers just smile serenely and ask a few questions back: "Would you rather be right or happy?" "Have you ever heard the phrase 'dead right'?" "Is this the hill you want to die on?" *"How important is it REALLY?"*

Now feeling anger in certain kinds of situations is a perfectly normal reaction. We're not saying that it's wrong or sinful to feel angry. What the twelve-step program does say is that it is vitally important to handle this anger in the right kind of way, and if it gets too big, or lasts too long, then we have to defuse it.

And we need to say something similar about fear. Some kinds of fear are healthy: The drunk says, "Whaddaya mean I'm drunk? I'm not drunk! Of course I can drive you home in my car." Healthy fear means recognizing that, whatever else happens, don't get in a car with that stumble-bum behind the wheel!

But there is another kind of fear, the sort which corrodes away and destroys our lives. Just as resentment takes different shapes, the kind of fear that causes us so much trouble takes different forms too: Afraid I'd be embarrassed or humiliated if I did what I really know is right for me. Being filled with so much anxiety in some kinds of situations that I can't think straight (like the student who knows the material, but walks into the exam, has a mind-paralyzing anxiety attack, and fails the test). Excessively afraid that "I might make a mistake." Afraid to say "no" when somebody asks me to do something I know is wrong, or when somebody is violating my essential personal boundaries. Being afraid to try something that I would actually like to try doing—in spite of the fact that, even if I tried and failed, it wouldn't be the end of the world. If I'm always trying to do things to prove that "I'm a real man," or "I'm a very feminine woman," that's always a reaction to some big underlying fear. Another form of fear produces constant worrying about the future, to such a point that my life becomes a total misery. Some people attempt to deal with this kind of fear by trying to plot and plan everything to death. What we call *shame* is the fear that "if anyone else ever found out," I would be totally disgraced as a person, and could never look anyone in the eye again.[16] And above all else, people who come into twelve-step programs are so often tormented by *the primal fear of being rejected and abandoned.*

Now since resentment and fear put my mind in such an inner turmoil, I find that I can't concentrate on anything good or enjoyable or positive. My inner life becomes a torment and a misery. But even worse, the internal turmoil is so great that I cannot maintain any strong conscious awareness of my higher power—my mind's just too busy thinking about the extremely painful resentments and fears. And if I try to pray, my mind won't stay still long enough to get through the prayers. Or even if I make myself mumble them mechanically, I don't feel as though the prayers are really "connecting" with my higher power. The old medieval term for this spiritual condition was *aridity*, which meant being spiritually "dry," like a plant that's gone too long without water.[17]

Now this puts me in a bind, because I have to figure out some way of consciously reconnecting with my higher power anyway, because that's the only way I'm really going to get out of the grip of those resentments and fears. Only the power of the universal spirit is great enough to still the waves on these troubled waters.

Spiritual Awakening No. 8
Waking up to the fact that the only way to genuinely heal the resentments and fears which torment my spirit is by drawing upon the healing and restoring energy of this higher spiritual power, even when my heart is troubled.

Newcomers to the twelve-step program often do things like come into a meeting and say, "I haven't been to a meeting for the last two weeks, because I was feeling too upset and down." Wrong! That's when we *most* need to go to meetings. They say things like, "I know you people tell me to pray to my higher power, but I'm so upset that when I tried to do that, I didn't feel any sense of anyone hearing me, so I just quit. It just wasn't working." Wrong! That's when we need to keep on praying *at all costs*. They say things like, "You tell me to pray for my enemies, but I hate that guy! He's a total jerk. I tried to pray for him, but I couldn't because it's too dishonest, I'd just be a hypocrite." Wrong! What were our instructions? Praying for our *enemies*, by definition, means forcing ourselves to pray these prayers for those whom we believe have hurt us the most deeply, which means those whom we hate the most.

One evening at the old Golden Key group, one of the newcomers said, "But prayer doesn't work unless you have faith, and on this issue I'm struggling with, I just don't believe that there's a higher power who could be talked into doing anything that way. I don't have that kind of faith, I just don't." One of the old-timers said, "Then pray for faith." The newcomer said, "But if you have to have faith before your prayers are answered, and you don't have faith, then wouldn't you have to have faith first before you could pray for faith? And then you wouldn't need to pray for faith because you already had it." The old-timers just started laughing at him, and finally red-headed Jane snorted and said, "Just pray. Just do it."

This eighth spiritual awakening is one of the most important of all for newcomers. *The whole program is deliberately designed to work while we're actually having the problems, not after we've already solved them.* The program is designed so that it works even when we're totally upset, or completely down and blue. The prayers work even when the mental static in our own minds keeps us from being aware that God is hearing us and responding to us: God *always* hears us, even when we can't hear him.

When we are asked to pray for our *enemies*, what the word "enemies" means is people we hate: It is automatically understood by God that the first time I make myself say the words, "God, please bless so-and-so," that what I actually want in my heart is for something really bad to happen to them! But God says, pray that prayer *anyway*, even if the first few times the words practically stick in your throat; I want you to *rehearse* acting like and talking like one of my children, even if you're just play-acting at first and feel like a total phony, until one day you'll be doing it, and it won't be an act any more. *If you practice the proper motion, you'll create the proper emotion.*

Now it is true that the more faith and trust we have in our higher power, the more we will be able to draw from his power and grace. But the faith that saves when the chips are down is a much more primitive kind of faith. It is the willingness to at least try. Faith means being willing to actually DO something even when I don't understand why. I don't even have to believe it will work, as long as I just honestly try to do it, and that means actually DOING it, no matter how I feel about it.

John Calvin, the sixteenth-century Protestant reformer, put a greater emphasis on faith as the means to salvation than just about any other theologian who ever lived. We are saved, Calvin said, *sola fide* and *sola gratia*, by faith alone and by grace alone. But in the section on faith in his *Institutes*, Calvin says bluntly that *there is no faith unmixed with doubt*.[18] If we had no doubts, then it wouldn't be faith, it would be knowledge. If we weren't phony, dishonest good-for-nothings, then it wouldn't be salvation by grace, because we wouldn't even need saving in the first place. We'd already be perfect little angels who had our lives under control and everything all worked out.

Remember what red-headed Jane said to the confused, babbling newcomer as she sat there laughing at him: "Just pray. Just do it." Do that and you will live.

Emmet Fox: Staying on the Beam and the Golden Key

The preacher Emmet Fox was a great favorite of the old-timers in the A.A. program back in the earliest days. They strongly recommended, for example, that all newcomers read his book on *The Sermon on the Mount*. One short piece that Fox wrote—I do not know where or when—was printed in the old Detroit pamphlet (a little booklet for newcomers written by the members of the Detroit A.A. group not long after it was founded).[19] It tells us what we basically have to do when resentment or fear start to overcome us.

Staying on the Beam
Today most commercial flying is done on a radio beam. A directional beam is produced to guide the pilot to his destination, and as long as he keeps on this beam he knows that he is safe, even if he cannot see around him for fog, or get his bearings in any other way.

As soon as he gets off the beam in any direction he is in danger, and he immediately tries to get back on to the beam once more.

Those who believe in the All-ness of God, have a spiritual beam upon which to navigate on the voyage of life.

> As long as you have peace of mind and some sense of the Presence of God you are on the beam, and you are safe, even if outer things seem to be confused or even very dark; but as soon as you get off the beam you are in danger.
>
> You are off the beam the moment you are angry or resentful or jealous or frightened or depressed; and when such a condition arises you should immediately get back on the beam by turning quietly to God in thought, claiming His Presence, claiming that His Love and Intelligence are with you, and that the promises in the [great spiritual books of the past] are true today. If you do this you are back on the beam, even if outer conditions and your own feelings do not change immediately. You are back on the beam and you will reach port in safety.
>
> Keep on the beam and nothing shall by any means hurt you.

Now it is important to note how Fox warned there at the end, that once you have turned to God in thought, you are back on the beam and are totally safe once again, "even if ...your own feelings do not change immediately."

When people first come into twelve-step programs, they want *instant mood altering*. If I'm feeling bad in any way, I just can't stand that bad feeling, and I've got to get into a good mood right this very second. Alcohol and drugs promise old Mr. Instant Feel-Good, and other people find the same magical lure dangled in front of them by a box of a dozen doughnuts, or a place where they can go cruising for sex, or by the prospect of making a list of all the faults of the person I live with, and then either planning out how to force or manipulate this person into changing, or at least being able to sit around smugly thinking about how much more superior and nobler I am than *that* jerk. Mr. Feel-Good can make your emotions and your mood change right away—he's not lying to you there—but the price you will pay is feeling even worse after Mr. Feel-Good goes away, and eventually totally destroying yourself.

What happens if you do what Emmet Fox suggests instead? Especially if you're a newcomer, you don't necessarily find the painful emotions *completely* disappearing *right there on the spot*. But you do get your head back together, and will become able to see a path appearing—a path you hadn't noticed before—which will lead you out of the unbearable situation. Since this takes you out of the total inner confusion and panic, and the feeling of being completely overwhelmed, it *does in that way* start to make you feel a little better almost immediately. And then as you begin actually working your way out of the problem, you start to feel a whole lot better about it. You talk to somebody in the program about how you're feeling, you maybe go to a meeting, you get a night's sleep, and when you wake up the next morning, you'll often find that the painful feelings and emotions are totally gone. At the very least, if you've done this honestly, you'll feel ten times better by then.

There is another famous little piece that Emmet Fox authored, a small leaflet which he wrote in 1931 for the Unity Church,[20] called "The Golden Key":

The Golden Key

Scientific prayer will enable you to get yourself, or anyone else, out of any difficulty. It is the golden key to harmony and happiness.

To those who have no acquaintance with the mightiest power in existence, this may appear to be a rash claim, but it needs only a fair trial to prove that, without a shadow of a doubt, it is a just one. You need take no one's word for it, and you should not. Simply try it for yourself.

God is omnipotent, and we are God's image and likeness and have dominion over all things. This is the inspired teaching, and it is intended to be taken literally, at its face value. The ability to draw on this power is not the special prerogative of the mystic or the saint, as is so often supposed.... Everyone has this ability. Whoever you are, wherever you may be, the golden key to harmony is in your hand now. This is because in scientific prayer it is God who works, and not you, and so your particular limitations or weaknesses are of no account in the process.... Beginners often get startling results the first time, for all that is essential is to have an open mind and sufficient faith to try the experiment. Apart from that, you may hold any views on religion, or none.

As for the actual method of working, like all fundamental things, it is simplicity itself. All you have to do is this: *Stop thinking about the difficulty, whatever it is, and think about God instead.* This is the complete rule, and if only you will do this, the trouble, whatever it is, will disappear. It makes no difference what kind of trouble it is. It may be a big thing or a little thing; it may concern health, finance, a lawsuit, a quarrel, an accident, or anything else conceivable; but whatever it is, stop thinking about it and think of God instead—that is all you have to do.

It could not be simpler, could it? God could scarcely have made it simpler, and yet it never fails to work when given a fair trial.

Do not try to form a picture of God, which is impossible. Work by rehearsing anything or everything that you know about God.

God is wisdom, truth, inconceivable love.

> God is present everywhere, has infinite power,
> knows everything,

and so on. It matters not how well you may think you understand these things; go over them repeatedly.

But you must stop thinking of the trouble, whatever it is. The rule is to think about God. If you are thinking about your difficulty, you are not thinking about God. To be continually glancing over your shoulder in order to see how matters are progressing is fatal, because it is thinking of the trouble, and you must think of God and nothing else. Your object is to drive the thought of the difficulty out of your consciousness, for a few moments at least, substituting for it the thought of God. This is the crux of the whole thing. If you can become so absorbed in this consideration of the spiritual world that you forget for a while about the difficulty, you will find that you are safely and comfortably out of your difficulty—that your demonstration is made.

In order to "golden key" a troublesome person or a difficult situation, think, "Now I am going to 'golden key' John, or Mary, or that threatened danger"; then proceed to drive all thought of John, or Mary, or the danger out of your mind, replacing it with the thought of God.

By working in this way about a person, you are not seeking to influence his conduct in any way, except that you prevent him from injuring or annoying you, and you do him nothing but good. Thereafter, he is certain to be in some degree a better, wiser, and more spiritual person, just because you have "golden keyed" him. A pending lawsuit or other difficulty would probably fade out harmlessly without coming to a crisis, justice being done to all parties concerned.

....You may repeat the operation several times a day with intervals between. Be sure, however, each time you have done it, that you drop all thought of the matter until the next time. This is important.

We have said that the golden key is simple, and so it is, but of course it is not always easy to turn. If you are very frightened or worried, at first it may be difficult to get your thoughts away from material things. But by constantly repeating a statement of absolute Truth, such as:

There is no power but God;
I am the child of God, filled and surrounded
by the perfect peace of God;
God is love;
God is guiding me now;

or, perhaps best and simplest of all,

God is with me

—however mechanical or trite it may seem—you will soon find that the treatment has begun to "take," and that your mind is clearing. Do not struggle violently; be quiet, but insistent. Each time you find your attention wandering, switch it back to God.

Do not think in advance what the solution to your difficulty will be. This is called "outlining" and will only delay the demonstration. Leave the question of ways and means to God. You want to get out of your difficulty— that is sufficient. You do your half, and God will never fail to do God's. "Whoever calls on the name of the Lord shall be saved" (Acts 2:21).

Now let's try to summarize what Emmet Fox said, to make sure that we understand it. Using this principle is very simple. I use a brief statement which I repeat in my mind as a mantra, until my thoughts are cleared and I am restored to harmony with the universe once again. He gives a number of examples of brief phrases which can be used, but I could easily make up one of my own if I wanted to:

The Golden Key

Stop thinking about the difficulty, whatever
it is, and think about God instead.
God is wisdom, God is truth, God is inconceivable love.
God is present everywhere, God has infinite power,
God knows everything.
I am the child of God, filled and surrounded by
the perfect peace of God.
God is love. God is guiding me now. God is with me.
There is no power but God.

In my own observation, *everybody I have ever met in the twelve step program who had a lot of serenity regularly used a technique that worked in some way that had the same practical effect.* They would stop thinking so much about the difficulty, whatever it was, and think about spiritual matters instead. Instead of thinking "poor me," maybe they would start thinking about something they could feel gratitude for, or something positive they could still do, or some way they could be of service to some other human being. When they became too angry over something, they would quietly walk outside and admire and enjoy the skies and trees and flowers—God's creation—until they regained their inner peace. Instead of being filled with self-righteous, superior rage and contempt, they would remember who they used to be, and how much God had forgiven them, and feel compassion and empathy for the other person instead.

When Submarine Bill's pigeons would phone him up, all upset over something—usually very late at night—he would finally tell them to go read the great passage on acceptance on page 449 of the Big Book, including the line that says: *"Nothing, absolutely nothing happens in God's world by mistake."* This is, of course, just another (perhaps even stronger) way of stating Emmet Fox's key phrase, "There is no power but God." And his pigeons would complain and grouse, but finally they would actually go read it, and immediately they would feel a whole lot better—maybe still unhappy about their situation, but certainly no longer feeling like they were totally overwhelmed and at their wit's end. And they found they could go to sleep now, instead of spending the whole night in totally pointless worry and outrage.

People with experience in the program find that, by facing all their problems with the basic assumption that God is good, and there is no power but God, they are able to simply turn the golden key—almost unconsciously and automatically after years of constant practice—and get their peace of mind back with amazing speed, and open the door to real solutions to whatever difficulties life was bringing them.

The Power of Grace

We talked about eight kinds of spiritual awakening. We can call them whatever we want to—sudden insights, moments of clarity, finally actually hearing something we have already been told for 4,285 times before without paying any attention—but the awakening process works, and it works for anyone who attends twelve step meetings regularly and actually does the steps. This is part of what has traditionally been called the work of grace: St. Augustine back at the beginning of the middle ages called it a kind of "illumination" (it played an important role in his general theory of human knowledge, and was a central topic for theologians and philosophers for centuries afterwards). Jonathan Edwards in the eighteenth century talked about it in detail in a piece called *A Divine and Supernatural Light.*[21]

But grace is even more importantly a kind of power where, as the Big Book puts it (p. 84), we find that "God is doing for us what we could not do for ourselves." This was the central teaching of the Apostle Paul in Romans 7:15–8:17, stressed even more strongly by St. Augustine and the medieval Catholic theologians, and rediscovered with enormous impact by John Wesley at the time of his Aldersgate experience, the event which sparked the eighteenth-century Methodist movement.[22] There is a power there to transform our lives, a higher power coming from outside ourselves. This is not just a theory: it really works, and it always has, for thousands of years. It is the basic key to the success of the twelve-step program, what gives it its power to genuinely change lives.

Again, *it truly works.* A new freedom and a new happiness are there for anyone who sincerely and honestly tries. There is no better or more satisfying life available on this earth, and it can be yours if you will become willing to accept a gift of *pure grace*—oh, you have to do the necessary footwork—but it is the divine grace that does the work. For those who have received this, there simply *are not words* for expressing the gratitude we feel towards the mighty hand and the outstretched arm of the one who reached down to save us.

Chapter IV

The Presence of God

1. Hearing the Word of God

Sought through prayer and meditation

The eleventh step says "sought through prayer and meditation to improve our conscious contact with God *as we understood Him*." At the bare minimum, this means that every morning I should pray "God, please keep me sober today" when I first awaken, and read in some book of daily meditations, and every evening I should pray just before I go to sleep, "God, thank you for keeping me sober today."

If I am not an alcoholic, and am using the twelve-step program to deal with some other focus issue, then I need to replace the word "sober" with some other *positive* word that describes in *positive* terms what I want to become. It doesn't work right if I use some negative phrase like "keep me from doing such-and-such" or phrases containing words like "no" or "not." The unconscious mind doesn't hear negatives in that kind of situation, so all I will be doing is encouraging my unconscious to continue living in the problem instead of living in the solution.

If I don't like the g-word, I can just leave out the word "God" or replace it with whatever I call my higher power.

Some newcomers worry because, they say, "I read my morning meditation, but I forget it immediately. If you asked me five minutes later, I couldn't even tell you what I read." They don't need to worry about this, because the reason for reading it as almost the first thing after waking up in the morning, is because the mind is especially susceptible to subconscious influence at that point. My conscious mind may have forgotten what I read, but my unconscious will have absorbed it just fine.

This is not theory, but is based on a kind of firsthand experience where you can check it out for yourself. Let us say that you start doing your morning prayer and meditation on a regular basis and keep it up for a few weeks. Then one morning you're in such a hurry that you jump into your day without doing your prayer and meditation. Before the day is over, you will notice that you feel irritable, on-edge, anxious, and spinning your wheels. As one old-timer put it, "When I miss my morning prayer and meditation one day, I notice it; when I miss it two days, my wife notices it; when I miss it three days, everybody who comes in contact with me notices it. 'What's going on with *him*? He was turning into such a nice guy. This is like the old jerk we used to avoid because he was such a pain in the neck.' "

The powerful effects of the morning prayer and meditation can be measured at the conscious level, even though the way it works is largely unconscious. In fact, an enormous amount of the program is actually absorbed at the unconscious level, which is why people who totally immerse themselves in the program make the most rapid progress: They go to meetings, and go out for coffee afterwards. They go to the potlucks and picnics and conferences and weekend retreats. They talk with people on the phone, and above all, they *hang with the winners*, drinking deeply at the unconscious level from the fountain of their serenity.

One other thing that needs to be mentioned here: When the Big Book was written back in 1939, its authors used the ordinary terminology of traditional western spirituality, where "meditation" meant reading something out of a spiritually-oriented book and then thinking about how the passage I read applied to my own specific life situation. In the years since then, many people in the United States have experimented with certain kinds of prayer brought over from Asia, like transcendental meditation (which came from India) and Zen Buddhist meditation (from Japan). In the terminology assumed by the Big Book and the twelve steps, these two techniques would have been called, not meditation, but *contemplation*.[1]

Now contemplation is one specialized form of prayer (there are also various Roman Catholic and Eastern Orthodox and Jewish ways of doing that), and there's no reason why people in the twelve step program cannot try out some kind of contemplative prayer if they want to. A lot of people experiment with it a little during their early period in the program. It strikes me however that, on the whole, the majority of people in A.A. who have long-term sobriety no longer use techniques that are structured quite like transcendental meditation. What they usually do instead is to practice the kind of prayer-without-words which the *Twenty-Four Hours* book describes, or they simply develop some sort of gentle relaxation technique: you can sit by a lake as you drink your morning coffee and watch the ducks, or take a walk in the park and look at the trees and the flowers, or sit in front of the fireplace and watch the flames dance lazily back and forth, or just go fishing without worrying about whether you catch any fish.

Hearing the Word of God in meditational literature

Now when I'm reading my daily meditation for the morning, or when I'm reading some work like the A.A. Big Book, on occasion an image, a passage, a sentence, or a single word will suddenly leap out at me. It suddenly "makes sense" of some problem I have been struggling with, or points out to me the real goal that I ought to be striving for in something that concerns me deeply, and somehow I know that this is God's truth *for me* that I am hearing. It "tells me what to do" in some specific situation, and somehow I know that this is God asking me to do it. Sometime the message makes me feel ashamed of my own attitudes and behavior, but at other times it gives me sudden comfort, or a new wave of hope.

It is a flash of insight, a moment of clarity, NOT about some grand theoretical issue, but about my own existential situation. It does not allow me to preach to other people about what they should do, or proclaim moral laws that everybody else has to follow, but it *does* tell me how I myself should actually act in certain kinds of real, practical situations. It does not allow me to set up some system of theological doctrines and dogmas that I can make everybody else follow—and burn them at the stake or something if they don't believe what I got "straight from God's mouth to my ear, by golly!"—but it *does* allow my heart to know better who God really is *for me*.

If I start learning how *to listen to this*, even more interestingly, I know within myself at some deep intuitive level that this is in fact the Word of God being spoken to me.

How do I know that this is from God? This is just my own personal opinion, but I think it's partly because I suddenly realize that what's being said there is *true*, and since God is simply the *verum ipsum*, Truth Itself, this small illumination or enlightenment must have come from him. And I also suspect that the medieval spiritual teachers may have been right when they said that there was a *scintilla* or little spark of the divine down at the bottom of the human soul.[2] The *Twenty-four Hours a Day* book refers to this in the readings for April 30 and March 4. Working on the principle of like being able to know like, the little piece of the divine within my own soul recognizes the voice of the great divine power, and instantly knows who is talking. I sometimes refer to this little spark of divine understanding within my spirit as "the scintillating center of the sober psyche," because that's a catchy little phrase that's easy to remember. In fact, it's more like a blessed inner haven of peace and calm and the kind of quiet wisdom the serenity prayer talks about.

I also think that there is a fundamental category of the human understanding (like the categories which the philosopher Kant talked about) which allows us to recognize the sacred or the divine wherever it appears, and put the right label on it once we learn to take this category of event seriously. This is the modification Rudolf Otto made in Kant's philosophy—Otto was probably the single most important and influential scholar in comparative world religions of the past century—and I myself think that Otto was right.[3]

But this is all just my own personal opinion, and it's all speculative intellectual stuff that can quickly lead people astray. When people who are intellectuals—or at least think they are!—start trying to work the twelve-step program, they frequently try to play rationalistic games, worrying over technical terms, and how to analyze this and that, so they can evade having to actually work the program the way it's written. It's all just one more form of denial or existential fleeing or avoidance—it's just a con game, in other words—and playing *that* game just keeps us on the road to doom.

Hearing the Word of God from the mouths of other people in the program

I think it can be safely said that anybody who goes to an even minimally decent twelve-step meeting will hear God talking to him through the mouths of other people in the program: words of warning, words of comfort and hope, or words of guidance. I think one good rule to follow is to remind myself that, after every meeting, I should be able to walk away with at least one thing *positive* that God told me. Not just don'ts and shouldn'ts and examples of catastrophes I need to avoid, but something strongly positive and uplifting that helps me point my own life into a more positive and worthwhile direction, and gives me the hope and courage to actually jump in and DO IT. If I haven't heard that, then I wasn't really listening to God, because that's the most important part of *every* message from him.[4]

Hearing the Word of God through the voice of my own conscience

Every person who comes into the twelve-step program still has within his or her spirit the *scintilla conscientiae*, the little spark of what I call deep conscience. Now sometimes, in order to see this little spark, you have to get in a dark room and use a magnifying glass—and squint hard too! The program doesn't get all preachy and moralistic with people like this, because it has been discovered that, sooner or later, as long as he continues to work the program, it will dawn on even a lifelong thief, for example, that every time he steals money or property from someone else, he always ends up paying the price in terms of it making his own inner resentment and fear even worse.

Nevertheless, if we take a simple set of basic moral rules, like that contained in the ten commandments for example—don't commit murder, don't steal, don't lie about other people to harm them, don't commit adultery, and so on—once we can fan that little spark of conscience up into a firm, steady glow, we find that we ourselves *know* at some deep inner level that this is the voice of God speaking the truth to us about how we have to live in order to free ourselves from the inner poison of resentment and fear.[5]

But some people get into trouble in the other direction. Some people come in filled with self-hatred and self-loathing, and feeling total shame about themselves, because they have set unrealistic and totally self-destructive goals for themselves. Some of the rules I was taught as a child, by my parents or by some of the religious leaders who instructed me, may not be good rules at all. A set of rigid, mechanical shoulds and oughts can be very destructive to the human spirit. Attempting to follow too many rules which use words like *always* and *never* will have the same effect. Trying to live by rigid, mechanical rules like this can be one of the causes of ordinary, garden-variety chronic depression.[6] Any set of moral beliefs which leaves me feeling like I'm a shameful person, who is permanently and fatally flawed as a human being, has something major wrong with it. I will be unable to hear the authentic voice of conscience when my spirit is poisoned by toxic shame of this sort.[7]

Someone brought up as a Roman Catholic may be terrified to work the steps, for fear that it will turn him into something like one of those horrible French saints who wore sackcloth and starved himself and slept on the bare stone floor of the church every night. A Protestant may be mortally afraid that it would turn her into someone like her moralistic grandmother, who went around singing hymns in her off-pitch, cracked voice all day long, and scolded her grandchildren for having any kind of innocent fun. A Jewish man stared with repulsion at the people who were twelve-stepping him and cried out, "You mean I'd have to start sitting around davening [rocking back and forth mechanically while you're praying], like those fanatical bearded rabbinical students who used to rent rooms in my grandmother's house?"

What does the Big Book say? "We are not saints.... We claim spiritual progress rather than spiritual perfection."[8] The goal God has in mind for *me* is a goal that is *right for me*, a unique goal that is in line with my own tendencies and talents and personal idiosyncrasies. God knows good and well that I'm not going to work hard and well for him unless he gives me a job that I myself can genuinely *enjoy* doing. Looking at the grand old-timers in A.A., I would say that some of them look and act like perfectly normal people (at least on the surface!), but I look at some of the others, and the only conclusion I can draw is that God must have a special fondness for lovable lunatics. It's clear that he doesn't much care what kind of crazy ways his children pick to enjoy themselves in their spare time, as long as they aren't harming themselves or anybody else while doing it.

If there are saints in A.A., they are the Laughing Saints—and sometimes the totally outrageous saints—the holy ones of God who chuckle and then throw all normal conventions and stereotypes to the four winds. They are those special few whom he chose out to send into places and situations where no one else dared go.

2. The Sacred Dimension of the World

Lori C., a psychiatric nurse who is in both A.A. and N.A., remembers her sponsor taking her over to the window—it was early evening, during the winter—and saying to her: "Make the sun rise."

Lori said, "Huh?"

Her sponsor said, "Make leaves grow on that tree."

Lori said, "Huh?"

Her sponsor said, "So you're willing to admit that there is something in this universe more powerful than you are?"

Many people who are currently in twelve step programs in this part of the country take the universe itself as their higher power, or feel this higher power most clearly when they are in contact with nature. The Al-Anon book which just came out in 1998, *Having Had a Spiritual Awakening*, has many readings that talk this way. An Al-Anon member in Germany wrote:[9]

I stopped asking, "Who or what is God?...I find contact with my Higher Power when I am walking by myself outside in nature. I'm aware of walking, I'm listening to whatever is around. Then, when I am looking, I can see what is around and in that moment I feel, I am here, and it is good that I am here—all is well! Sometimes I call my Higher Power "The Life," and whatever life brings up, I have to find an answer.

An Al-Anon member from Australia wrote about taking her breakfast outside one spring morning, and soaking up the warmth and just relaxing while listening to the birds chirp. "As I meditate, I feel very peaceful and want to stay calm and serene forever."[10]

A woman in that book tells how her Cherokee grandfather used to take her for walks when she was a little girl:[11]

I learned that the spirits of my ancestors are still alive in the hawks and eagles that fly over their lands. Often while walking to the hill above the house, my papaw would point to a red-tailed hawk and tell me, "There's your great-grandmother."

Now that she is in the Al-Anon program, she finds strength from recalling those feelings.

I love to go barefoot, to feel the heart of Mother Earth beneath my feet, keeping me grounded and connected to Her and to the land. When I look up and see "Father Sun, Grandmother Moon, and Sister Stars" that Papaw told me of, I feel connected to them, also. I feel a kinship with the hawks.... I know my papaw is at peace, soaring and happy that I am renewing the interest that he sparked in that little girl who loved to walk with him to the meadows he loved so dearly.

Now some might say to this last passage, "Oh, but that is primitive Native American belief, and not at all like the higher western spiritual tradition." Well then, let's look at a few verses of St. Francis of Assisi's famous "Hymn of the Sun," and see if you can tell that much real difference:[12]

> Be praised, O Lord, for all your creation,
> And especially for Brother Sun,
> Who brings forth the day and gives it light.
> For he is glorious and splendid in his radiance,
> And it is your likeness, Most High, which he bears.
>
> Be praised, O Lord, for Sister Moon,
> And for the stars in the heavens;
> You have set them out all bright and sparkling
> and beautiful.
>
> Be praised, O Lord, for Brother Wind,
> For the air and for the clouds,
> For calm days and stormy days,
> For through these you sustain all living things.
>
> Be praised, O Lord, for our sister, Mother Earth,
> Who nourishes us and governs us,
> And brings forth the various fruits,
> And the bright flowers and the plants.

Like the Cherokee woman whose words we read earlier, another Al-Anon in that book also talked about learning to recover an early childhood experience:[13]

> My earliest recollection of the presence of God in my
> life was after it snowed at night. I would experience feel-
> ings of peace, contentment, beauty, and holiness. Even
> though it was nighttime it would be so bright outside. I
> felt so connected to God through the beauty that He cre-
> ated; an overpowering love would swell up in me.... Now
> I realize that what I felt was unconditional love for others,
> the kind of love that God has for us.

Notice how this reading speaks of the holiness of nature, the awareness
of the *sacred* in nature. It is the perception of something much like what
some philosophers have called the sublime. The feeling of the sublime is a
mixture of awe, together with an awareness of great beauty and goodness.
But if perceived correctly, it also gives us inner calm, and a quiet kind of
simple joy. From this inner spirit of calm and joy, real love can spring.[14]

Although these are all Al-Anons talking here, my own observation is
that an incredible number of A.A. people in this area of the country regularly make contact with their higher power in similar ways. It's something
that works, and works for an awful lot of people, from naturally gentle
souls all the way to the really tough guys.

3. The Sacred within My Soul

Bill W. the tailor came into the A.A. program in Chicago in 1945 as
one of Chicago's earliest black members. He came over to South Bend,
Indiana in September 1999, now 96 years old—sober 54 years—to sit on
a panel of old-timers and answer questions from the audience.[15] A young
man named Dave asked how he understood the phrase "having had a
spiritual awakening," and his answer was reminiscent of something St.
Augustine, the great African saint, had said when he wrote his *Confessions*:
Knowledge of God is already present in my mind, locked away in forgotten

memories and unused mental faculties, that I have allowed to fall dormant. Bill the tailor said to the young man:

> Spiritual awakening. I've always had that, but about what?…I'm a Christian, I accepted Christ in 1911 as a child. But it's just certain things that I didn't *know*. See, I didn't know what alcoholism was, and is. See, I was taught that it was a habit. And spiritual awakening would take care of that. I went to my minister, and they said, "We'll pray for you." I went to the doctor, he said, "Well, I don't know what to do about it." He didn't know.
>
> But a spiritual awakening is something that you *know*, that *revives* within you. And I learned that that part of me was the part of God. See, a man is a two-fold being: spiritual and carnal. The carnal man didn't know, but the spiritual man was in there, *so when I awoke the spiritual man that was in me, then he understood what that meant:* a spiritual awakening.
>
> It had been me, but it'd been dormant. It was laying over in the corner someplace, and I hadn't been using it for the right reason. I had been using it for one thing, but not for the 'nother.
>
> And then when I camed and realized, and it was awakened within me, then that told me *who God was, what he was, and what he could do for me if I asked him.* And I turned my will and life over to the care of God as I understood—[no], not as I *understand* him. I still don't understand God. I don't understand God, I don't know why he could do something for somebody that didn't want to do something for themselves. I don't know *why*, but he *does*. He does that because he's God.

And God is a spirit, and those that worship him, worship *in spirit* and in truth. And I'm a part of that, because I'm a part of what God made. So this spiritual awakening is a-raising something that's already there, but has been sitting over here in the side of my heart, dormant. Like you've got some things at home you don't use?—it's been laying in the closet, but the clothes, they're there. But they're laying in the closet. Well, I wasn't *using* this part of me, the spiritual part, that took care of that. (Or I don't think spiritual is a part, it's a whole.) But I wasn't *using* it.

So it just laid there within me until God arised in me, and I asked him to give me what I needed. And he gave it to me, this spiritual awakening, and I have been able to give it to others. It isn't something that you get like you get this cup [of coffee I have in my hand]. That isn't it. It's a *gift* from the God of your choice, and he awakeneth it within you. He was already there—but I didn't know it, I wasn't woke....

Has to be something to awaken that, and then we'll be able to use it.

Another black old-timer from Chicago was also there, a flamboyant character named Jimmy H., with a long grey beard. When he speaks to large audiences, he literally jumps around the stage as he carries on a kind of rhyming jive patter. But underneath is a great profundity of thought. He told about his childhood in the old south:

I had a little white boy friend. We rambled around together in Shelby, Mississippi. He was gon' peep in that church, and I knew if I got caught looking in a white Christian church, what would happen to me.

To his mostly white audience, he said

> I'm not degrading nobody, I'm talking about the experiences that I've had that brings me to you.
>
> Not drinking! I'm finding out drinking and sniffing [cocaine] wasn't really the basis—the first, the primary cause—but it was in here [pointing to his own heart]. That [drinking] was a symptom. And I found out what a symptom was. A symptom presents one thing, but indicates the evidence of something else.
>
> That's what I am, and I made grammar school, that's all I had. But I'm in the greatest school for this fool!
>
> And I heard about Tennyson. Who was Tennyson? He was an English literary giant, high-level and *worse! You* know more about Tennyson than I do. And Tennyson made a statement to me, through the universal laws, 'cause he's left here, and he made a statement, you told me.
>
> He says that this God that his nation believe in—talking about who God is, and where he is—*is way up yonder in heaven somewhere.* He said that even went over his head, or something similar to it…. He said, but the God he believes in was "*nearer than breathing,*" and "*closer than hands and feet.*"
>
> So they locked me out of a church in Shelby, Mississippi. I couldn't sit in a Christian church. See, this is important to me. It ain't locked away from nothing. I seen God when I looked down here. I see God. He said "nearer than breathing," and I believe God is in all his creation. They don't talk, but "little cat, a bat, a gnat, a rat…." I know people get a headache with me!—but I believe this. If I didn't believe that, I couldn't believe in nothing. So…I see God right there, I see God in that white boy sitting

over there, all the whites that I see it, blacks, browns, yel-
lows and red, and dinosaurs, and everything else. I have
to!...

I know who the devil is too! I found out where the devil
was, in that fourth step [when I looked inside myself]. I
don't want to get caught up on that, but I see the devil
don't bother me no more. Because of you, helping me how
to handle the devil right here.

Like Bill the tailor, Jimmy H. saw a deep division within his own soul. Bill
called it the conflict between the spiritual and the carnal parts of our
minds. Jimmy personified it more strongly, as a war between God and the
devil.

Early Christianity took the demonic very seriously too: back in the
fourth century frequent references were made to this in St. Macarius' *Fifty
Spiritual Homilies*, in the writings of St. Gregory of Nyssa and Eusebius of
Caesarea, and so on.[16] Even if many program people do not turn the
demons into vividly felt personal entities as they did (and as Jimmy H.
does) we can nevertheless see what can only be described as *a demonic style
of behavior* in some segments of human society, and in individual human
beings as well. For there is real evil in the world: implacable, blind, irrational, and totally heartless. Like a disease, you can catch it from other
people who are caught up in this kind of evil if you hang around them too
long.

Different demons have different personalities, different basic evil games
they like to play, but the fourth-century spiritual writers agreed that this
demonic element always had certain underlying characteristics. It was jeal-
ous and envious (*phthonos*). It was *misokalos*: it hated all that was fine and
beautiful and good, instead of admiring and appreciating it. It was *philo-
ponêros*: it loved that which was evil. The demonic has become fascinated
by the lure of evil, and is pulled towards it like a moth drawn into a candle
flame. And above all, the demonic is *pseustês*, a liar. Any truly demonic evil

is based on beliefs that are not true at all. Once we unmask them, they can easily be seen to be total lies, and often unbelievably foolish and simpleminded to boot.

The important thing to remember is, that I am not caught in this battle alone: there is also a divine and totally good power which I can discover, or call into, my soul. This good divine power is far stronger than anything the demonic can summon up, and when the battle is over, God will always have won.

There are other ways to feel the presence of God within my own soul. One of Submarine Bill's pigeons once called him at two o'clock in the morning, all upset and going to pieces. Bill told him to go lie down in bed, and try to visualize himself simply being held in the arms of a loving God, and see if he couldn't go to sleep. Bill's pigeon did that, and his inner mental torment gradually began to lessen, and finally he drifted off to sleep. When he woke up in the morning, he was able to handle the problem without coming to pieces again. He found the truth of the famous passage (Deut. 33:27), "The eternal God is your refuge, and underneath are the everlasting arms."

"God is love," and the entire creation—including my own mind and heart—are held in being every moment by the continuous, never-failing energy of this force of creation flowing into us. I can call on this as a countervailing force when my own inner negative and self-destructive forces are threatening to overwhelm me. It doesn't matter at all what name I put on these two opposing forces:

The spiritual part of my own soul

vs.

the carnal part.

The God who is "nearer than breathing
and closer than hands and feet"

vs.

the devil within my own heart.

An angelic or bodhisattva-like messenger
(or some divine avatar)
of compassion and enlightenment
vs.
the false desires and illusions which send me
down the karmic path to destruction.

The creative love-energy flowing out of the divine ground
vs.
the imaginary monsters I have allowed to crawl out of
my own inner closet of anxieties.

At the practical level, it all works out the same. And the people we have quoted here are typical of many in the program who find, by going down within their own hearts, not only the character defects and attitudes and delusions which were destroying them, but also the higher power which can save them from their doom.

Chapter V

Two Classical Authors of A.A. Spirituality

1. Practicing the Presence of God: Richmond Walker's Twenty-Four Hour Book

The second most popular A.A. author in total book sales, second only to Bill W. himself, was Richmond Walker. He was a man from the Boston area who managed to get sober in 1939 in the old Oxford Group, but then went back to drinking two and a half years later. He joined A.A. in May of 1942, and finally found lasting sobriety there. In 1948 he wrote the book of daily meditations called *Twenty-Four Hours a Day*, which for many years was the basic meditational book for all A.A.'s. Hazelden offered to print it for him in 1954, when the job of distributing it all over the country became too big for him to handle by himself.[1] It is still widely used by A.A.'s and A.A. groups today.

Soul-balance

One of the principal spiritual goals, Richmond said, was attaining a kind of *soul-balance*. We put our lives into a kind of quiet rhythm where we alternated between working in the world and retiring back for quiet moments with God (Jan. 15):

> I will learn soul-balance and poise
> in a vacillating, changing world.
> I will claim God's power and use it....
> As long as I get back to God
> and replenish my strength after each task,
> no work can be too much.

It is the time when I am by myself, in quiet communion with God, which gives me the power, when I go back out into the tasks of everyday life, to *wear the world as a loose garment* (Mar. 29):

> I must live in the world and yet
> live apart [from the world] with God.
> I can go forth from my secret times of
> communion with God
> to the work of the world.
> To get the spiritual strength I need, my inner life

must be lived apart from the world.
I must wear the world as a loose garment.
Nothing in the world should seriously upset me,
as long as my inner life is lived with God.

Seek inner calm in order to do good and avoid evil

Allowing too much resentment and fear to upset my soul prevents me from living my life as it ought properly to be lived—*serving as a channel for God's spirit*—and doing God's work in the world (Jan. 26):

I will try to keep my life calm and unruffled.
This is my great task,
to find peace and acquire serenity.
I must not harbor disturbing thoughts.
No matter what fear, worries and
resentments I may have,
I must try to think of constructive things,
until calmness comes.
Only when I am calm can I act
as a channel for God's spirit.

Too much resentment and too much fear are far more dangerous to me than any external threat whatsoever: *Uncalm times are the only times when evil can find an entrance.* (Feb. 21)

I will be more afraid of spirit-unrest,
of soul disturbance,
of any ruffling of the mind,
than of earthquake or fire.
When I feel the calm of my spirit

has been broken by emotional upset,
then I must steal away alone with God,
until my heart sings and
all is strong and calm again.
Uncalm times are the only times
when evil can find an entrance....
I will try to keep calm,
no matter what turmoil surrounds me.

God inside, God outside, God above

In the great spiritual teachings of the world—Europe, Asia, ancient times, the middle ages, at all times and places—we find some people seeking the divine or sacred within their own souls. Others have sought the divine in the world around them. Yet others saw the great power as far above and infinitely removed from both ourselves and the physical world around us:[2] ancient Greek Neo-Platonic philosophers, Hindu religious thinkers like Shankara, and some Christian spiritual teachers too, like St. Bonaventure for example, said that we had to free the mind of all external sense impressions, all internal thoughts and concepts, and all thoughts even of the self, before we could achieve the vision of the ultimate transcendent ground.[3]

Now it should also be said that some of the best of these spiritual teachers said that all three routes led to the same divine power, and that we could take any of these routes, or even all three of them, to seek out contact with that higher power.

Trapped in a box of space and time

In some passages, Richmond Walker seems to have chosen the third route, placing his higher power far above and behind the universe and all that is in it. Using Kantian philosophical language, he talked about the way our minds are locked within a box of space and time, with God (who is infinite and eternal) existing outside that box. Our human minds, by their very nature, attempt to structure all the universe in terms of myriads of physical objects (sense phenomena) set at specific locations in three-dimensional space, moving sequentially through chronological time, and rigidly obeying natural laws—that is the only way we can ordinarily think at all.[4] Since God in his essential nature necessarily has to lie outside that framework, he is therefore normally blocked from our direct perception (Mar. 24):

> We live in a box of space and time, which we have man-ufactured by our own minds and on that depends all our so-called knowledge of the universe. The simple fact is that we can never know all things, nor are we made to know them. Much of our lives must be taken on faith.

So we cannot "point out where God is" in the same way we could point our fingers and say, "You see that really tall mountain-top behind you? That's Pike's Peak, the top is 14,110 feet above sea level, almost three miles high." We also cannot fit God smoothly into our laws of physics, because these laws deal with finite physical objects.

God must touch me with his spirit for me to know him

So how can I have any kind of knowledge of God at all, or contact with him? Richmond Walker says that I must start by blocking off the world of external sense perceptions: I must begin by remembering that God is not a physical object out there in the external material world. I cannot measure his length, weigh his mass, describe his color or shape, or draw a picture of him. What I feel when his spirit touches mine can therefore only be described in metaphors or analogies or symbolic language (Mar. 10):

> My five senses are my means of communication with the material world. They are the links between my physical life and the material manifestations around me. But I must sever all connections with the material world when I wish to hold communion with the Great Spirit of the universe. I have to hush my mind and bid all my senses be still, before I can become attuned to receive the music of the heavenly spheres.

We don't have any good words in English for describing what is happening when God touches us, although some of the German philosophers and theologians of the nineteenth century developed some technical terms for talking about this. We "feel" God (the German word for feeling is *Gefühl*) rather than sense him as we would a physical object. We apprehend him as a hint, an intuition, the awareness of a presence (where the German word for this is *Ahnung*).[5] Richmond Walker described it as a spirit-consciousness or a spirit-touch. It is a very subtle thing in the sense that it is over on the fringe of normal consciousness. It is not some overwhelming ecstatic washing away of normal consciousness, but a quiet feeling which touches us gently (Apr. 27 and Feb. 27):

> We know God by spiritual vision. We feel that He is beside us. We feel His presence. Contact with God is not made by the senses. Spirit-consciousness replaces sight. Since we cannot see God, we have to perceive Him by spiritual perception. God has to span the physical and the spiritual with the gift to us of spiritual vision. Many a man, though he cannot see God, has had a clear spiritual consciousness of Him. We are inside a box of space and time, but we know there must be something outside of that box, limitless space, eternity of time, and God.

This is the time for my spirit to touch the spirit of God. I know that the feeling of the spirit-touch is more important than all the sensations of material things. I must seek a silence of spirit-touching with God. Just a moment's contact and all the fever of life leaves me. Then I am well, whole, calm and able to arise and minister to others. God's touch is a potent healer. I must feel that touch and sense God's presence.

Sometimes Richmond described God's spirit as being like a deep, flowing river of peace and healing (Jan. 5 and Jan. 3):

> I believe that God's presence brings peace
> and that peace, like a quiet-flowing river,
> will cleanse all irritants away.
> In these quiet times,
> God will teach me how to rest my nerves.

> His spirit shall flow through me and,
> in flowing through me,
> it shall sweep away all the bitter past.

In his meditation for April 6, he described it as acting like the warmth of the sun touching a little flower. Elsewhere he described God's spirit as something we can "breathe in" as a breath of fresh air (Mar. 13): "Gently breathe in God's spirit," he said, "that spirit which, if not barred out by selfishness, will enable you to do good works." If we take pains to dwell near God, the power of his spirit will automatically be quietly absorbed into us at a level below our conscious awareness (Jan. 23).

Take time alone with God

To make this work, I must take time alone with God on a regular, scheduled basis (Feb. 14):

> I must keep a time apart with God every day. Gradually I will be transformed mentally and spiritually. It is not the praying so much as just being in God's presence. The strengthening and curative powers of this I cannot understand, because such knowledge is beyond human understanding, but I can experience them.... My greatest spiritual growth occurs in this time apart with God.

If something happens during the day which throws me into unmanageable resentment or fear, then I must also go off someplace where I can be alone and spend a few minutes alone with God (Apr. 15):

> I must keep calm and unmoved
> in the vicissitudes of life.
> I must go back into the silence
> of communion with God
> to recover this calm
> when it is lost even for one moment.
> I will accomplish more by this calmness
> than by all the activities of a long day.
> At all cost I will keep calm.
> I can solve nothing when I am agitated.

The prayer without words

In order to enter this place of peace and calm, I need to stop most of the inner dialogue within my mind. When the kind of people who need a twelve-step program get upset, their minds become filled with nonstop arguments. Some people refer to this as "holding a committee meeting in my head." One part of my mind says "do this" while another part says "no, do that." One part of my mind obsesses anxiously about all the things which could go wrong in the future, while another part obsesses bitterly about bad things that happened in the past. I devise endless theories, and try to analyze everything to death.

When I go off to take some time alone with God, I need to stop this. What Richmond Walker was talking about was a kind of contemplation which some of the early Christian spiritual writers called *the prayer without words* (Jan. 7): "In silence comes God's meaning to the heart.... God's word is spoken to the secret places of my heart."

This sounds a little bit like the Hindu technique called transcendental meditation, but that particular technique was designed to cut off all emotion, all feeling, all real contact with the world of sense impressions. Richmond Walker was describing something totally different, with a subtle but rich, and in fact, extraordinarily powerful feeling tone.

You can do what Richmond was talking about while you are looking at some beautiful flowers in a vase, or walking through the park, or sitting in an easy chair just enjoying feeling relaxed and comfortable. You're not trying to cut off all emotions and feelings. Instead, you're letting yourself feel loved, and surrounded by peace and calm, and warmed by the glow of the spirit. You're letting yourself feel something moving through you, healing you and washing out all the disturbing elements. And if you look at the things around you, and feel a feeling of enjoyment and appreciation, and even gratitude towards the divine creator of these things, that just makes it work that much better.

Faith

Richmond Walker said that what he was talking about would not work without faith. Hebrews 11:1 said that "faith is the foundation upon which hope can be built, the way we evaluate the truthfulness of things we cannot see" with our physical eyes. Love and trustworthiness and compassion are things that are perfectly real, but they are not physical objects where we can describe what color they are, or how much they weigh, or how many inches long they are.

So Richmond described faith in this sense (Mar. 28) as "the confidence in things unseen," a confidence that there was a "fundamental goodness and purpose in the universe." Faith meant (Apr. 22) "a belief that God is the Divine Principle in the universe and that He is the Intelligence and the Love that controls the universe."

Without faith, I can go off and be alone all I want, and I will feel no presence but my own. *Without* faith, I will then return to my work in the world and still be as irritable and anxious and upset as I was before. So I must develop some kind of faith. Once I have faith, this technique will start working, and resentment and (particularly) fear will start to melt away (Jan. 21):

> I will take the most crowded day without fear.
> I believe that God is with me,
> and controlling all.
> I will let confidence be the motif
> running through all the crowded day.
> I will not get worried,
> because I know that God is my helper.
> Underneath are the everlasting arms.
> I will rest in them,
> even though the day be full of
> things crowding in on me.

When we begin working the twelve steps, our faith is always very small. But if it is great enough just to try a few of things that are suggested to us, we will see that some of these actually work for us. And so, the next time, our faith will be a little stronger (Apr. 17):

I gain faith by my own experience of God's power in my life. The constant, persistent recognition of God's spirit in all my personal relationships, the ever-accumulating weight of evidence in support of God's guidance, the numberless instances in which seeming chance or wonderful coincidence can be traced to God's purpose in my life. All these things gradually engender a feeling of wonder, humility and gratitude to God. These in turn are followed by a more sure and abiding faith in God and His purposes.

The Friends of God

The bible describes people like Moses and Abraham as the Friends of God, and tells how Moses used to talk with God "as a man talks with his friend."[6] By the time people have been in the twelve step program for a while, many find themselves talking to God all day long inside their heads. They discover, to their surprise, that God does not strike them dead if they sometimes swear at him and ask him, "Why did you do that?" Not only do they talk to God about what they're doing, at some level they sense what God is saying back to them. "Why do I have to do *this*? Oh, O.K., because it's the responsible thing to do, and I'll feel good about it after I've done it."

Richmond Walker makes the very interesting suggestion that God may enjoy being friends with me just as much as I enjoy being friends with him (Feb. 6):

> God finds, amid the crowd,
> a few people who follow Him,
> just to be near Him,
> just to dwell in His presence.
> A longing in the Eternal Heart
> may be satisfied by these few people.

> I will let God know that I seek
> just to dwell in His presence,
> to be near Him, not so much for teaching
> or a message, as just for Him.
> It may be that the longing of the human heart
> to be loved for itself
> is something caught from the
> great Divine Heart.

Guidance

So we become friends with God, and we talk with God during the day. And somehow, we often know at some level what God is saying back to us. We discover, in fact, that by regularly spending time alone with God, we can receive guidance from him, at least to the extent of knowing what is the next right thing to do.[7] But as I keep on doing that, one step at a time, and if I also look carefully to see the direction of God's providential leading, I will end up being guided even in the big things which take weeks and months and years to accomplish (Feb. 5 and Mar. 14).

> I must trust in God and He will teach me. I must listen to God and He will speak through my mind…. There will be days when I will hear no voice in my mind and when there will come no intimate heart-to-heart communion. But if I persist…God will reveal Himself to me.

> Persevere in all that God's guidance moves you to do. The persistent carrying out of what seems right and good will bring you to that place where you would be. If you look back over God's guidance, you will see that His leading has been very gradual and that only as you have carried out His wishes, as far as you can understand them, has God been able to give you more clear and definite leading.

You are led by God's touch on a quickened, responsive mind.

This becomes smoother and easier for us "as our consciousness becomes more and more attuned to the great Consciousness of the universe" (Apr. 23).

Eternal Life

Richmond Walker interpreted the words eternal life in what modern theologians call the Johannine sense.[8] He believed that God had prepared a place for us in his heavenly realm after our death,[9] but the phrase eternal life also referred, even more importantly, to our ability to participate here and now in the eternal life-force, the creative power which continuously brings life into being within this universe (Jan. 25):

> I do not look upon this life as something to be struggled through, in order to get the rewards of the next life. I believe that the Kingdom of God is within us, and we can enjoy "eternal life" here and now.

When we commune with God, and come in contact with his eternal divine calm, and come to rest in him, we ourselves participate in that eternal love and acceptance and peace (Mar. 17):

> The eternal life is calmness
> and when a man enters into that,
> then he lives as an eternal being.
> Calmness is based on complete trust in God.
> Nothing in this world can separate you
> from the love of God.

Where is the Kingdom of Heaven? The Kingdom of Heaven is within us and among us. Open your spiritual eyes, and see where you are, and where you can be.

This is the fundamental spiritual awakening produced by working the twelve step program. The good life can be here and now. I can feel at ease and simply *at home* in that grand harmony of life that extends through both earth and heaven. I can deal with trouble and disturbance and *real* fear and *real* grief without losing my head and feeling overwhelmed with blind panic. I can learn when to hang tight and when to let go. I can regain the quiet center of peace and calm within. I can regain my own soul.

A warning from the unwritten tradition

A word of warning needs to be inserted here. To fully understand the spiritual teaching of any spiritual discipline it is necessary to go, not only to the formal written texts which the founders of that movement published, but also to the tradition which developed among the early members explaining how the rules and suggestions and principles were actually interpreted and carried out at a practical level. Within this tradition it was eventually discovered that something needed to be added to what Richmond Walker had said about serenity in the *Twenty-Four Hours* book. Submarine Bill often phrased it like this when he spoke about this part of the teaching of the good old-timers:

> When I first came into the program, I thought serenity meant going around never feeling any kind of disturbance or upset of any sort, a kind of perfect inner peace all the time. What I think serenity is now, is when you're wading through shit up to your chin, and you tip your head up so

you can breathe, and you can keep on doing what has to
be done.

In other words, you use your program so you can keep cool enough to continue making the best decisions that it is actually possible to make. You may feel hurt or frustration or disgust or grief, or a number of other very painful and unpleasant emotions. But you keep your inner sense of *soul-balance*. You don't take out your frustrations on other people around you by attacking them, or playing blaming games ("It's all your fault we're in this situation," and so on and so forth). If other people are behaving badly—selfishness, gross irresponsibility, totally egocentric attitudes—you try to work around it as best you can, and you *keep your own side of the street swept clean*, no matter what the other person is doing. You look for positive solutions, and try to move things that way as much as the other people and the situation itself will allow it. The fullness of serenity means keeping your soul-balance, keeping centered, even amidst that kind of emotional maelstrom.

2. The Myth of Perfection: Father John Doe's Golden Books

If the second most popular A.A. author has been Richmond Walker, the third most widely read has probably been Ralph Pfau from Indianapolis, the first Roman Catholic priest to get sober in A.A. In addition to three long books and thirty recorded talks, he wrote (under the pen name of Father John Doe) a series of fourteen little booklets called the *Golden Books*, which have been the most widely read of all.[10]

At the end of *The Golden Book of Resentments* he put a long section called "The Myth of Perfection."[11] He began it with a quote from St. Augustine, the ancient African saint who supplied so many of the basic ideas of the medieval Catholic church, the Protestant Reformation, and

Bill Wilson's interpretations of the twelve step program: "*Let us admit our imperfections so we can then begin to work toward perfection.*"

St. Augustine spent a number of years after his conversion to Christianity trying to be perfect, and attempting to flee from *all* ordinary human emotion into a supernatural vision of the divine ground of being. When he was made bishop of a port city on the coast of Africa, he finally had to admit that the people who crowded into his church every Sunday morning were simply never going to be perfect in that sense—and neither was *he*—and that trying to develop a spiritual life on that basis was not even relevant to the real everyday problems which both he and the members of his congregation actually had to face.[12]

St. Augustine bequeathed to all subsequent western Christianity the fundamental principle which Father Ralph puts in this form: "*There ain't nobody perfect in this world.*"

> "There ain't nobody perfect in this world".... All of our lives we expected perfection, and when we again and again found instead imperfection, faults, failings, even serious ones, we became "disillusioned"—which in reality was only a vicarious form of self-pity....
>
> We first thought our parents were perfect. Then we found out they weren't! Frustration number one. Then we met the gal (or guy) of our dreams. And think we to us: *here* is perfection. And then we married her (or him)! Frustration number two....
>
> Then along came our children. And without doubt they were perfect. "Isn't he the most perfect thing that ever lived?" And then the policeman brought T. Jonathan home one day.... *Our* child? Never! But it *was* our child. More frustration....

But we held on to the mirage to the very last: *We were perfect*, and if you didn't believe it, all you had to do was to ask us!…

The truth? *No one is perfect*…. Like a little Scriptural proof? "If anyone among you says he is without sin, he is a *liar* and the truth is not in him."[13] Just a longer way of saying: *There ain't nobody perfect.*

Perfection is a myth based on spiritual pride. But in fact we will never have a perfect family, perfect friends, perfect business associates, or a perfect body. Sometimes we'll get sick, or have aches and pains. We will also never have perfect emotional lives. Father Ralph comments:

> How many come to us and complain: "I have been try-
> ing so long—for years—to control myself and I still get
> upset, I still get jittery, I still get angry, and I still get nerv-
> ous." Well, what did they expect? Perfect control?
> *Perfection?*

This is the alcoholic mind at work, Father Ralph says, the "persistent struggle to reach that *smooth* feeling." When alcohol stops doing it, some people then turn to drugs. Sedatives like the barbiturates and bromides were the drugs alcoholics most often turned to in the early days of A.A., then there was the tranquillizer era, followed by the marijuana era, and so on. But what do we discover when we finally see that the Myth of Perfection is just that, nothing but a myth?

> There will be days when we will be feeling wonderful
> and there will be days when we will be feeling lousy; and
> there will be days when one is quick to anger and days
> when nothing upsets; and there will be days when we feel
> mean as all get out and days when we feel like doing a

good turn even for our worst enemy. But then, life and
emotions are like that, very uneven and *imperfect*, even in
the best of men.

We also need to remember that perfection is a myth when we get too worried about the wandering thoughts running through our heads. "We may
live to be a hundred, but we shall still have distractions, and 'bad'
thoughts, and 'screwy' thoughts, until we're dead."

This will be true even in prayer or meditation. Father Ralph refers to
the classic tale about St. Francis de Sales to make his point. The way I
myself originally heard the little story, it went this way: That saint rode
around doing missionary preaching, and the only thing he owned was the
horse he rode. One day another priest bragged that he could pray for
hours without any distracting wandering thoughts. "Oh," said St. Francis,
"I'll bet you my horse that you can't pray for even five minutes without
having some distracting thought pass across your mind." The priest got
down on his knees and started praying, but after a few moments suddenly
looked up at St. Francis and asked, "Does the saddle and bridle come with
it?"

In fact, the Myth of Perfection teaches us a major lesson about the spiritual life in general: we will fail to meet our highest goals over and over
again. "For the myth of perfection tells us that in the spiritual life above all
else, burdened with fallen human nature, we will fall and fall and fall again
until 'two days after we're dead'!"[14]

The goal of the twelve step program is progress, not perfection. In traditional theological language, growing towards sainthood, spiritually and
morally, is called becoming *sanctified*. Father Ralph makes the startling
statement that "anyone who tries the best he can to do the will of God in
all of his affairs—day in and day out—and keeps on trying in the face of
repeated falls and failures" is *fundamentally sanctified*, because what God
measures us by is not whether we perfectly succeeded, or even succeeded
at all, but *whether we tried*.[15]

With God's help, an alcoholic *can* avoid drinking, one day at a time—this is about the only absolute in the program. With God's help, a drug addict *can* avoid using, one day at a time; someone with an eating disorder *can* avoid going on a food binge or whatever, and likewise for compulsive spenders and people who are driven into destructive sexual compulsions, and all the rest. That we *can* do.

Past that point, we do the footwork, and we turn our frailties over to God, and we let *God* do the healing at whatever speed *God* knows to be best. And we work on developing *humility*, because we are human beings, not gods. God loves us in our very humanness and frailness and fragility. As long as you don't forget that, and stick with the program, you're O.K. Your life will be blessed, and blessed beyond your present wildest imaginings. That's the greatest spiritual awakening of all: to realize with overwhelming gratitude the way God has blessed my life with grace upon grace in a glorious journey that just keeps on going to greater and greater heights.

Chapter VI

Resentment

Resentment is the number one killer of alcoholics

As it says on page 64 of the Big Book, "Resentment is the 'number one' offender. It destroys more alcoholics than anything else."[1] And this applies to all versions of the twelve-step program: resentment fills my life with pure poison. If I am an alcoholic, it is not what the other person did to me which drives me back to the bottle, it is the resentment which I am feeling. If I am a compulsive overeater, it is the resentment and self-pity I am feeling which are driving me to stuff down a dozen doughnuts. If I am a codependent,[2] it is my own unbearable feelings inside myself which are driving me back into even more frenzied (and futile) attempts at caretaking, controlling, manipulating, and rescuing.

"But look what so-and-so did to me!" I will say if I am an alcoholic for example. That's an excuse, and it's time to stop making that kind of excuses if I want to stop drinking myself to death, because I have almost no control over what other people do. If I keep on making that kind of excuse to myself, I will just keep on drinking myself to death (and that's not just some highfaluting theory, simply go to A.A. meetings and look at the people who keep on going back out and drinking again, and *listen to the way they talk about their problems*). It's the resentment I'm feeling which is making the bottle of booze look so unbearably desirable, and I DO have some kind of control over what I myself am feeling—by the aid of God's grace and the help of the other people in the program, and a little bit of footwork on my part.

"But look at what so-and-so did to me!" I will say if I am an alcoholic. And as I let that resentment build up inside me and become greater and greater, I will keep making the situation I am in worse and worse. And that's not a theory either, just go to A.A. meetings and look and listen to the people who *aren't* making it. The longer I let the original resentment fester inside me, the more I will create even worse problems for myself in the outside world, and the more additional items I will add to my inner list of resentments. If I'm stuck in a hole, the more I just keep digging the hole deeper and deeper, the more painful and laborious it's going to be to climb back out again. And the sooner I start climbing out of the hole, the easier it's going to be. I've seen people dig themselves holes so deep that they became paralyzed with total despair, and finally committed suicide— they looked up at the little patch of light at the top of the hole they had dug for themselves, and it was so far away, and the climb back up so agonizingly hard, and they were so totally *overwhelmed* by all the additional miseries and resentments they had brought on themselves by refusing to let go of the original resentment, that they gave up—the wrong way.

Can you still get out of the hole if you've dug it that deep? Of course you can, but the deeper the hole, the more completely you're going to have to surrender to God as you understand him, and the more totally you're going to have to abandon yourself to his care—and that was the part that you didn't *want* to do in the first place! But some of the most impressive of the good old-timers talk in their leads about the incredibly deep holes they had dug for themselves before they finally surrendered and turned their wills and lives over to the care of God, and they just shrug and say, "It takes what it takes to get here." In this program, we don't shame people, and we don't heap guilt on their heads—we absolutely DO NOT do that, because the real God does not *ever* do that to us.

Resentment is the number one killer of people in the twelve-step program. Even with Al-Anons, it's the resentment that finally drives them into total craziness at the end. Have you been seriously contemplating suicide? That's a guaranteed sign (even if you're totally blocking it from your conscious awareness) that the resentment bottled up inside you has gotten to the lethal point.

Resentment: re-feeling the pain over and over, and feeding its flames higher and higher

So what do we really mean by a resentment? Ralph P. (Father John Doe), one of the three most important early A.A. authors, was a Roman Catholic priest who knew his Latin well. He pointed out that, like a lot of words in English, the word resentment originally came from a Latin word, the verb *sentio*, which means "I feel" or "I experience emotionally." We get a lot of other English words from that same Latin root, like sentimental and consent and sensation and sensitivity. In the English word resentment, we take that basic Latin root and put the *re-* prefix in front of it, which means to experience something *emotionally* over and over again.[3]

So somebody does or says something to me that makes me feel hurt, or makes me angry, or makes me feel some way I don't like to feel. Instead of just acknowledging to myself that "that didn't feel good," and moving on, I start to rehearse the painful emotion over and over in my mind. "How could anybody have dared do something like that to me!" "But I was trying so hard to help him and rescue him by my love." "But I was right, and he was wrong—anybody can see that—I can *prove* it to you!" "I ought to go tell her off." "Boy, I'd like to punch him in the nose." "I just want to cry all the time, I hurt so much." And every time I rehearse and re-feel that painful emotion in my mind, it grows even more painful. *Practice makes perfect*, and I finally work myself into a state of perfect rage, or perfect frustration, or whatever.

Learning to use the natural instincts properly

Now feeling anger is one of the normal human emotions, so that in itself is not what is doing the harm. In the ordinary course of everyday life, sometimes people will say or do things that make me angry, and that's perfectly O.K.—that is the sane, well-balanced human response—as long as I handle that natural human reaction in the right kind of way. One of the most important principles of the twelve-step program is contained in the chapter on the fourth step in *Twelve Steps and Twelve Traditions*.[4] That chapter begins by stating the fundamental principle (p. 42):

> Creation gave us instincts for a purpose. Without them we wouldn't be complete human beings. If men and women didn't exert themselves to be secure in their persons, made no effort to harvest food or construct shelter, there would be no survival. If they didn't reproduce, the earth wouldn't be populated. If there were no social instinct, if men cared nothing for the society of one another, there would be no society. So these desires—for the sex relation, for material and emotional security, and

for companionship—are perfectly necessary and right, and surely God-given.

We want a certain amount of personal security; we want a certain amount of material things like food and clothing and a warm place to sleep at night; we want a few other people around us for companionship and mutual help; and most people (though not all, and they are O.K. too) would like to have a warm and caring relationship with a spouse or mate. If these are threatened, anger is a natural surge of emotion telling us to take some kind of action (if we can) to push back the danger, or regain a position of safety.

That chapter in the *Twelve Steps and Twelve Traditions* tells us that the problem for people who come into the twelve-step program is that they have invariably let these natural instincts get out of hand: they wildly over-react (or dangerously under-react), or they try to grab too much of this or that and drive themselves crazy in the process. They start living in fantasy demands and illusory solutions, and lose touch with the real world. And then they start obsessing about their disappointments, and brooding about them over and over, and resentment starts to poison their spirits, and eventually they destroy themselves.

So no one in the twelve-step program is telling us that we should *never* feel anger, and that we are "bad people" if we *ever* get angry. But for starters, I need to learn how to restrain myself from out-of-control scream-ing, yelling, attacking, name-calling, hitting, stabbing, or shooting the other person. The best way to handle anger is to begin by letting myself feel the anger, and admitting to myself that it's anger I'm feeling, and that it's *my* emotion in *my* head—it's something in me, not the other person. Then I need to control my response if I have to; sometimes I may need to walk away and calm down a little bit before doing anything at all. And then I need to move on and *let the emotion die naturally*. If I can do some-thing positive and constructive to solve the problem, then I need to do it, and if I can't do anything about it, then I need to accept it, to detach from it, and to just shrug the problem off my shoulders and move on to something I can do something about.

It's the same thing when someone does something that makes me feel very hurt: feel the hurt, keep cool, and then move on and let the emotion glide out of my mental processes. The sense of anger and hurt will die off by itself by normal natural processes—that's the way the human mind is designed to work—unless I start doing something *to lock myself into the painful emotions*. It's amazing how many angry and hurt feelings will wash away after a single good night's sleep.[5]

I myself sometimes like to visualize the teeming angry and hurt thoughts in my head as being something like a swarm of unpleasant flying insects: tiny little things that are not really dangerous, but obnoxious and annoying. And then I visualize the swarm of black flying specks being slowly blown out of my center of consciousness by a gentle breeze which gradually forces them to drift over to the side and out of sight. Or I visualize myself walking down a street, and turning over into a side street, and then suddenly realizing that this side street leads into a very nasty and unpleasant neighborhood, where I don't want to go on this particular walk. And it's my choice (no one else's) which journey I want to take in my own thoughts inside my own head. So I turn back down the route I was already planning to walk, which leads to pleasant scenes and delightful experiences.

The gradual poisoning of my whole life

The point where I get into trouble, is when I start rehearsing the painful feeling over and over in my mind, and can't get rid of it, because I refuse to let myself get rid of it. I try to do useful work, and I keep being distracted by the painful memories coming back into my head and taking over. I try to do something which requires me to be cool and calm, and I'm still so emotionally upset that I make constant mistakes, and miss things that are obvious. If you don't believe this, just try doing really precision work sometime, something which takes a totally steady hand—like threading a needle or something like that—when you're in a total rage.

A resentment poisons everything else in my life too. Let's say that I'm cherishing and rehearsing a major resentment one day; then someone else comes in to talk to me—a totally innocent party—and he does something minor that I don't like, and suddenly I'm dumping all my anger at the original offender on this person who's done something really trivial. You know how it works: the boss unfairly yells at a woman at work, she comes home in a foul mood and starts screaming at her husband over something really small, he turns around and sees his little boy walking around with one shoe untied and starts attacking the poor little boy (who didn't even realize that the shoe had come untied) and starts yelling at him and telling him he's careless and no good, and will never amount to anything, and the little boy goes outside and deliberately kicks the family dog who's minding her own business snoozing in the sun. The dog—who feels she's got a really legitimate grievance here—goes off to try to pick a fight with the family cat, who then gets so outraged that she runs over and deliberately slashes with her claws at the arm of the best couch back in the living room, right in front of everybody's eyes. And then things *really* start to go down-hill from here!

And what's the most dangerous thing of all about hanging on to resentments? Let's suppose the woman is a new member of a twelve-step group, and goes off to a meeting later that evening, still seething with resentment. The next thing she knows, she's screaming that "There is no God, and if there is one, he's done nothing but dump crap on me all day long."

Resentment is the number one killer of people in twelve-step programs, most of all because *nobody* can be feeling the presence of God, or be consciously thinking about God and the spiritual dimension of things, when his or her mind is filled with nonstop resentment. It wasn't just God whom this woman couldn't see; she couldn't see that her husband—who loved her very deeply—was in fact glad to see her when she first walked in the door (although probably not after she began opening her mouth). She couldn't see the blessing of her little boy running around the house enjoying himself and being happy (at least at first) that his mommy was home. She couldn't even enjoy the dog and the cat, who liked nothing better than to snuggle up to her and be affectionate.

It's all linked together: When I can't see God, I can't see lots of other good things too; and vice versa, if I let resentment blind me to all the other good things, I won't be able to see God either. And what makes it most dangerous is that it tends to just keep on getting worse and worse.

Resentment is a vicious cycle, which feeds on itself, and in the process grows more and more poisonous. It involves circular thinking, where I keep on re-thinking the same thoughts and phrases over and over, like a hamster running on one of those little wheels they put in hamster cages. The little hamster can run on the rotating wheel as fast and hard as he wants to: he'll never actually get anywhere. "But if I just try harder, I can get somewhere." Not if you're on this kind of hamster wheel.

It can be easier to see from the outside. If someone who has a major resentment comes to spend the afternoon with me to share his or her tale of woe, past a certain point the person will just be saying the same thing over and over again: no new ideas appear, and it's just the same phrases and tiresome complaints and self-justifications repeated and repeated and repeated without end. People like this are *locked into* their resentments, and won't let themselves figure any way out.

Breaking the cycle

So we have to break the repeating circles at one point or another, and the twelve-step program gives us lots of devices for breaking the cycle.[6] It doesn't really matter which point in the repeating circle I pick to act to break the cycle. If I can disrupt it at any point in the repeating sequence, the whole cycle will break down, and I'll be able to get out of it. So the old-timers tell us all sorts of techniques which will short-circuit the obsessive revolving thoughts of anger and hurt and self-pity:

For starters, did I bring this painful situation on myself? This has to be the very first question of all. Was I totally ignoring the effect of my own behavior on other people? Did I myself actually begin the conflict by trying to mind other people's business, and by trying to control everything they thought and did? There is always a backlash to that. Was I an arrogant know-it-all, "Mr. Big Shot," who spent my time criticizing them and putting them down, who always had to "be right" and have the last word? People finally get fed up with that and start attacking back. Did I demand that they all immediately jump on board each of my continually shifting "instant crusades"? Did I fall into a rage if they failed to give me *exactly* what I wanted? "And right now too, on the spot! And why did I even have to tell you, why didn't you read my mind?" Was I trying to grab off too big a chunk of everything for myself and attempting to squeeze them out? Maybe they finally decided to start squeezing me back. Did I walk into the situation with a chip on my shoulder, daring anybody to cross me? There will always be somebody who will take up that kind of dare, so it's just like having a big sign saying "please kick me" on the seat of my pants. If I behave in certain kinds of ways, other people will eventually be so enraged they will retaliate. *If this is what is really going on, it is my own behavior that I need to start changing, because it's me who is the real problem—and once I start to honestly do that, the repeating cycle will be broken, and my resentment will disappear.*

However I answer that first basic question, the best long-term cure is to do a fourth step on the resentment: I need to discover what character defect in me creates such an overpowering reaction.[7] That kind of obsessive resentment *always* means I have some kind of underlying character defect producing the overreaction.[8] The resentment towards the other person or the external situation will start to disappear automatically once I truly admit to myself, down in my gut, that the real underlying problem lies in my own attitude, and I start praying to God to change *me* instead of the external circumstances.

Keep reminding myself that if I am in the grips of a really powerful resentment, I am bleeding from an artery, spiritually. It doesn't *matter* who was right and who was wrong: I'm the one who's bleeding to death in either case. So I need to quit "playing courtroom" and rehearsing over and over all the logical reasons I can make up for why "the judge" should rule that I was right and the other person was wrong, so that then I can be "justified" in holding that resentment. That's part of the circular reasoning that keeps the resentment going. There is no "judge" who can *make* the other person do right, no matter how good my arguments are, and I'll be darned if I can think of any kind of reason at all that I could feel "justified" in sitting there bleeding to death and doing nothing to save myself.

Above all, quit being part of the problem, and start being part of the solution. Maybe I need to call my sponsor, and start talking about positive ways I could solve the problem, or keep it from occurring in the future. John S., an old-timer from Gary, Indiana, talked about how he would fly into a rage because his children would squeeze the tube of toothpaste in the middle instead of from the end, until one night at a meeting, someone said to him, "John, get your own tube of toothpaste—it isn't that expensive—and put it in another drawer. You can put a *lock* on that drawer if you want to, so nobody else except you can use it." The real solutions are frequently much simpler than we like to think.[9]

The twelve-step program is a program of progress, not perfection. You don't have to work it perfectly in order to enormously improve your ability to deal with resentment. An alcoholic, for example, who can handle a resentment without drinking over it or physically assaulting anyone, has made an enormous improvement. An alcoholic who can also avoid screaming and cursing at anyone or doing anything grossly self-destructive has made an even greater improvement. An alcoholic who can take a hellish resentment and mute it down to a dull ache (which is uncomfortable but manageable) has improved even more. An alcoholic who has learned how to go through large parts of the day simply doing ordinary things and enjoying the world around him, has moved even further forward, even if thoughts of the resentment still flare up now and then.

An alcoholic who has learned how to banish resentments from his mind fairly quickly—and who can then go back to just relaxing and enjoying life and making positive and responsible decisions, and who can continue to show compassion and tolerance—is in an advanced state of grace, and should utter prayers of enormous gratitude to God for leading him to such a state of blessedness.[10] And yet there are many such people in the twelve-step program everywhere I have travelled—it is certainly not an unattainable dream.

The good old-timers who have arrived at that state of grace did so because they also showed gratitude to God, at every point in their journey, for helping them make all the other slow, tiny steps along the way: for each of these improvements in their ability to deal with resentment was a gift from God which made their lives just that much happier and more satisfying. Continue, continue, continue. Show gratitude, don't ever turn back, and head towards the dawn.

Keep your own side of the street swept clean

But let us suppose I really was right, and the other person really was wrong. What do I do in circumstances like that? I myself first heard a lot of this old-time A.A. advice from Submarine Bill, in Osceola, Indiana, who learned his A.A. almost a quarter century ago from some really outstanding old-timers, but I've heard many of these things since then from a variety of other experienced program people—these sayings and suggestions are all part of the old tradition.

Bill is apt to say to his pigeons in this kind of situation, rather brusquely, "keep your own side of the street swept clean." If I use the fact that the other person did me wrong in an attempt to "justify" doing angry and revengeful things back to him, then I will just work myself deeper and deeper into the cycle of poisonous resentments: if I retaliate with this attitude, the other person will then counter-retaliate, and I will counter-counter-retaliate, and then he will counter-counter-counter-retaliate, and we'll both be dragged deeper and deeper into the old Hatfield and McCoy mountain feud spirit of "you shot my eighteen-year-old son, so I'll set your log cabin on fire and then shoot and kill your wife and six-year-old daughter as they run out the door."

If the other person *genuinely* did me wrong—but I allow myself to be overcome by such an overpowering resentment that *I start doing equally bad and wrong things back to him*—then how could I call upon God to step in and take care of me and protect me while I'm acting that way? I'm not allowing God any chance to work, because I've fallen back into my old self-destructive habit of trying to be my own God: "judge of all men, smiter of the wicked, and avenger of the innocent." That's the kind of stupid guff that got me into the twelve-step program in the first place! I cannot be practicing the third step—"made a decision to turn our will and our lives over to the care of God"—unless *I keep my own side of the street swept clean*, regardless of what the other fellow or gal is doing.

What fuels the cycle of resentment and supplies the psychic energy that keeps it running is some kind of deep, underlying fear. One of these fears can be a feeling of being totally helpless in the situation. The other person seems to have me totally within his control, where he can make me dance to his tune at all levels. Since one of the three or four fundamental existential anxieties is the anxiety of powerlessness and helplessness, feeling like this can so paralyze my mind that I cannot think clearly anymore. On the other hand, if I deal with the painful situation in such a way that I can walk away saying "Well, at least I kept my own side of the street swept clean, and I can feel pretty satisfied about that, because it wasn't easy," then I can emerge from it with a feeling of real triumph, and having been put back in some sort of control once again. I wasn't totally powerless: I did have options, I did have choices, and *I took the right ones*. The real power of the resentment will often start to die off quickly once I start acting that way.

When I keep my own side of the street swept clean, and otherwise turn the matter over to God, I allow God to take control of the overall basic situation once again, and *there is no safer place to be, than to be in a situation where God is totally in control.* The more I can concentrate on that, the less fear and anxiety I will feel, and the less resentment I will feel.

When Submarine Bill gives his blunt order to his pigeons, "Keep your own side of the street swept clean," he will sometimes add one further line: "Remember that what goes around comes around." If the other person is really that kind of rotten stinker, who goes around treating other people like that on a regular basis, then he will generate what the Hindu religion in India calls a chain of bad karma, which will turn back around on him and bite him in his own rear end sooner or later. In my life, I have never seen a person who was that kind of real stinker who didn't end up paying and paying dearly by the end of the game, and usually they ended up seeing everything they really cared about and wanted utterly destroyed before their eyes at the end of the tale. I would be willing to almost one hundred percent guarantee this in terms of what I have myself seen over the past forty years. My warning to you is that *you don't want to go* where that other person is going, so don't let him drag you with him.

I need to remind myself that as long as I continue to stew and steam over this resentment, "I'm letting the other person live rent-free in my head." Submarine Bill is apt to add a personal note to that old program advice: "I'm a person who always likes to win, and as long as the other person has that kind of grip on my mind and my thoughts, he's the one who's winning, because he not only did me one wrong, now he's continuing to ruin my life and make me miserable." There can be a kind of perverse glee in shrugging off the deliberately mean and spiteful thing that the other person said or did and going on about my business cheerfully, while *the other person* is left standing there stewing and steaming and feeling frustrated and powerless. Now after we've made enough spiritual progress, maybe we'll feel pity instead of pleasure, but if you're a beginner, take your pleasures where you can!

Submarine Bill said that when he first came into A.A., he had an in-law whom he really hated, so his sponsor made him do one favor every day for that person for an entire year. So in wintertime, for example, when he took out his snowplow to clear the driveway on his own farm, he would go over and plow out the brother-in-law's driveway too. Totally against his own will, the strategy worked—he says that he considers this person his best friend now! And to go along with this, Bill says that for over a year, he read the St. Francis Prayer from the *Twelve Steps & Twelve Traditions* every morning when he first got up:[11]

Lord, make me a channel of thy peace
—that where there is hatred, I may bring love
—that where there is wrong, I may bring
the spirit of forgiveness
—that where there is discord, I may bring harmony
—that where there is error, I may bring truth
—that where there is doubt, I may bring faith
—that where there is despair, I may bring hope
—that where there are shadows, I may bring light
—that where there is sadness, I may bring joy.

Lord, grant that I may seek
rather to comfort than to be comforted
—to understand, than to be understood
—to love, than to be loved.

For it is by self-forgetting that one finds.
It is by forgiving that one is forgiven.
It is by dying that one awakens to Eternal Life.
Amen.

Another old-timer worked out a variant on that method one winter for changing his underlying attitude towards other people: whenever he got off work and went out to the parking lot and had to scrape the snow and ice off the windshield of his own car, he did the same for the car parked next to it—an automobile belonging to some stranger whom he didn't even know, and who would never know who it was who did him that favor, so he couldn't have said thank you even if he wanted to.

When I myself begin treating other people differently, I will discover to my surprise that I will run into a lot fewer situations where other people seem to be wronging me without cause—the inner attitude that I "radiate" towards the world seems to act almost like a magnetic field attracting certain kinds of behavior on other people's part.

Prayer, acceptance, detachment

When I'm in the grips of a resentment, it wouldn't hurt to try one of the following simple techniques which people in the program have been using successfully for years. The reason these standard methods have been used so often is because they so often actually work!

Pray for the person who offended me.[12] This has worked for a lot of program people in a lot of situations, even though it won't work for everyone in every situation. For tough cases, the old-timers said, give it the thirty-day prayer treatment: every day, pray a short prayer asking God to give that other person all the good things I would want for myself, and repeat that prayer every time I start to think angry or hurt thoughts about that other person. At the very least, this takes all the fun out of being resentful!

Father John W. is a Catholic priest who has been in the A.A. program for many years; he is still living, but very elderly now. He worked a delightfully simple but very effective program. He was one of many who recommended this tool: Make myself a "God box," and write down my problem on a little piece of paper, and put it in my God box, and turn it over to God. If I start thinking about it again, then I have to take the piece of paper back out of the box and hold it in my hand until I get tired of thinking about the resentment and am ready to give it back to God again. Does this sound too childishly simple-minded? Don't knock it if you haven't tried it. As Louise Hay says, the universe loves symbolic gestures.[13]

Emmet Fox (whom the A.A. old-timers really loved to read) advised us to apply the Golden Key to the problem.[14] Every time I start to think about the resentment, start thinking about God instead, by repeating some simple phrase that reminds me of God's love and power: "There is one who has all power, that one is God" or "God is love" or "All is going to be well."

Or start thinking about the program instead, by saying some simple-minded old program slogan again and again to myself (Take It Easy, First Things First, One Day at a Time, Let Go and Let God, Think Think Think), or by repeating the first three steps to myself over and over, until I start to hear what those words are really saying.

Go read the famous passage on acceptance in the Big Book (page 449 in the third edition).[15] None of us likes to be told to read that when we are in the grips of a resentment which is driving us totally mad—our first reaction is to scream back with rage and frustration at our sponsor or whoever suggested it—but if we can force ourselves to sit down and actually read it through, we will at least start the process of cooling off and *coming back to our senses* once again.

Or take a walk, and say the Serenity Prayer over and over to myself until I start actually hearing the words. In that prayer, I ask God to grant me (1) the serenity to *accept* the things I cannot change, (2) the *courage* to change the things I can, and (3) the wisdom to know *the difference*.[16] If I'm wasting time trying to change things that simply *cannot* be changed (about people, places, and things) then I will work myself up into a massive resentment. Can anything be more obvious? Trying to do the impossible means I will always necessarily fail and end up totally frustrated. I get out of that resentment by (1) finally admitting to myself, down in my gut, that I may not *like* such-and-such, but I'm never going to be able to change it. And then I need to start looking for (2) what I have to do next in order to survive, and I need to pray for the *courage* to do what has to be done. If I've lost my job, then I need to start writing a resumé so I can look for another job, and I will need to pray for the courage to wait until replies come, and the courage to remain calm and undisturbed at the job interviews. If my husband keeps spending all the family's money on alcohol and drugs, including both his paycheck and my own, and refuses to go to A.A. or N.A. and get clean and sober, and my children and I will soon have no roof over our heads or food to eat, then I will eventually need to pray for the courage to kick him out and make it on my own. *Of course* this is frightening to someone caught in that situation, which is why I will need to pray for God's help to find the courage to do it, because that's the only way I'll be able to carry it out successfully.

People in the Al-Anon program sometimes don't like the word acceptance—they've gotten in trouble too many times by believing that they had to accept unacceptable behavior or they wouldn't be "good people"—so they prefer to use the word *detachment* instead. This means removing the emotional and spiritual links, and becoming an observer instead of a participant. That can sometimes be a good word for people in A.A. and N.A. too: Detach, detach, detach. Learn to wear the world like a loose garment. And detach the person or situation permanently from your life if you have to.

Some more tools for breaking the cycle of resentment

But there are many other tools in the program toolkit. Ask yourself, "how important is it really?" People who come into the twelve-step program tend to be incredibly thin-skinned, and are experts at taking instant offense over incredibly petty issues. They are also experts at making mountains out of minor-league molehills. I've heard many program people say, "I never trip over mountains, it's the molehills I trip over."

Also ask yourself, "how important will it be tomorrow? next week? next year?" Think back into your own past, when similar annoyances occurred: Did I even remember things like that the next day? Brooklyn Bob F. says that, at the age of eighty, he cannot think of a single thing he fretted and fumed over back when he was in his thirties and forties—and thought the whole world depended on, and drank over continuously—which matter to anyone or anything at all today. "Everyone involved is *dead* now except me," he once mused at a meeting. The things of the material world are like a dream which passes away; what I accomplish in terms of my own spiritual growth is what is real and solid and lasting. The only thing that I can ever grasp which will not ultimately crumble between my fingers is the eternal God. Me and God—that's all there ever will be at the end—but if I have that, I have everything.

A good Al-Anon sponsor I know will sometimes snap at her pigeons, "Is this the hill you want to die on?"[17] I must ask myself that question seriously: Is it important enough to lose everything over it? Is it important enough to face the possible consequences of taking that stand, or charging into that situation?

Finally getting sick and tired of being sick and tired is one good way to let go of a resentment. Holding onto a resentment is exhausting and draining. It's all right to let go of it, and the only reason I need to give is "just because I'm tired to death of feeling this way all the time." For many years, A.A. groups have been holding weekend spiritual retreats at a place in Ohio called Yokefellow. There is a big ox yoke hung over the fireplace, with an obvious reference to a famous scriptural passage (Matthew 11:28–30).

Come unto me, all you who labor and are heavy laden,
and I will give you rest. Take my yoke upon you and learn

from me, for I am gentle and have a humble heart. For my
yoke is easy and my burden is light.

Paradoxically, the twelve-step path IS the easier, softer way in actual practice. Why not just let the burden of resentment slide off your weary shoulders and let it drop?

There was a man in the program (let's call him Fod, which was his old
childhood nickname) who went to a psychotherapist to deal with bottled-
up resentments and rage that went back to his early childhood. He was the
intellectual type, who had to analyze everything and give complicated
explanations for everything. So the therapist, to short-circuit this, made
Fod go out to an athletic supply store and get a set of spring grips that
were used for building up the gripping muscles in your hands. Every day,
for five minutes, he had to hold the spring-loaded handles shut while he
concentrated on all the resentment and rage he felt. After a couple of
weeks, Fod told the therapist in dismay: "My grip should be getting
stronger, but instead, every day it's getting harder and harder to hold the
grips closed for the full five minutes." The therapist laughed at him, and
said, "You think you're failing at this, don't you, when you're really being
very successful? You're finally getting tired of holding onto all that resentment and rage, aren't you, down deep? Your body, your subconscious, and
your will are all telling you, we're tired to death of holding onto this
resentment. And though you've been trying as hard as you can to focus on
that resentment, and hang onto it, they're finally beginning to get their
message through to you. And that's a sign that the therapy is finally starting to actually work."

If I want to try this technique, keep it simple: Maybe say to myself, "I
am now willing to release the need to continue feeling this resentment."
Surprisingly, I don't actually have to *know* exactly what the deep, dark
subconscious need really is for this to work. I don't need to analyze and
psychoanalyze and dissect my inner child. I just say to myself calmly,
whenever I start to feel the resentment again, "I release the need to continue
feeling this resentment," and if I speak these words to myself with total

seriousness, where I actually mean it, and then just let myself breathe out and relax, this will frequently work all by itself. Or I can say: "I'm going to quit feeling all this resentment, because I've grieved enough over it, and I'm just worn out." It is frequently necessary though *to first do the grief work* before I will be able to let go in this way.[18]

If I am being overwhelmed by some resentment, I can call my sponsor, and vent my anger in this safe context. But remember, it's *not* my sponsor's job to *force* me to let go of the resentment, because no one else can let go of my resentment except me. I'm calling my sponsor to try to get a more objective view of the problem, and so I need to listen to my sponsor: If my sponsor thinks I'm making a mountain out of a molehill, and that the thing that has me so disturbed isn't really important at all, then I need to listen to that and hear that. If I really am in serious danger, and I really do need to take strong and decisive action, then a decent sponsor will tell me that too, right away. But I'm misusing my sponsor if I just keep on arguing, and saying things like "but don't you see that I was right and he was wrong," and things like that, and just use the phone conversation to continue rehearsing and refeeling and building up my resentment to even greater heights. The object is to *break* the continually mounting cycle of resentful thoughts.

The same thing applies to going to a meeting and talking about my resentment: if all I'm doing is just rehearsing the resentment one more time, and working myself up into an even greater sense of rage and hurt and self-pity and righteous indignation, then I'm making things worse, not better. I can talk about my resentment at a meeting to do some safe venting, but I also have to pay attention to how other people are reacting (especially those who have a lot of serenity). And it's useful to say right out, when I first start talking about it, something like "I know that resentment is the number one killer, and I know that this is doing me great harm, but I need to talk about it some, and not just try to stuff it, so I can help myself figure out some way of getting out of these feelings before they get me into even bigger trouble." And I also need to pay attention to what other people at the meeting say, because at least *one* of these people will say at least one *positive* thing that I very much need to hear to help me find a workable way out of my resentment—that's guaranteed, because that's part of the magic of the spirit of the tables.

If I'm in A.A. or N.A., it sometimes helps a lot to *go do something to help someone else*, and start thinking about something outside myself for a change. In the cycle of resentment, I become locked into looking just at myself and my own problems with such a ferocious tunnel vision, that anything that will genuinely get me out of myself for a while can break the repeating circle of resentful thoughts.

If I'm in Al-Anon, or I'm extremely codependent, *go do something nice for myself*, like taking a warm bubble bath or buying myself some ice cream or going bowling with my friends, and start thinking about positive and good things I can do to make my own life more enjoyable and happy regardless of the other problem. The cycle of resentment can be a form of self-torture game where I keep on willfully wallowing in and increasing my own inner pain, so making myself deliberately do something which will give me innocent, harmless pleasure can sometimes help break the repeating circle.

Tools for codependents and others who betray themselves

Particularly if I have problems with being too codependent,[19] I need to ask that first question that was mentioned at the beginning of this part of the book: "What is my role in creating this situation?"[20]

I am responsible for myself, not for everybody else in the whole world. I am not the Savior of the World. We have padded cells with locks on the doors for people who seriously think that they are Jesus or Napoleon or whatever—you know, "I have to save the whole world" or "I have to rule the whole world and set everybody else straight, because they aren't capable of running their own lives."

Did I create the problem by being unwilling to set proper boundaries for myself? If I let the other person intrude into what is really my space or my business, then I may need to practice saying "no." *It is not my responsibility for keeping the other person from feeling anger or resentment in this kind of situation.* Maybe the other person needs to start working a twelve-step program too—but that's his or her business, not mine.

Bubbly Diane used to say at almost every meeting, "If someone else is wallowing in his shit, I don't have to sit down and wallow in it with him. And I don't need to clean him up, or try to haul him out of his own shit. When he feels like getting up and walking out of his own shit, he'll do it."

We all need to learn to say "no" at the right time and place, but of course, there are better and worse ways of saying this. A man who was a fireman in a town near me came into a meeting one night, and said that the fire chief had asked him to do something that was not in his job description or part of his responsibilities. "So I told him to eat shit and howl at the moon. Then he told me that I was suspended for eighteen days without pay. Now that I've cooled off a little, I realize that I could have just said 'no.'"

I also need to ask myself: Did I let the other person just use me for weeks and months before I finally built up this massive resentment? If so, maybe I need to start developing a greater sensitivity, in advance, of when I'm starting to get into situations where the other person is going to try to use me, and put a halt to it before it even starts. There is one kind of newcomer who *will* do this if he thinks he can (in the A.A. and N.A. programs in particular, but you can see these people walking in the doors of any twelve-step program), and these people have developed looking needy and helpless and sincere to an art form: they are professional users, and they will use and bleed other program members if they can con them.

Start looking around, and seeing if you can learn how to spot the telltale symptoms of a user in advance, because the basic cons and manipulations they use are all pretty standardized. There will be easily identifiable road signs put up, telling you which way that road is actually going (along with some other bogus billboards erected beside the road, saying "I am so needy," "I am so helpless," "I swear to you that I'm really trying so hard this time," and so on—but that's the basic trick to the con game they're playing).[21] Once users of this sort get a hook into you, their requests and demands will just keep growing bigger and bigger. It's *your* choice when you're going to finally say no—why not learn to see the *real road signs*, and just quietly say no before your own resentment grows too big? "If he fools me once, shame on him; if he fools me twice, shame on me."

An ancient Greek myth told of creatures called sirens, who looked like beautiful women and stood along rocky coasts, singing a totally irresistible song which lured passing sailors in to their doom. A theologian named Denny Groh told me many years ago (tongue in cheek) that he had talked once with one of those sirens, who was retired now, he said, and living in a little apartment in Chicago, and he asked her what the song was that they sang. He could not help but wonder what kind of song it was, no matter how beautiful, that could conceivably make accomplished professional sailors steer their ships onto what were obviously the rocks of total self-destruction. "Oh," she said to Denny according to his tale, "it was a simple-minded little ditty—*only you can save me*—but it worked every time."

And in addition to trying to play caretaker and rescuer, there are also other ways we can betray ourselves. The sentence which prefaces the Twelve Promises in the Big Book says (p. 83): *"As God's people we stand on our feet; we don't crawl before anyone."* When I am whining, begging, and groveling before someone else, and pleading "Oh, please, please take me back!" or "Oh, please, please love me!" the underlying resentment is just going to keep building up. I have to have the courage to stand on my own feet, and stop crawling and begging—if that is what I have been doing—before the suppressed resentment will start to go away. Please note that *making amends* is not pleading with someone else to forgive me or love me. When I make amends to someone else, if I'm doing it in the right spirit, the other person's reaction (positive or negative) will be totally immaterial to me.

When Larry W. came into the program, one of his first sponsors was a white-haired old man who had had Dr. Bob himself as his first sponsor.[22] Larry still remembers the first night he met that old man, many years ago, and one of the first things he said: "Larry, you don't need to betray yourself any longer." Is this really where my resentment is coming from? Have I been *betraying myself* as a true child of God, over and over again? When I develop the courage to stop betraying myself, the resentment will lose its power over me.

Rage, temper tantrums, and learning to recover my calm and control

When I get too hot and I'm about to explode with rage, I need to pick something innocent and enjoyable to do for a while, so I can cool down some. One man in the A.A. program goes and plays computer solitaire for a while. After a few games, his mind is clear enough again to start making calmer decisions, and he can start doing something useful, something that needed to be done anyway, instead of endlessly stewing over that resentment in his mind. The dean of a theological seminary whom I knew many years ago, would go home and spade in his garden until he cooled down, and one of the church historians who taught there would go work out on a punching bag he had set up in his family room at home—you see, "normal" people have to do this too.

Doing something else to allow the anger a little time to cool down is *not* the same as turning into a work-oholic who attempts to work nonstop every waking hour of the day to continually flee from having to feel his own feelings and think his own thoughts—what I'm recommending here is a short-term emergency therapy (a half an hour to an hour maximum), and it seems to work best if it's something enjoyable (or something that will let me work my muscles) but relatively mindless and mechanical and not particularly useful.

I must resist the impulse to scream and hit. And that means using every last ounce of my will power if I have to. There is a woman in a town not far from where I live—let's call her Claudia—who talked in a step meeting once about how she behaved when she first came into the program. She would fall into rages over small things and beat her little children savagely. She told her sponsor that she was trying to follow the fifth step, and that she was "ready to have God remove" this defect of character. But God hadn't decided to remove that character defect yet, so there was just nothing she could do about it. Now Claudia's sponsor was a fierce old Scotswoman who had been in the Royal Air Force during World War II, and took no nonsense from pigeons (or anybody else), and she fixed a steely gaze on Claudia and delivered a blunt order: "*You will resist! You will resist!*" And if prayer, meditation, and the power of God's grace aren't working, then that's what we have to do, and *there are no excuses.*

When Green Berets are in training, and the trainees are told that they have to go out into the jungle and catch a snake or a lizard and eat it raw as survival training, one of the recruits will often start complaining. And the person in charge will say, "I'm sorry, you don't understand. We didn't say you had to like it. We just said you had to do it." So we don't give in to rages, and we don't have screaming temper tantrums, and if holding back my tongue and my fists is as difficult as making myself eat a raw lizard, well then, if I'm lost in a jungle, eating a lizard raw is better than starving to death. And if I do not yet understand that the twelve-step program is about life and death and my very survival, I'd better start getting more serious about my program. I don't have to like it, I just have to do it.

Life isn't fair and people don't act right

A pigeon comes to his sponsor, complaining about some situation he's in, or something somebody else has done to him. His sponsor just shrugs his shoulders and says, "Life isn't fair and people don't act right." Is this a cruel and unkind thing to say? Not in the long run: if I cannot figure out how to be reasonably happy ever when things are not completely going my way, I will ultimately be miserably unhappy most of the time, because in the normal course of everyday life things will almost never go exactly my way. A creative and inventive person can always figure out something to complain about. Like the Three Bears: "This soup is too hot." "This soup is too cold." And Mama Bear finally said, "You two sort it out—the stove is that white thing with the knobs on it. I'm going to an Al-Anon meeting."

When people first come into the twelve-step program, there is an elementary and very simple fact of life which they are doing their best to avoid seeing. And yet it is so simple that even a very simple person can understand it. It is impossible to be happy, joyous, and free—AND to be filled with seething resentments—at the same place and the same time. If you want to be happy, you're going to have to ditch all your most treasured resentments. There are no other choices here. This is not Goody-Two-Shoes moralistic preachy stuff, just a blunt fact of life.

Now when we first come into the twelve-step program, we like to pretend that there is a third alternative, which if it existed in the real world, would clearly be a much better deal. "But I would be happy as a little lark if the other people around me would just start acting differently." So in other words, if you were just given God-like power, you'd be happy. So what you're really trying to do is play God, and since you aren't God, life isn't working out for you terribly well. That's a shame, but since we folk in the program don't know how to teach you to be a God—that's way beyond our expertise—the only thing that ignorant people like us can share with you is the real happiness we discover whenever we stop trying to play God, and start working on more realistic life strategies.

"But I *love* to hate." Is that what's really going on? Do I actually *love* to feel that anger and hatred so much that I won't let go of it, or do any kind of sensible work to get rid of it? That's a perverted kind of love, and the twelve-step program is trying to teach all of us a higher, better, and ultimately far more satisfying kind of love.

Or is it that I'm scared to let go of my anger?—scared that other people will beat me up if I don't frighten them off with the threat of a crazy, out-of-control retaliation and revenge? Many of us in our childhoods were caught in situations where that was our only realistic chance for survival. But as an adult, I have more choices, a better sense of judgement, and more control—enough to make other, better options usually possible, if I start thinking about things more instead of just acting on blind impulse.

The underlying fear

Every resentment is built on some underlying fear: fear of being humiliated in public, the anxiety of powerlessness and helplessness, the anxiety of rejection and abandonment, or perhaps the fear of losing something that "I *can't live* without." (Actually, most of the time, I certainly can survive without it, regardless of what my emotions are trying to make me believe.) This overwhelming fear is what supplies the psychic energy that keeps the cycle of resentment turning. So I can make myself much more resentment-proof if I start each morning with a prayer or meditation which affirms that God will take care of me as long as I just turn my life over to his care and stop worrying so much.

But I have to *work* at this, and I have to practice it every day—there's no magic prayer or meditation which I can say once and have it instantly switch off a type of resentment which I have been rehearsing and practicing in my mind for years. There are all sorts of good meditations of this sort, like saying the Twenty-Third Psalm every morning for a month, or reading a passage like one of the following every morning for a month (these are taken from the *Twenty-Four Hour* book):[23]

August 5
God is your healer and your strength.
You do not have to ask Him to come to you.
He is always with you in spirit.
At the moment of need He is there to help you.
Could you know God's love and His desire to help you,
you would know that He needs no pleading for help.
Your need is God's opportunity.
You must learn to rely on God's strength whenever you need it.
Whenever you feel inadequate in any situation,
you should realize that
the feeling of inadequacy is disloyalty to God.
Just say to yourself:
I know that God is with me
and will help me to think and say
and do the right thing.

August 7
You should never doubt that God's spirit
is always with you, wherever you are,
to keep you on the right path.
God's keeping power is never at fault,
only your own realization of it.
You must try to believe in God's nearness
and the availability of His grace.
It is not a question of whether God can provide
a shelter from the storm,
but of whether or not you seek
the security of that shelter.
Every fear, worry or doubt is disloyalty to God.
You must endeavor to trust God wholly.
Practice saying:

"All is going to be well."
Say it to yourself
until you feel it deeply.

When I begin to trust God more deeply, I will find that all my resentments will have less and less power over me.

Making a gratitude list

One of the very best ways to break the repeating cycle of resentment is to *make a gratitude list*, and pull that list out and read it, and then start thinking about all the things I'm grateful for instead. It is absolutely impossible for a human mind to be feeling deep resentment and profound gratitude simultaneously. The two emotions cannot coexist in the same mind at the same time.

If I'm resentful towards my spouse for one thing, make a list of all the other things about my spouse for which I feel grateful. That will put everything in a saner perspective. If I'm resentful about something at my job, then make a gratitude list on that. People in twelve-step programs all too often have magnifying minds where, even in an almost ideal situation, they will spot *one tiny flaw*, and start obsessing so much about that, that they become totally blind to how well off they are.[24] Any idiot can imagine how the best possible situation could be *even more perfect*, so he can start playing the self-torment game full tilt (and intelligent people are even more talented at this!). When I'm falling off the bicycle one direction, I need to lean the opposite direction to regain my balance. A gratitude list can do wonders when I'm starting to tumble off on the resentment side of the bike.

This was one of the most important *spiritual* teachings of the old-timers, which is the reason why this chapter is in this book: When I start to feel grateful again, and my mind returns to being calm and clear, then whenever I want God, I will be able to sense him more clearly. It was a simple truth they were trying to point out to us: resentment blocks my ability to see God, and gratitude helps me see God.

A NOTE TO CHAPTER SIX

The only strategies which will make me more resentment-free in the long run are to do a fourth step on the resentment, and to work systematically to alter some of the underlying character defects (such as selfishness, co-dependency, or lack of faith and trust in God) which produce resentment and fear as their fruit.

Remember page 42 in the *Twelve Steps and Twelve Traditions*, along with page 65 in the Big Book: a character defect takes the form of a lack of balance in my natural instincts. My survival instinct prompts me to strive for food and shelter and material security. My social instinct prompts me to build personal relationships with other human beings, and to seek not only companionship but some kind of respect and recognition (of one sort or another) within that network of social relationships, so that I can have a sense of meaningful self-esteem and some feeling of emotional security. The sex drive is also a worthy natural instinct, which we are not trying to deny or destroy.

So *selfishness* is a lack of balance in one direction in my desire for material security: I want too much to ever be happy. *Laziness and irresponsibility* are a lack of balance the other direction. *Vanity* is a lack of balance in one direction in my desire for emotional security and a sense of self-esteem: I demand too much from other people, and drive them crazy. *Low self-esteem* is a lack of balance the other direction, where I let other people walk over me and use me as a doormat. *Over-controlling* means that I want the balance tipped totally my way in my personal relationships: I insist on trying to make all the decisions for other people. An *inability to establish firm personal boundaries*, on the other hand, is an imbalance the opposite direction. A *codependent* (who tries to do too much caretaking) can only create sick personal relationships with people who are *over-dependent*, that is, out of balance the other direction, where they expect someone else to take all the responsibility for them, no matter how irresponsibly they are acting.

If I can start correcting the underlying character defect, I will no longer be involved in trying to do things which will inevitably put me in the grips of resentment and fear. This is the only true long-term cure for resentment and fear.

It is important to remember here that Pride (trying to play God myself) and Fear (refusing to trust God and turn my life over to his care, so I can start acting with more courage), are the basic character defects which seem to underlie all the others for people who come into the twelve-step program.

Chapter VII

Gratitude

This chapter is based in part on a sermon originally given on May 28, 2000 at Zion United Church of Christ in South Bend, Indiana.

Father John, who died several years ago, was a Roman Catholic priest over at the University of Notre Dame. Their campus, which is very beautiful, with big trees and lakes and fine old golden-tan-colored brick buildings, starts just four blocks north of where I live. Father John had been in the A.A. program for many years, and was deeply loved. He gave a talk several months before his death, on the nature of the spiritual life.

He said that when he was young priest, he was assigned to hear the confessions of a group of elderly people at a retirement home over a long period of time. And he said that he noted that nearly all people, at the end of their life, fell into one of two categories: the *grateful* and the *resentful.* The grateful people looked back over their lives with joy and appreciation, and a sense of real satisfaction—and they still enjoyed the world around them even in the present. The resentful people, on the other hand, were filled with bitterness. They talked continually about all the negative things that had happened to them over the course of their lives. When they talked about other people, they complained about what terrible people they were, and how they had done this and that. You could bring up the name of anybody they had ever known, and they would start putting that person down and filling your ear with all the bad things that person had done. They were so filled with grudges that they still felt deep hurt and resentment at things that had happened ten years ago, twenty years ago, forty or fifty or sixty years ago.

And then the priest who was talking about this—who knew now, many years later, that he himself was dying—said that he hoped that he had learned how to be one of the grateful people.

Now I am very sensitive to this issue, because over the past several years, I spent a good deal of time with a woman who finally died last December at the age of 87, and she was unfortunately one of the resentful ones. Anything anybody tried to do for her, she would find something wrong with what they were doing, somehow or some way, and would bitterly criticize and attack them. She ended up driving away every one of her old-time friends: One friend tried to drive her places (like the grocery store or the doctor's office) and she drove that person away by continually criticizing her driving. And another one she attacked for this trivial thing, or accused of some other minor thing, until finally no one wanted to be around her any more.

She had a younger brother, but refused to have anything much to do with him. Why?—because, as she would explain every time his name was brought up, when she was fourteen years old, he had told their rigid Methodist mother about it, when she had gone dancing with a boy, and gotten her in trouble over it. She would continually bring up the story of how she had been sick when she was six years old, and an uncle had brought her some candy, and someone had come in and taken it away because they thought it would be bad for her.

And on and on, over all the years of her life, every single memory of the past had become so tainted by her cynicism and resentment and bitterness, that she could no longer talk about anything positive at all. All joy and pleasure had departed from her life by the end, all sense of satisfaction and appreciation had left her, and she simply sat around in misery, filled with anxiety and fear and loneliness.

The Two Great Commandments

I hope you see how much is at stake here, in this world as well as the next, because it is not just a this-worldly issue. The Apostle Paul, in his letter to the Romans, says that those who do not have the Bible (those who are neither Jewish nor Christian) will be judged at the last judgment on how well they have followed two simple commandments: When they stand before the throne of judgment, they will be asked, first: did they genuinely follow their own consciences, and act in accordance with what they themselves knew about the difference between right and wrong? (Rom. 2:14–16) They will then be asked, second: did they honor the higher power which created this universe, and give grateful thanks to him for all the good things of their lives? (Rom. 1:20–21) *In other words, did they practice gratitude?*

Suppose you were brought up Jewish or Christian—are the rules any different? No, because for Jews and Christians there are two great commandments, which supersede all the others in their importance: "You shall love the Lord your God with all your heart and all your soul and all your might, and you shall love your neighbor as yourself."

In fact, it's really just the same two rules. For non-Jews and non-Christians, the first and primary rule of the natural conscience is, to treat other people the way I would like to be treated, which is exactly the same thing as saying "love your neighbor as yourself." And I can hardly say that I love God with all my heart and soul, if I show him no gratitude for all the things in this beautiful and good universe which he has created for my benefit.

It's not two different sets of rules, just two different ways of phrasing what are essentially the same two requirements. And the one I want to talk about today, is the one that says that *we are expected to show gratitude to the God who created this world we live in, for all the things of this world.*

Learning to appreciate new things

Let me talk about something I did when I was a college student: I decided I wanted to learn how to appreciate classical music. At first, it all sounded the same to me; I couldn't really appreciate the difference between one piece and the next. But I kept on listening to different composers, and eventually I started learning how to appreciate Vivaldi—one of his pieces, the Four Seasons, you will hear played fairly often on the radio, and other places—it's a very simple but still very beautiful piece of music. And I kept on listening to classical music, and within a year or two, I started learning how to appreciate some of Tchaikovsky's music, like the 1812 Overture, and then I started to enjoy some of Bach's work—oh, things like the St. Matthew Passion. And slowly, over the years, I learned how to appreciate some other composers also—Stravinsky, Berlioz, and so on. About ten years ago, I began to develop a great passion for Mozart: the Magic Flute, the Requiem Mass, and many of his other pieces.

This took *work and practice.* I had to start on simple composers like Vivaldi, and slowly work my way up to composers like Mozart.

Practice makes perfect

We've already mentioned Father Ralph Pfau, who was a priest for many years down in Indianapolis and southern Indiana, and was one of the three most popular A.A. authors who have ever written. In one of his Golden Books, he talked at one point about an old saying among the German-speaking people there in one part of southern Indiana, along the Ohio River, where he once served a parish: *Die Übung macht den Meister.* In English, we usually say that as "practice makes perfect." But the German literally says, "Using something makes me the master of it."

A good concert musician—a violinist, or a pianist, or a trombonist—has to practice a minimum of three hours every day in order to stay in shape. Father Ralph talked about one great concert violinist who said, "If I miss my practice period for a single day, I can tell the difference. If I miss practicing for two days, my wife can tell the difference. If I miss for three days, everybody can tell the difference."[1]

Practicing gratitude

In light of this, let's ask again: which group of people do I want to be in at the end of my life? The resentful people or the grateful people? The resentful people end up in an inner hell of their own making. They are so filled with grudges, and keeping score on all the wrongs of the past, and cynicism, and bitterness, and despair and disgust, that their hearts can know no rest. In Psalm 95, the first part is a hymn of thanks and praise by the grateful people, and then the very last part talks about the other kind—the resentful people—and God says to them there at the end of that Psalm, "You shall not enter my rest," either in this life or in the next.

The grateful people, on the other hand, live in the sunlight of the spirit. They know how to smile and laugh and appreciate everything around them, and enjoy life, and wear the troubles of this world as a loose garment. They already have more than a taste of heaven in their hearts even while they live on earth. But that is because *they practice gratitude.*

Die Übung macht den Meister, "practice makes perfect." It would do no one any good at all for some pastor to preach a sermon at them telling them that they must be grateful instead of resentful, as though you could simply decide, here and now, that you were going to be grateful from now on instead of resentful. It's not a matter of simply sitting there and scrunching up your face really hard, and saying, "By golly, I'm going to totally change my behavior by pure will power, here and now, and from this point on I'm going to be grateful instead of resentful."

How many people reading this book can play the violin? Probably not all that many. Well, could any of the rest of you decide, here and now, that you were going to be violin-players, just by exercising your will-power? Could you get up from wherever you're sitting, reading this book, and simply pick up a violin and play beautiful music on it, right this very moment, just by exercising some will-power? Of course not! Some things take practice: days and weeks and months of practice.

Practice makes perfect. You have to *practice gratitude* in order to turn into a grateful person—and you have to deliberately and consciously work at practicing it, particularly in the beginning.

What kind of practice helps?

Learning how to practice gratitude doesn't have to be complicated, but it does have to be done deliberately and systematically. For example, some people go about it something like this: When I get up *in the morning*, first thing, pray a short prayer something like this: "Lord, help me to appreciate the good things in my life today, the gifts you have given me." Then *just before I go to sleep at night*, pray a prayer something like the following: "Lord, thank you for the good things you gave me today. I appreciate them." I must do this consistently, every morning and evening, over a period of weeks and months. When I first awake, and just before I go to sleep, are points where my subconscious is particularly susceptible to suggestion.

Then one day, I will be in such a hurry that I will forget to pray that morning prayer. By the middle of the day, I will realize that I am tense and uptight and nervous and irritable, and nothing seems to be going right. Why? Because I forgot that morning prayer. I will suddenly realize that it was doing a whole lot more good for me than I ever thought. But cheer up—if I forget, I can stop at any moment during the day, and say that prayer, and start my day over again.

I know a woman in Al-Anon who had to drive past a Roman Catholic church on her way to work every morning. She was Methodist, and had never been in that particular Catholic church in her life, but seeing the steeple of the church would remind her—did I say my prayer this morning? And if she had forgotten, she simply said it right then and there, while she was driving her car to work.

There are some A.A. and Al-Anon sponsors who have been very effective at teaching other people how to practice gratitude, who insist that their pigeons work on what they call a *gratitude list*. There are different ways of doing this. One way is to make a list of ten things you feel gratitude for, and then read that list over every morning for a month. Another way is to get the list out every evening, and put one new thing on that list that happened to you today, for which you feel gratitude. Then review at least part of that list every morning as part of your morning prayer.

I know one woman—let's call her Karen—who had been tremendously filled with anger and resentment. But when she started practicing gratitude, she eventually got to such a point that when she went outside, the birds and the wild animals would sometimes come up to her, just like the old stories about St. Francis. Karen said as she went through her day, she would simply say a little silent thank you to God for everything she could think of. If she shut the refrigerator door and it stayed closed, she would say thank you. Does this sound silly? Before Karen started doing this, she was so filled with anger and resentment and feeling sorry for herself that her life had literally become unbearable. And nobody else around her could stand her either! But she lives a pretty happy life now, most of the time. She's not a saint yet, but she's a basically happy person.

But I don't have anything to feel grateful for, you may say. Well then, you aren't really putting your own mind to work on this wholeheartedly yet: Hold your hand in front of your mouth—are you breathing? Are you going to have *something* to eat today? Are you going to have a bed to sleep on tonight? Are you only grateful for steak and lobster dinners? Maybe you ought to start practicing learning how to truly enjoy the taste of a good peanut butter or tuna salad sandwich. Practice makes perfect. Don't scoff until you've practiced it for a while. You have an old, beat-up car. Perhaps you need to practice being grateful when you climb in the car and turn the starter and it actually starts. And if it doesn't start, then you need to start practicing being grateful that you can somehow scrape the money together for a new starter or a new battery. Or if the car finally quits entirely, then you need to start practicing being grateful you can still walk.

Gratitude in spite of pain

A few years ago, I slipped coming down the stairs in my own home, and broke my back. I got to the hospital, they x-rayed it, and told me that if the crack had gone one eighth of an inch further, I would have been paralyzed from the armpits down. I immediately started praying prayers of gratitude to God for that. I was able to lie in my bed at home, and continue giving the lectures for my classes over the telephone by setting up a speaker phone in the classroom over at the university. And I was grateful for that. I was eventually able to get up and walk, as long as I didn't try carrying anything heavier than a single file folder. And I was grateful for that. Then I was able to carry a small briefcase, as long as I did not have to walk too far. And I was grateful for that. After six months, I was back to normal, and could lug heavy suitcases around and all that sort of thing. And I was grateful for that.

Because I continued to be grateful, and to pray prayers of gratitude, what some would regard as a major accident was something that I don't look back on as all that painful or all that big a deal. *An attitude of gratitude changes the whole dynamic of how we experience anything at all.*

Forgiveness

In the middle of the Lord's Prayer, it says "forgive us what we owe you, just as we forgive other people what they owe us." I can have no true gratitude as long as I am still tormented inside by grudges against other people for things I believe they did to me back in the past. Am I myself a hard-hearted, unforgiving person? Well, whenever I think about so-and-so, what thoughts come to my mind? "I'm still so hurt because he did such-and-such to me." When I am arguing with my spouse, how do I argue? "And furthermore, I'll never forget such-and-such, which you did twenty years ago," or forty years ago, or whatever.

What do hard-hearted, unforgiving people say when they are challenged on this issue? "But you don't understand! He really did do that!" Or they'll say, "But you don't understand! I was right and he was wrong!" I don't care, and God doesn't care. You're the one who's totally sick with resentment inside. You're the one who keeps on rehearsing this wrong inside your soul—whether it was real or imagined—and it's your soul which is being poisoned by it.

Of course, if the person is still doing it, I may have to take actions to protect myself. But there's a difference between simple common sense, and the kind of person who seethes with resentment and self-pity, and who can't simply move on, and live life today.

This is not a chapter on how to practice forgiveness—because you also have to *practice* that to get good at it—but when people start practicing gratitude on a systematic, daily basis, they find that learning forgiveness comes a whole lot easier.

When I learn how to see all the things around me, every day, with which God has blessed me, it finally starts to dawn on me that the things I don't like aren't really important at all, most of the time. And even the bigger things become manageable, when I can learn how to look at the universe as a universe which is alive with God's light and grace and love.

Start looking around you with new eyes

Let's start practicing right now! Look around the room or place you're in right now: what are you grateful for here? If you're grateful for one of the people you came into contact with today, say a little prayer of thanks to God for that person right now. Actually *look* at the trees and the flowers as you walk outside: are they beautiful? then say a little silent thank you to God as you enjoy them. Or if it's snowing or raining, learn to appreciate the beauty of snowflakes and raindrops, and then start saying thank you.

I went back home to Texas several years ago, with a colleague from this part of the world (the lush green fields of Illinois and Indiana), and as we drove in the airport limousine from the airport to our hotel, and passed through the Texas countryside, he said in horror: "This is the most God-forsaken country I've ever seen in my life." And I suppose that was his honest reaction at one level—it was scrubby little mesquite trees and prickly pear cactus, black dry earth and chunks of flint rock, with an occasional blade or two of grass, burnt brown and dry, sticking up here and there—it certainly wasn't the incredibly fertile farmland of Illinois or Indiana. But *God-forsaken*? For heavens sakes, of course not! I didn't try to argue with him though, because I'm sorry to say that he was one of the most resentful people I've ever known, and an enormously unhappy person as a result: I just settled back and gazed out the windows and enjoyed myself, and sighed and said, "No, *it's home*."

Father John, the priest who was dying, understood it all. There are basically only two kinds of people—the resentful and the grateful—so which group do you tend to fall into? Examine your soul very carefully before answering this question: the life of your soul is at stake here.

If what I'm saying here strikes home with you, and you discover that you can't honestly put yourself in the category with the unquenchably grateful people, you can't turn yourself from a resentful person into a grateful person here and now, right this very moment, just by exercising some mighty act of willpower. *Practice* makes perfect. You get better at it only by practicing it, over and over, until you get the hang of it.

But if what I'm saying here strikes home with you, you *can* do something about it during the next twenty-four hours: you can *make a start* at it. Before you go to bed tonight, think of at least one thing you're grateful for, and pray a prayer of thanks to God for it. And write it on a slip of paper if you have to, but remember tomorrow morning to start off first thing with a little silent prayer to God, asking him to help you to practice more gratitude for the rest of that day. I absolutely guarantee you that everybody whom I have ever known who has done this regularly and consistently has quickly found their lives filled with such a new spirit as a result, that they will assure you that this is not just some hokey, unrealistic theory. It gets real results, and you yourself will be the one who will feel that and know it.

God's grace is real, and he gives it, in overflowing abundance, to any human being who will simply ask him for it, in the simplest possible words, and will truly accept the gift which God so willingly gives. And accepting gifts from God properly means *appreciating* these gifts, which makes us react with true gratitude. This is life which you are being offered: please accept that gift. Amen.

The hard-hearted who know no rest

When a lot of the material in this chapter was originally given as a sermon at Zion United Church of Christ about a year ago, the scripture reading which was read was Psalm 95 in the Old Testament (one of the most important holy books of the eastern Mediterranean world), a song written and sung among an ancient race, almost three thousand years ago, about the two kinds of people we've been talking about:

One kind of person is filled with joy and happiness and appreciation, and continually gives thanks to God for all things, great and small, and lives in *gratitude* all day long. When the Lord judges them, he will say, these are my sheep, they are part of my flock, I will make them to dwell in my house forever.

The other kind of person is *hard-hearted*. They have hearts of stone, and know neither love nor forgiveness nor thankfulness. Whenever God judges them, he will be forced to say, "They shall not enter my rest." It is precisely because they are so hard-hearted, and their hearts are so filled with resentment instead of gratitude, that their hearts can never receive any rest or any inner peace. It's like the theologians said in the middle ages, not even God could make a square circle, because nothing could be both perfectly square and perfectly circular simultaneously. So unfortunately no one, not even God himself, can enable these poor hard-hearted and resentful people to enter the deep calm and serenity of his eternal presence.

Psalm 95

O come, let us sing unto the LORD;
    let us make a joyful noise to the rock of our salvation.
Let us come into his presence with thanksgiving;
    let us make a joyful noise to him with hymns of praise.
For the LORD is a great God,
    and a great king above all gods.
In his hand are the deepest places of the earth;
    the mountain peaks are his also.
The sea is his, because he made it,
    and the dry land, molded by his hands.
O come, let us worship and bow down,

let us kneel before the LORD, our Maker.
For he is our God,
> and we are the people of his pasture,
> and the sheep of his hand.

Oh, if only you would listen to his voice today!
Do not harden your hearts, as at Meribah,
> as on that day at Massah in the wilderness,
when your ancestors tested me
> and made me prove myself,
> though they had seen what I could do.
For forty years I loathed that generation
> and said, "They are a people whose hearts go astray,
> who do not know my ways."
Therefore in my anger I swore
> that they would not enter my rest.

On this same topic, it was the great African saint, St. Augustine, who said sixteen centuries ago: "You have made us for yourself, and our hearts are *rest*-less until they find their rest in you."[2] We will find no inner rest, by day or by night, until we turn to God and learn to practice gratitude, and learn to live in the sunlight of his spirit, where all our tears will be wiped away.

A prayer

Then I ended the Sunday morning service back in May of 2000 with the following pastoral prayer. This is the prayer that I now pray today for you, the reader:

O Lord, your messengers have taught us the nature of true love. Our hearts are filled with gratitude for your love for us. Even when we have fallen short, you have accepted us just as we were. You came to us with your help when we were in need. You came in quietness and gentleness, and sent us humble messengers who opened their hearts to us. Even when we turned away from you, you treated us with respect, and waited until we ourselves were willing to accept your help.

You sought only what was our own true, highest good—what would be good and healthy for us, and would allow us to feel true satisfaction with our lives. You were patient with us, and taught us that you will still love us even when we are angry with you. We asked you for forgiveness when we went astray, and you turned the page and let us start over with a clean slate.

You taught us to seek only the truth, about ourselves and about the world, and to be totally honest with you, as you are totally honest with us. You shielded us and protected us. You trusted us, and taught us to trust ourselves. You put your hope in us.

Even when we could not hear you or feel you, you were always there. Your everlasting arms held us up: You, the living God, who are eternal, and can never falter nor fail: to you be the glory forever! Amen.

So let us now let us go forth in peace, hearts filled with gratitude and thanksgiving, knowing that the sunlight of God's spirit shines all around us, and that his grace can conquer all things and transform our lives from glory unto glory, filling our souls with peace and joy and faith and courage.

May the blessing of God Almighty be upon you, and remain with you always. Amen.

Chapter VIII

Being at Home

Agapê love

When Jewish rabbis began to translate the Old Testament into Greek in the third century B.C., they discovered that there was no Greek noun that meant "love" in the sense in which it was often used in the bible. Pagan Greek had a word which referred to lust and erotic love, or any love where a powerful desire for the beloved played the dominant role; they also had a word which meant friendship, or simply liking somebody at a deep level; but neither of these words seemed totally appropriate to many parts of the bible.[1] These creative rabbis therefore decided to invent a special term. The word which they created seemed so perfect, that the early Christians took it over and used it throughout the New Testament. What the rabbis did was to take the Greek verb *agapaô*, and make a noun out of it. The verb meant to greet with affection, to welcome into one's home, to be completely contented with something or someone, to cherish the presence of the person or thing, and to be deeply pleased by it. So the noun *agapê* which they invented meant something like welcome-home-love.

Welcome-home-love is the word which is used repeatedly in the New Testament to describe the kind of love which Jesus and the Apostle Paul were so often talking about, the love with which God welcomes us back when we return to him and ask him for help.

Coming back home

I myself will always remember the first time I visited Dr. Bob's house in Akron, Ohio. I walked up the long steps to the front porch and stood at the front door; a young man I had never seen before came to the door and opened it, and simply said quietly, "Welcome home."

And I just said "Thank you," and walked into the house, an ordinary middle-class two-story residence with living room, dining room, and kitchen downstairs and bedrooms upstairs. The rooms were fairly small—it was in what was a respectable neighborhood in those days, but it was never the kind of truly grand home that would catch the eye by its class and distinction and size. South Bend, Indiana, where I live, is filled with thousands of houses much like it from that same era (I live in a similar house myself, built around the same time as Dr. Bob's house).

Eventually I went back to the kitchen, and someone there quietly asked, "Would you like some coffee?"

"Sure," I said.

There was a coffee pot beside the kitchen stove, so I poured myself a cup of coffee and sat down on one of the plain chairs around the little wooden table, and sipped some coffee, as I thought about the many recovering alcoholics who had sat in that same kitchen, drinking coffee and talking with Dr. Bob and his wife Anne.

Then I went back out on the brick front porch that stretched across the front of the house and sat down on the porch swing there, and continued drinking my coffee as I looked out at the lawn, completely relaxed and content just to be there. At one point, another visitor—again, someone I had never seen or met before—also came out, and sat on the porch railing, and she and I chatted quietly for a while, as though we were old friends who had known one another forever.

And that was the spirit of the house: the chairs, the beds, the bathroom sink, were simple and inexpensive, with nothing grand or pretentious, and yet it was a place where I just felt instantly at home. It was like the best part of my parents' home, and my grandmother and grandfather's house, and my Aunt Jenny's, and all the places I had ever been where I had some-how known that I could relax and feel at home there—but without any of the stress or tension which I also sometimes felt in those places from my own childhood.

Feeling at home

I also remember the first time I was invited to attend the monthly Old-timers Lunch Group for the A.A. people from Elkhart and Goshen, Indiana. It is held on one Thursday each month at an Amish-style restaurant and buffet, halfway between the two towns, with hearty, home-cooked food prepared by Mennonite women in prayer bonnets. There at a long table were fifteen or twenty silver-haired men, old in years but young in heart, chatting and smiling and joking quietly with one another. Their eyes sparkled, and they laughed at themselves, and they were just old men, but they seemed somehow to glow with some strange light which can only be discerned by the eyes of the spirit. My own inner tensions and anxieties began to die off as I began to absorb a little bit of their spirit of relaxation and calm and serenity. Each of these men was a person who was at home with himself, and therefore at home in the world. There is a power to heal the soul just from being around such people.

Seeing so many gathered together in one place was especially impressive, but any one of them, by himself, would have irradiated the same spirit of being-at-home-in-the-world no matter what situation you placed him in. There is an incredible strength in such a human being: even in the midst of great crisis and confusion, with other people running here and there, yelling and arguing and screaming, and even in the midst of death and dying, such a man or woman stands out above the rest, acting in clear-headed fashion, and making wise and practical decisions based on responsibility and compassion.

If you call up one of these men or women in the middle of the night, you find that you can talk completely openly about what has terrified you or put you in a rage, and they will genuinely listen to you, with kindness and compassion. They will not shame you or tell you that you are a bad person. But they also will continue to retain their own inner calm and serenity, and will finally say something simple like, "How important is it, really?" or "Well, you can't do anything about it tonight, so why don't you go read the passage on acceptance on page 449 of the Big Book, and then go to sleep?" or "You're right, it is unfair what so-and-so is doing to you, but the important thing to remember is to keep your own side of the street swept clean—as long as you do that, it'll work out the way it's supposed to work out." And so you hang up the phone, and you're still upset, but somehow not as much, and to your surprise you discover that you can lie down and go to sleep now, and that their strange magic has worked.

The "flavor" of twelve-step spirituality

Each of the great spiritual traditions of the world has its own "flavor" or "feel," in spite of the fact that they are all, underneath, so often saying the same things. We can read stories about the Zen masters doing whatever they felt like doing and ignoring all of society's normal conventions while they posed their preposterous paradoxes to their puzzled disciples, and get something of the feel of this kind of Buddhist spirituality. St. Teresa of Avila's nuns, on the other hand, had ecstatic visions and experienced strange things like out-of-body soul travel, and eventually reached a state called the spiritual marriage where they were bound body and soul to their Lord. Or you can go to a certain type of Protestant revival and see people lying on the floor, twisting spasmodically and crying out "Praise Jesus! Praise Jesus!" while others are speaking in tongues or shouting "Hallelujah!" at the top of their lungs. The monks of Mt. Athos in Greece chanted the Jesus Prayer silently in their minds over and over, all day long, until they were caught up in the vision of the Uncreated Light that penetrates from beyond this created world and fills us with the divine glory. St. Gregory of Nyssa, St. Denis, and St. John of the Cross talked about the look down into the bottomless abyss of No-thing-ness, and the sudden, gut-level, totally disorienting awareness of the complete incomprehensibility of the Ultimate.

People who enter the twelve-step program have frequently seen or at least read about spiritual disciplines with this sort of flamboyant "flavor," and keep trying to experience things like that, and can end up completely missing the point of what it is they are trying to do in the twelve-step program. Sometimes they continue trying to hype themselves up yet more, or drive themselves yet harder in perfectionistic ways, so that their inner anxieties and resentments just keep on growing greater and greater.

Sometimes you want to say to some of these newcomers to the program, "What you really need to do is to learn to relax a little." Submarine Bill warns his pigeons frequently, "Don't take yourself so seriously." His sponsor, Don H., would just ask his pigeons quietly, "How important is it, really?" Brooklyn Bob F. often repeats a line which an old-timer named Roger Stanz used to say at meetings many years ago, a little formula which is simple yet says so much: "Don't hurry, don't worry, don't compare." All of them were trying to say the same thing: learning how to relax—so the fear and resentment can start to dissipate—is one of the most important goals in the program.

A major goal of twelve-step spirituality is to learn to-be-at-home-with-myself, so I can learn to-be-at-home-in-the-world. In the fourth step I learn who I myself truly am, in the fifth step I quit hiding the secrets, in the eighth and ninth steps I clean away the wreckage of the past (where I can) so that I can start over with a clean slate, and in the twelfth step I begin living this new way of life every hour of every day in a new, outreaching kind of way. But the only way to accomplish this often frightening spiritual journey is to start learning how to-be-at-home-with-God, because only that can give me the strength to do the other things that have to be done.

As I progress along the way, I end up learning more and more about how to feel all three ways of being at home—being at home with myself, in the world, and with God—but the best and greatest of these is being-at-home-with-God. Because God is everywhere, and is always with us wherever we go, being with God is being at home in the most ultimate and satisfying sense. And if I have learned how to clear away the barriers within my own mind which block me from feeling God's presence, I will automatically know how to start feeling at home with myself, and totally and unselfconsciously at home in the world around me, wherever I am.

The good old-timers in A.A. are just as much in a state of *satori* as any Zen master, it just "feels" different on the surface. They don't hit foolish disciples over the heads with bamboo poles; instead they zing them with a well-chosen sentence that stops them in their tracks. The good old-timers walk continually with God just as much as anyone who ever achieved St. Teresa's spiritual marriage, and they go on twelve-step calls into dangerous places with the same fearlessness as frontier Methodist circuit riders journeying into the trackless forests of the American wilderness. They know the radical incomprehensibility of the ultimate abyss as well as any follower of St. Gregory of Nyssa or St. John of the Cross; and they speak with the *parrêsia*, the total boldness of speech, of the ancient Egyptian desert monks. They have the simplicity of the eighteenth-century Hasidic followers of the Baal Shem Tov and the total abandonment to God of the original followers of St. Francis of Assisi.

But the "flavor" is different in the twelve-step program. It is a great spiritual tradition all its own which has already, in less than seventy years, produced two great classic works on the spiritual life, and a number of respectfully good lesser books and writings—and it has demonstrated over and over again that it actually works if you work it, and it works amazingly deeply and amazingly quickly compared to any other of the great classical spiritual traditions I myself have studied. If you wish to receive its fruits, however, you need to work towards what it actually promises as its reward.

So you need to ask yourself: what do you, the reader, really *want* out of life in order to be truly *happy?* Not what mama wants or papa wants, or hubby or wifey wants, or what magazines and television shows try to make you want. What do *you* want to be happy? If it's continuous ecstatic visions or trance states, or endless mind-blowing experiences of the unutterable, or the self-torture of sleeping on a bed of nails or wearing a haircloth shirt, or sitting cross-legged and staring at your navel while you try to empty your mind of all content, there are religious groups which will teach you how to do that. But what do you yourself really want to be happy with your life?

Welcome home

I have been at twelve-step meetings where a newcomer stumbled in, weeping and crying, as he choked out his story past his sobs. And finally someone in the group said quietly, "Welcome home." What does that little phrase mean? It means you're O.K. now, you're not lost anymore, you're not going to have to cry *that* way anymore—though it's perfectly O.K. to cry—but you're safe now, and we're going to get you all well again.

Wouldn't it be great to-be-at-home-with-God, where all your tears will be wiped away? To-be-at-home-with-yourself? Simply to-be-at-home-in-the-world, wherever you go? Because then you can enjoy anything and everything else that's really worth enjoying and appreciating. The theologians stood around outside and talked about God; the desert monks sat inside and dined with God. The twelve-step program is not talk-about God, but a way of living that leads us to being-with God.

One of the most powerful passages in the Big Book is the section called the Twelve Promises:[2]

> If we are painstaking about this phase of our development, we will be amazed before we are half way through. We are going to know a new freedom and a new happiness. We will not regret the past nor wish to shut the door on it. We will comprehend the word serenity and we will know peace. No matter how far down the scale we have gone, we will see how our experience can benefit others. That feeling of uselessness and self-pity will disappear. We will lose interest in selfish things and gain interest in our fellows. Self-seeking will slip away. Our whole attitude and outlook upon life will change. Fear of people and of economic insecurity will leave us. We will intuitively know how to handle situations which used to baffle us. *We will suddenly realize that God is doing for us what we could not do for ourselves.*
>
> Are these extravagant promises? We think not. They are being fulfilled among us—sometimes quickly, sometimes slowly. They will always materialize if we work for them.

As Brooklyn Bob F. says to newcomers who walk into their first A.A. meeting, if this is the way you would really like your life to be, "this is not the best place for you to be, it is the *only* place for you to be." Why must it necessarily be a completely spiritual program? Because of the realization that comes in the twelfth promise above: everything else was secondary, for it was only God working secretly within our souls, who—often without us even being aware of it—did for us what we could never in a million years have done for ourselves.

Listen to the gentle laughter and look at the smiles on the faces of the good old-timers and hear the simple words with which they greet you when you arrive at their door: "Welcome home." They are but earthly channels, for it is God himself speaking to you, and telling you that you can lay down your burdens now, for you—the wandering, lost child— have come home at last. Amen.

Notes

CHAPTER I. DISCOVERING A HIGHER POWER

1. Glenn F. Chesnut, *The Factory Owner and the Convict: My Story Is My Message—the Words of Early Pioneers in the Alcoholics Anonymous Movement in the St. Joseph River Valley*, 1st ed. (South Bend IN: Hindsfoot Foundation [P.O. Box 4081, South Bend IN 46634], 1996).

2. Or "I am who I am," Exodus 3:14. For the Christian tradition, see Etienne Gilson, *History of Christian Philosophy in the Middle Ages* (New York: Random House, 1955), p. 368. Thomas Aquinas, along with Augustine, John of Damascus, and Anselm, regarded this phrase as the necessary starting point of any philosophical theology: the only true name we could give to the ultimate ground of being was HE WHO IS, or simply HE IS. For Augustine this meant that it was the ground of eternally unchanging truth, that which we were perpetually seeking in our quest for knowledge. For John of Damascus this name implied that the ground was an infinite ocean of beinghood, and for Anselm that it was the nature-of-being itself. Aquinas said that it meant that God was the act-of-being itself: God's essential reality was simply "to be" (*esse*) as that underlying ground which *had to exist* by internal necessity, in order for anything else at all to exist. We could not say that God "is this" or "is that," because that would be to limit him and turn him into just a part of the created universe. So any other names we gave God (or any other attempts to describe him) had to be only analogies, symbols or metaphors, which *pointed towards* that divine ground but did not describe it literally. Our problem was that, on the one hand, if we claimed they were literally true, we would be falling into idolatry. But on the other hand, if we refused to use such names and descriptive language, we could

not think or talk about God at all or establish any meaningful relationship with him.

So what the twelve-step program says is, that we must each pick our own names, symbols, and metaphors for talking and thinking about God—ways of visualizing and relating to this higher power which make sense to us—but we absolutely cannot force our own favorite terminology on other people. Even language taken directly from the Hebrew Bible, the New Testament, the Koran, or some great Asian religious text, still represents only one of many metaphors or analogies or limited historical ritual traditions. We can tell which members "know" God by seeing whose lives are being transformed in extraordinarily positive directions by drawing on the power of the divine grace.

3. Chesnut, *The Factory Owner and the Convict*: Nick Kowalski's story is told in chs. 9–11 (pp. 45–65) and 14–16 (pp. 85–104). The quote is from ch. 15, p. 94.

4. Sue C. (South Bend IN), see chapt. 3, n. 7.

5. Plato talked about the Good in his parable of the cave, in the *Republic*, 2 vols., trans. Paul Shorey, Loeb Classical Library (London: William Heinemann, 1935-7), 7.1.514A-3.518B. In 7.3.517B–C he said that the bright sun shining outside the dark cave stood metaphorically for "the idea of the Good" (*hê tou agathou idea*), which was that which enabled us to see what is right (*orthos*) and beautiful (*kalos*), to recognize truth (*alêtheia*) and intelligible meaning (*nous*), and to act in a manner which was sane and sensible (*emphrôn*). On Philo, see Erwin R. Goodenough, *An Introduction to Philo Judaeus*, 2nd ed. (New York: Barnes and Noble, 1962). On Augustine see, for example, Frederick Copleston, *A History of Philosophy*, Vol. 2. *Mediaeval Philosophy: Augustine to Scotus* (Westminster MD: Newman Press, 1950), pp. 62 and 82 (on God as the Good Itself and its connection with Plato's parable of the cave) and pp. 68–71 (on God as Truth Itself).

6. Sue C. (South Bend), see chapt. 3, n. 7.

7. The three authors within the ranks of A.A. whose books have sold more by far than anyone else are Bill Wilson, Richmond Walker and Ralph Pfau. For Bill W., see passages like *Alcoholics Anonymous*, 3rd ed. (New York: Alcoholics Anonymous World Services, 1976), p. 46: "Our own conception [of God], however inadequate, was sufficient to make the approach and to effect a contact with Him…. We found that God does not make too hard terms with those who seek Him."

For Richmond Walker, see *Twenty-Four Hours a Day*, Compiled by a Member of the Group at Daytona Beach, Fla., rev. ed. (Center City MN: Hazelden, 1975). Rich, who wrote this little meditational book, came into the A.A. program in May 1942; he wrote the book in 1948 and printed and distributed it to A.A. members himself until the task became too big, and Hazelden offered to print it for him in 1954. In the reading for June 1, he said:

> You were born with a spark of the Divine within you. It had been all but smothered by the life you were living. That celestial fire has to be tended and fed so that it will grow eventually into a real desire to live the right way. By trying to do the will of God, you grow more and more in the new way of life. By thinking of God, praying to Him, and having communion with Him, you gradually grow more like Him. The way of your transformation from the material to the spiritual is the way of Divine Companionship.

See also the readings for April 30, "there is a spark of the Divine in every one of us," and March 4, "we start out with a spark of the Divine Spirit but a large amount of selfishness."

Ralph Pfau, a Roman Catholic priest, came into the A.A. program on November 10, 1943. Four years later, he published the first of a long series of books and pamphlets on twelve-step spirituality, using the pen name "Father John Doe" to preserve his public anonymity: *The Golden Book of the Spiritual Side* (Indianapolis IN: SMT Guild, 1947). On p. 12 of that little book, Father

Ralph quoted with hearty approval a passage from p. 55 of the Big Book: "Deep down in every man, woman, and child, is the fundamental idea of God. It may be obscured by calamity, by pomp, by worship of other things, but in some form or other it is there."

There are summaries of the medieval teachings about this divine spark in *Dictionary of Latin and Greek Theological Terms: Drawn Principally from Protestant Scholastic Theology.*, ed. Richard A. Muller (Grand Rapids MI: Baker Book House, 1985), s.v. *scintilla animae, scintilla conscientiae, conscientia,* and *synderesis.* It is "a divine spark deep within the soul...that provides the point of union between God and man." In some late medieval Catholic spiritual writers, it was viewed as a spark of the uncreated light of God himself present within the human soul.

In the eighteenth century, John Wesley, "The Original, Nature, Property, and Use of the Law" 1.3, in his *Standard Sermons,* ed. Edward H. Sugden, 4th ed., 2 vols. (London: Epworth Press, 1955–6) gave this teaching more of a classical Protestant interpretation. God gave this understanding of his moral law (and therefore who he was) as a *special gift of grace* to the first human beings on earth, "...not wrote indeed upon tables of stone or any corruptible substance, but engraven on his heart by the finger of God, wrote in the inmost spirit of men and angels, to the intent it might never be far off, never hard to be understood, but always at hand, and always shining with clear light, even as the sun in the midst of heaven" (note the reference both to the covenant of grace passage in Jeremiah 31:31–34 and to Plato's parable of the sunlight of the Good shining outside the door to the cave). When a human being fell totally from grace, this tiny spark of the inner sunlight of the spirit was lost, but God reimplanted it inside his heart by new, specific acts of grace directed towards that particular person, so that no human being was ever totally without it for very long. So for Wesley the *scintilla* was always there, but as a gift which God's grace gave over and over again (no matter how hard we tried to destroy it or deny it) rather than as a natural human capacity. Also, the spark was not God himself actually present in the soul, but an image or likeness of God which he created for us down here within the created realm.

These various historical interpretations are given merely as examples. The twelve-step program of course allows people to interpret ideas like this in any way they wish.

8. The hymn of the seraphim comes from Isaiah 6:3. On the kabbalistic doctrine, see A. E. Waite, *The Holy Kabbalah* (New Hyde Park NY: University Books, n.d.).

9. M. Scott Peck, *The Road Less Traveled: A New Psychology of Love, Traditional Values and Spiritual Growth* (New York: Touchstone/Simon & Schuster, 1980).

10. The idea of the knowledge of God in the mirror of the soul appeared in Greek patristic literature as early as the fourth century, see St. Gregory of Nyssa, *From Glory to Glory: Texts from Gregory of Nyssa's Mystical Writings*, ed. Herbert Musurillo (New York: Scribner, 1961). The introduction (pp. 1–78), by Jean Daniélou, is an excellent summary of some of the major themes in Gregory's teaching.

In the thirteenth century, St. Thomas Aquinas said that the statement that God was Being Itself was the only literal statement we could make about God. For him, even the statement that "God was good" was an analogy; it was not a univocal (simple literal) statement, but was based on what he called the analogy of being. See Frederick Copleston, *History of Philosophy*, Vol. 2, *Medieval Philosophy: Augustine to Scotus*, (Westminster, Maryland: Newman Press, 1950), ch. 25, "St. Thomas Aquinas—V: God's Nature," pp. 347–362; Josef Pieper, *Guide to Thomas Aquinas*, trans. R. and C. Winston (New York: Mentor-Omega Books, New American Library, 1962), ch. 11, pp. 119–130; and Thomas Aquinas, *Summa Theologica* 1.13.5.c.reply to obj. 1 in Vernon J. Bourke, ed., *The Pocket Aquinas* (New York: Washington Square Press, 1960), "Analogy in Predication and Being," pp. 163–5.

11. As it says in the Old Testament, in Genesis 1:27, "So God created a human being in his image, in the image of God he created human beings: male

and female he created them." The idea of the image of God in the human soul—the *eikôn tou Theou* or icon of God in Greek, the *imago Dei* in Latin—has been a fundamental motif in nearly all Christian thought, including Roman Catholic, Eastern Orthodox, and Anglican theology, as well as Protestant theology of all sorts. See for example s.v. *imago Dei* in the *Oxford Dictionary of the Christian Church*, 2nd ed., ed. F. L. Cross and E. A. Livingstone (London: Oxford University Press, 1974) and in *Dictionary of Latin and Greek Theological Terms: Drawn Principally from Protestant Scholastic Theology*. Or see s.v. image of God in Van A. Harvey, *A Handbook of Theological Terms* (New York: Macmillan, 1964). For the idea of the image of God as it has appeared in discussions of the person and work of Christ down through history, see Glenn F. Chesnut, *Images of Christ: An Introduction to Christology* (San Francisco: Harper & Row/Seabury, 1984).

For the Greek patristic (and later Orthodox) doctrine see Vladimir Lossky, *In the Image and Likeness of God*, ed. J. H. Erickson and T. E. Bird (Crestwood NY: St. Vladimir's Seminary Press, 1974) and also Lossky's *The Vision of God*, trans. A. Moorhouse (Crestwood NY: St. Vladimir's Seminary Press, 1963), pp. 56–7, 86, 115 and 117; John Meyendorff, *Byzantine Theology* (New York: Fordham University Press, 1974); and Jean Daniélou's introd. to Gregory of Nyssa, *From Glory to Glory: Texts from Gregory of Nyssa's Mystical Writings*, sect. 2, "Gregory's Doctrine on the Image of God in Man" (pp. 10–23).

Some of the best ancient pagan Greco-Roman thinkers also insisted that the truly good man or woman needed to live and act as God's image here on earth: see Glenn F. Chesnut, "The Ruler and the Logos in Neopythagorean, Middle Platonic, and Late Stoic Political Philosophy," in H. Temporini and W. Haase, eds., *Aufstieg und Niedergang der Römischen Welt: Geschichte und Kultur Roms im Spiegel der neueren Forschung* 2.16.2 (Berlin: Walter de Gruyter, 1978), pp. 1310-32.

12. John Wesley, "The Original, Nature, Property, and Use of the Law" 2.1. in his *Standard Sermons*. The moral law gives us a picture of who God is at the deepest level, for it shows us God's own basic moral character.

[It is] an incorruptible picture of the High and Holy ONE that inhabiteth eternity. It is he whom, in his essence, no man hath seen, or can see, made visible to men and angels. It is the face of God unveiled, God manifested to his creatures as they are able to bear it—manifested to give and not to destroy life, that they may see God and live. It is the heart of God disclosed to man.

It shows us *the character of God's personality*, to use modern language. In a Greek phrase borrowed from a christological passage in Hebrews 1:3 and applied here in a slightly different context, Wesley says it is the *charactêr tês hypostaseôs autou*, a phrase which Wesley himself translates as "the express image of his person." The Greek word *charactêr* meant the image stamped on a coin or carved in an official seal, and hence a characteristic distinctive mark, or sometimes any sort of likeness or representation of a thing.

13. *Twenty-Four Hours a Day*, Nov. 16 (quoting Matthew 18:20): "'Where two or three are gathered together in My name, there am I in the midst of them'…. Where any sincere group of people are together, reverently seeking the help of God, His power and His spirit are there to inspire them." See also Nov. 29.

14. As St. Augustine insisted, what is important is "the inner spiritual history of each individual human soul, as God providentially arranges each external historical situation in which the soul finds itself, in order to chasten it, comfort it, reward it, warn it, [or] divert it from future spiritual dangers." Glenn F. Chesnut, "The Pattern of the Past: Augustine's Debate with Eusebius and Sallust," in John Deschner, Leroy T. Howe, and Klaus Penzel, eds., *Our Common History as Christians* (New York: Oxford University Press, 1975), pp. 69–95, on p. 81 which also quotes (in this context) from Augustine's *City of God* 1.8:

For as the same fire causes gold to glow brightly, and chaff to smoke…thus it is that in the same affliction the wicked detest God and blaspheme, while the good pray and praise. So material a difference does it make, not what ills are suffered, but what kind of man suffers them.

15. I have hesitated to use the word *empiricism* in this work, because empirical testing can often mean performing one isolated experiment, recording the immediate result, then performing another carefully isolated experiment, and so on. The object is to build up a body of easily repeatable test observations where, under controlled laboratory conditions, anyone who sets up the same experiment will be guaranteed to find exactly the same results, in ways that can be measured and quantified. In this book however, we are looking at how human beings come into contact with God's grace, and God (who is *super*-natural in the original meaning of the word) refuses to let himself be domesticated by our science, and sends his grace where, when, and how he wishes, in often unexpected fashion. The term I have chosen to use instead is the word *pragmatism*, although I do not mean it in quite the same way as that word was sometimes employed by the early twentieth-century philosophers who make up what is called the "American pragmatist tradition." When I use this term pragmatic, I am referring to what we might call the practical wisdom of accumulated personal experience.

But see Ernest Kurtz, *Not-God: A History of Alcoholics Anonymous* (Center City, Minn.: Hazelden Educational Services, 1979), pp. 164 and 181, where he points to the linkage between the ideas of William James (one of the founders of American pragmatist philosophy) and early A.A. thought.

16. Alan M. Turing, "Computing Machinery and Intelligence," *Mind* 59, No. 236 (1950), repr. in Alan Ross Anderson, ed., *Minds and Machines* (Englewood Cliffs, N.J.: Prentice-Hall, 1964). See also the discussions of Turing's argument in Douglas R. Hofstadter, *Gödel, Escher, Bach: an Eternal Golden Braid* (New York: Vintage/Random House, 1979), pp. 594–599 *et passim*.

17. It was not until twenty years after he and Dr. Bob founded Alcoholics Anonymous that Bill W. told the detailed story of his ecstatic experience of the great white light, the mountain top, and the wind of the spirit blowing upon

him. See *Alcoholics Anonymous Comes of Age: A Brief History of A.A.* (New York: Alcoholics Anonymous World Services, 1957), p. 63, and Ernest Kurtz, *Not-God: A History of Alcoholics Anonymous*, pp. 19–20 and n. 41.

18. Stephen Arterburn and Jack Felton, *Toxic Faith: Understanding and Overcoming Religious Addiction* (Nashville: Oliver-Nelson/Thomas Nelson, 1991). Pp. 99–101 and 112–4 discuss the linkage between becoming addicted to religion and the subsequent development of compulsive over-eating and/or workaholic behavior. Pp. 143 and 149 discuss forming dual addictions between religion-oholic behavior and either secret compulsive drinking or the covert practice of some sexual addiction. See also p. 157 on "searching for another fix," i.e. the intensification of such dual addictions in the later stages of religious addiction.

19. *Alcoholics Anonymous*, 3rd ed. (New York: Alcoholics Anonymous World Services, 1976) pp. 63 and 76.

20. *Ibid.* pp. 64–68.

21. The twelve-step program uses an ancient concept of serenity. The goal of the good life, in pagan Greek and Roman Stoic teaching, was to achieve a kind of serenity which they called *apatheia*—no longer being at the mercy of the *pathê*—or in other words, freedom from the power of obsessive thoughts and compulsive behaviors. Early Christian teaching in the eastern (Greek-speaking) end of the Mediterranean later used this same term *apatheia* to describe the goal of the Christian life as well. For a good study of ancient Stoic philosophy, see R. D. Hicks, *Stoic and Epicurean* (New York: Charles Scribner's Sons, 1910). See also Seneca's *De ira* (On Anger), in his *Moral Essays*, ed. and trans. John W. Basore, 3 vols., Loeb Classical Library (Cambridge MA: Harvard University Press, 1928–35). In the tragic drama Seneca wrote about King Agamemnon's return from the conquest of Troy, he showed us how the king's wife Clytemnestra and

the even more vengeful Aegisthus were finally driven by obsessive resentment into violently murdering the unsuspecting Agamemnon.

The Stoic teacher Epictetus explained how we gained *apatheia* (serenity) once we obtained the wisdom (*sophia*) to know the difference between *ta ouk eph' hêmin* (the things we cannot change) and *ta eph' hêmin* (the things we can)—an ancient wisdom passed down through the centuries and encapsulated for our time in Reinhold Niebuhr's Serenity Prayer. See Epictetus' *Discourses and Manual*, 2 vols., trans. W. A. Oldfather, Loeb Classical Library (Cambridge MA: Harvard University Press, 1959–61).

Classical Greek had a contrasting word pair, *praxis* and *pathos*: The first word, which meant "action," came from the Greek verb *prassô*, which meant to do, act, practice a business or way of life. The word pragmatic came from that same root. The second word, *pathos* (plural *pathê*), fundamentally referred to "something which I suffer as a passive victim," since it came from the verb *paschô*, which basically meant to suffer or be affected by something, as opposed to acting for myself. Ancient Stoic philosophy therefore used the word *pathos* as a technical term to refer to a kind of mental state which held me at its mercy, where this malfunctioning of my own mind drove me to act irrationally and self-destructively. The precise meaning of *pathos* as a Stoic technical term was often not appreciated or understood even in the ancient world, where some people mistakenly thought that it referred to the emotions in general, and believed that the Stoics were teaching that salvation came from becoming totally unfeeling and emotionless. Even modern classicists usually translate the *pathê* as "the passions," which is still not on target, because the English word passion simply refers to an especially intense emotion, particularly when love and sex are involved. The *pathê* were not really emotions at all, but ways of thinking about the world that were inevitably self-defeating, extremely destructive, and incapable of achieving their stated goals. These peculiar mental states did however drive us into out-of-control emotional states, such as rage, fury, panic fear, overpowering lust, and so on, because of the way they made our minds malfunction. What the *pathê* were in fact was what a modern psychologist would call *patterns of obsessive thoughts which finally drove us to compulsive behavior.* So the word *a-patheia* ("serenity") simply meant not-having-*pathê* in that destructive sense.

22. Matthew 13:45–46.

23. John Herman Randall, Jr., *Aristotle* (New York: Columbia University Press, 1960), pp. 251, 268, and 271.

24. Compare Emmet Fox, *The Sermon on the Mount: The Key to Success in Life* and *The Lord's Prayer: An Interpretation* (San Francisco: HarperSan Francisco, 1938), p. 4: "Men built up absurd and very horrible fables about a limited and man-like God who conducted his universe very much as a rather ignorant and barbarous prince might conduct the affairs of a small Oriental kingdom. All sorts of human weaknesses, such as vanity, fickleness, and spite, were attributed to this being."

CHAPTER II. BEGINNER'S BLOCKS

1. *Alcoholics Anonymous*, 3rd ed. (New York: Alcoholics Anonymous World Services, 1976).

2. *Dr. Bob and the Good Oldtimers: A Biography, with Recollections of Early A.A. in the Midwest* (New York: Alcoholics Anonymous World Services, 1980); *Pass It On: The Story of Bill Wilson and How the A.A. Message Reached the World* (New York: Alcoholics Anonymous World Services, 1984); Mary C. Darrah, *Sister Ignatia: Angel of Alcoholics Anonymous* (Chicago: Loyola University Press, 1992).

3. Glenn F. Chesnut, *The Factory Owner and the Convict: My Story Is My Message—the Words of Early Pioneers in the Alcoholics Anonymous Movement in the St. Joseph River Valley*, 1st ed. (South Bend IN: Hindsfoot Foundation [P.O. Box 4081, South Bend IN 46634], 1996): Nick Kowalski's story is told in chs. 9–11 (pp. 45–65) and 14–16 (pp. 85–104); the professional burglar is Raymond I., who spoke occasionally during the interviews with Jimmy M. recorded in chs. 17–20 (pp. 105–129). The nationally-known Al-Anon speaker is Mary Pearl T., whose tape-recordings are available from the organizations which tape record the leads at A.A. and Al-Anon conferences; one of her best talks was entitled *12 Step Study for AA's and Al-Anon's*, given at the Edisto Beach Roundup on April 13, 1995, available from Dicobe Tapes, Box 200, Bellevue NE 68005. On sexual addiction, see above all Patrick Carnes, *Don't Call It Love: Recovery from Sexual Addiction* (New York: Bantam Books, 1991), a treasure trove of case histories, along with carefully compiled statistics about percentages of those who have this or that symptom or traumatic background, the average length of time for each stage of recovery, and so on. Many of these numerical figures would apply fairly well, in my own observations, to people with other kinds of addictions, especially alcoholism, where some sexual problem (gross promiscuity, offering sex to get drinks or at least pretending to be sexually available to get strangers to buy you drinks, excessive use of pornography, using prostitutes or being one, and so on) are nearly always present. See the section in *Alcoholics Anonymous* on pp. 68–70,

emphasizing that resentments and fears in this part of our lives *have* to be included in the fourth step, and that shameful incidents which we have kept as secrets revealed to no one *have* to be brought into the light in the fifth step: we are as sick as our secrets, and people do not begin to get well until they have "told someone else *all* their life story" (p. 73). Patrick Carnes has written a number of other useful books—his first work (which appeared in 1983) helped to open up this field of study and is now in a second edition: *Out of the Shadows: Understanding Sexual Addiction* (Minneapolis MN: CompCare Publishers, 1992).

4. The metaphor of the good physician who comes to heal the sick was used for example in Luther's lectures on Paul's epistle to the Romans which he gave at the University of Wittenberg in 1515, the point at which he discovered the basic principle of justification by faith alone, two years or so before he nailed the Ninety-Five Theses to the door of the castle church at Wittenberg (October 31, 1517) and started the chain of events which led to the Protestant Reformation. One of the clearest systematic accounts of Luther's theology is still Philip S. Watson, *Let God Be God! An Interpretation of the Theology of Martin Luther* (Philadelphia: Fortress, 1947).

Luther was a Catholic priest and college professor, a member of the religious order called the Augustinian Hermits, who taught theology and scripture at the University of Wittenberg. He recognized above all that "faith" as mere intellectual belief could not save anyone: the only kind of faith which could save was a willingness to put your whole *trust* in God. He regarded himself as a defender of St. Augustine's teaching on grace and our necessary human imperfections (the heart of traditional Catholic belief for most of the previous thousand years), and a foe of the merit theology of late medieval nominalists like Gabriel Biel (with all their distinctions between *meritum de condigno* and *meritum de congruo*, and so on). It was these nominalists (beginning with William of Occam in the early 1300's) who had taken over the Catholic universities of Europe during the fourteenth and fifteenth centuries. For Luther in Germany, Archbishop Thomas Cranmer in England, and John Calvin in Switzerland alike, the nominalist teaching that we had to "merit" or earn our salvation was a principal target of their Protestant reforms: God's grace was always a pure gift, and we did not ever have to earn his love, simply accept it.

It should also be noted that Luther was deeply influenced by the Dominican spiritual tradition of Meister Eckhart and Johann Tauler. This particular tradition, which had been deeply influenced by the great spiritual writer who wrote around 500 A.D. under the name of Dionysius the Areopagite (often referred to simply as "St. Denis" in the middle ages), represented one of the more important strands of fourteenth-century Catholic thought *in the monasteries and convents* (as opposed to the universities and parish churches). These works are very useful for understanding what Luther meant by trust, and abandoning oneself completely to God. In 1518 Luther himself supervised the production of the first printed edition of the *Theologia Germanica*, a late fourteenth-century work from that same tradition.

It is important to recognize that Luther's basic ideas about faith and grace (particularly in his earlier period) were not at all alien to an important part of the medieval Catholic tradition. There is no necessary quarrel *at all* between good Protestantism and good Roman Catholicism when we attempt to work and live the spirituality of the twelve steps.

5. For St. Thomas Aquinas's conception of God see chapt. 1, nn. 2 and 10.

6. Chesnut, *The Factory Owner and the Convict*, ch. 30, p. 200, gives transcriptions from the tape recording of Goshen Bill's lead given at Life House treatment center in Elkhart, Indiana in 1981. The tape is in the archives at the A.A. Central Service Office in Elkhart.

7. The story of Abraham or Abram, the ancestor of the Jewish people, is given in the book of Genesis, see espec. Gen. 12:1–4 and 15:6. This is referred to in the New Testament in Galatians 3:6–7, Romans 4, and Hebrews 11:8 as a primary example of the kind of faith which saves us; compare Acts 7:2–5, and the warning in James 2:21–24 that, even in Abraham's case, faith without works would have been dead. See also Rabbi Kerry M. Olitzky and Stuart A. Copans, M.D.,

Twelve Jewish Steps to Recovery: A Personal Guide to Turning from Alcoholism and Other Addictions (Woodstock VT: Jewish Lights Publishing, 1991). These two modern American Jewish authors use the same motif, echoing the biblical stories of Abraham leaving Haran and Moses and the Israelites making their exodus from Egypt, but with the additional poignant invocation of the way in which so many present-day American Jews are alive only because their grandparents somehow got out of Poland or Germany or Hungary as the onslaught of the Nazi holocaust swept through central Europe:

> Our grandparents! In the darkness of night, they packed their bags and fled in fear for their lives and those of their families. Yet, somehow our people always have known that they had to take the first step if they were to improve their lot. Powerlessness does not have to be passivity. As Jews, we do not believe in chaos. Rather, order is what anchors us in this world…. When the world we have built and the family we have nurtured are threatened because of our dependence [on some addictive substance or behavior], we should act.

8. Bill Hoover's story is told in chs. 17–20 (pp. 105–129) of Chesnut, *The Factory Owner and the Convict.*

Ludwig Wittgenstein, the Austrian philosopher who taught and wrote at Cambridge University in England in the earlier part of the twentieth century, talked about learning what words actually meant as a kind of "language game." Ludwig Wittgenstein, *Preliminary Studies for the "Philosophical Investigations": Generally Known as the Blue and Brown Books* (Oxford: Basil Blackwell, 1969), see e.g. pp. 2 and 14 of the *Blue Book.* How do people learn the language when they go to a foreign country? Verbal definitions do us no good if we are beginners who do not know any words of that language at all: Suppose a native speaker tells us that the word "*ubunga*" means a "*babalooba magooba-bonga.*" That's not very helpful at all. What you *can* do, is have someone who already knows what the words mean give you an "ostensive definition" by pointing at an object (say a yellow wooden pencil) and saying the correct word several times, such as "*ubunga,*

ubunga." But at first, you cannot know whether that strange word *ubunga* means yellow, or long, or cylindrical-shaped, or wooden, or what have you. So you point at something else yellow, say a large lemon, and say "*ubunga?*" and then notice your teacher scowling, and realize you've gotten it wrong. So, as the editors of the *Blue and Brown Books* put it (p. vi), learning the meaning of a word requires "training." Wittgenstein points out that even in one's own native language, knowing the meaning of a word is not at all the same as being able to give a *verbal definition* of what that word means. Does the fact that you would have enormous trouble giving a precise verbal definition of what you meant by a perfectly ordinary word like "leaf" or "green" or "grass" mean that you do not know what those words actually mean when you use them?

Words like grace, detachment, ego-deflation, and humility have no more real meaning to most people who enter the twelve-step program than would words like *ubunga* and *magooba-bonga* from some strange new language. We have to go to meeting after meeting and receive slow, gradual *training* from the people there who already know that language.

9. The little story which follows is based on Jimmy M.'s account of how Ruby (another real old-timer) came into her first A.A. meeting, see Chesnut, *The Factory Owner and the Convict*, ch. 18, p. 116.

10. See for example *Alcoholics Anonymous*, 3rd ed. (New York: Alcoholics Anonymous World Services, 1976), p. 58 "the result was nil until we let go absolutely," p. 59 "we asked His protection and care with complete abandon," p. 68 "we trust infinite God rather than our finite selves," and p. 76 "we would go to any lengths for victory over alcohol." See also Harry M. Tiebout, M.D., "The Act of Surrender in the Therapeutic Process: With Special Reference to Alcoholism," *Quartery Journal of Studies on Alcohol* (Yale University) 10 (1949): 48-58; "Surrender Versus Compliance in Therapy: With Special Reference to Alcoholism," *ibid.* 14 (1953): 58-68. See also his paper on "Conversion as a Psychological Phenomenon," read before the New York Psychiatric Society on April 11, 1944, on the disappearance of all the alcoholic defiance when real sur-

render occurs. All three articles are available as reprints from the National Council on Alcoholism, 733 Third Avenue, New York NY 10017. On Tiebout's role in early A.A., see *Pass It On: The Story of Bill Wilson and How the A.A. Message Reached the World*, pp. 211-212, 295-297, 326, 336, and 358; also the photograph of the psychiatrist on p. 296.

11. Viktor E. Frankl, *Man's Search for Meaning*, rev. ed. (New York: Washington Square Press/Simon & Schuster, 1984. First published in Austria in 1946, not long after he was released from the concentration camp, under the title *Ein Psycholog erlebt das Konzentrationslager*.

12. This is part of a long unwritten tradition. A.A. sponsors first began developing the technique of having their pigeons write gratitude lists (and re-read them every morning when they first got up) as one effective way of dealing with the self-hate syndrome described so vividly in the chapter on the fourth step in *Twelve Steps and Twelve Traditions* (New York: Alcoholics Anonymous World Services, 1953) p. 45:

> If temperamentally we are on the depressive side, we are apt to be swamped with guilt and self-loathing. We wallow in this messy bog, often getting a misshapen and painful pleasure out of it. As we morbidly pursue this melancholy activity, we may sink to such a point of despair that nothing but oblivion looks possible as a solution. Here, of course, we have lost all perspective…. this is not a moral inventory at all; it is the very process by which the depressive has so often been led to the bottle and extinction.

The image of the bog or swamp also appeared in Dante's *Inferno*, Canto 7, ll. 106-126, where the people struggling on the surface were dominated by the deadly sin of Anger (*ira*), and the people who had sunk totally into this cesspool were afflicted with the deadly sin of Accidie (*acedia* or *tristitia* in medieval Latin). Those who had fallen below the surface of the mire cried out:

> *Tristi fummo*
> *nell' aere dolce che dal sol s' allegra,*
> *portando dentro accidioso fummo:*
> *or ci attristiam nella belletta negra.*

Translating Dante's Italian rather literally (and reading the second *fummo* as it is, as part of an atypical medieval Italian compound verb used in this awkward colloquialism much like *stare* with a gerund in modern Italian, rather than altering it to *fumo*, "smoke," which does not fit the wet, muddy poetic imagery): "we fell into *tristitia*, when we were in the sweet air made happy by the sun, we put ourselves into a state of *accidie*; now we put ourselves into this state of *tristitia* in the black muck." With acute psychological insight, Dante saw that Accidie was simply deep-set resentment finally falling into terminal despair. The Italian text is taken from Dante Alighieri, *Inferno*, Italian and English, ed. Terence Tiller (New York: Schocken Books, 1966).

Accidie is still often translated as "Sloth," which can be very misleading, because in modern English that word has come to mean simple laziness. That can be part of the problem, but in present-day psychological terminology, we would say that the medieval concept of Accidie also included many forms of clinical depression, neurotic procrastination, and disastrously low self-esteem. In older English literature, much the same range of severe psychological problems were often referred to as "melancholy," a word which Bill W. also used in the passage quoted above.

13. The *Twenty-Four Hour* book prefers to call these periods "the gray days," "the dull, dark days," when you feel like there is "a shadow on your life." *Twenty-Four Hours a Day*, Compiled by a member of the Group at Daytona Beach, Fla. [this was Richmond Walker, in 1948], rev. ed. (Center City MN: Hazelden, 1975), December 15 and 16.

One classic spiritual author who described some of the aspects of the Dark Night of the Soul was of course St. John of the Cross, see for example his *Ascent of Mount Carmel*, trans. and ed. E. Allison Peers (Liguori, Missouri: Triumph Books, 1991), with the famous poem that begins: "On a dark night, / Kindled in love with yearnings / —oh happy chance!— / I went forth without being observed, / My house being now at rest." We can in fact undergo some of our greatest spiritual growth in the process of finding our way through these dark periods.

For a classical Protestant evangelical treatment of this theme, see John Wesley, *The Works of John Wesley*, Vol. 2. *Sermons* II: 33-70, ed. Albert C. Outler (Nashville: Abingdon Press, 1985), Sermons 46 and 47, "The Wilderness State" and "Heaviness through Manifold Temptations," espec. 46.3.12, where he argued with those Roman Catholic spiritual writers who he believed were attempting to make the dark night more positive than it actually was, and who seemed to be saying in places:

> "But is not darkness much more profitable for the soul than light? Is not the work of God in the heart most swiftly and effectually carried on during a state of inward suffering? Is not a believer more swiftly and thoroughly purified by sorrow than by joy? By anguish and pain and distress and spiritual martyrdoms than by continual peace?"

In fact, we get through the dark night of the soul best, Wesley argued, by *doing whatever is necessary* to regain our sense of the presence of God and his peace as quickly as we can—"a strong consciousness of this will do more in an hour than his absence in an age"—and by recovering the naturally happy and joyful state which is the mark of the full inward presence of God's spirit.

Both sides have their point, for we can undergo enormous spiritual growth during these periods, but the growth comes principally in two ways: First, as we work our way out of the darkness, in the process we will learn new and even more powerful ways of drawing on God's grace to return us to serenity and a sense of his love and immediate presence. Second, our faith is made stronger as we have impressed on us ever more convincingly that, if we hold fast to the program and keep working the steps, we will eventually find our way back to serenity, peace, and true inner happiness and satisfaction—and in an even higher form than anything we have experienced before. We become more and more "panic proof" as we see that we can survive anything as long as we keep turning back to God for help.

(The darkness motif was also used from the time of St. Gregory of Nyssa onwards, and in St. John of the Cross over and over again, to talk about the paradoxical fact that the more I learn about the higher power and real spirituality, the less I find myself able to put what I know and feel into words—but this is a different aspect of the darkness metaphor, based on the story of Moses' vision of God in the dark cloud at the top of Mt. Sinai in Exodus 19.)

14. In his autobiography, Father Ralph Pfau (the Father John Doe of the Golden Books which are still read by so many in A.A.) used this old Catholic terminology when he talked about the events leading up to his first nervous breakdown back at the end of the 1920's, while he was still in seminary. See Ralph Pfau and Al Hirshberg, *Prodigal Shepherd* (Indianapolis IN: SMT Guild, 1958), pp. 30-31. When the totally distraught young man told his spiritual advisor, Father Anselm, that he felt completely unworthy of the priesthood, the priest told him that "this is just a matter of scruples"—a diagnosis which Ralph came to recognize was correct after he came into the A.A. program around fifteen years later, but which did him no good at that time. See chapter five of this present work on the way Ralph later described what happened to him as falling prey to the "Myth of Perfection." In classical Latin, a *scrupulum* was a very small weight or measure, and a *scrupulus* was a small, sharp stone, like one which might nag at you painfully when you got it lodged in your sandal; the adjective *scrupulosus* (which was passed down to medieval Latin) could reflect either or both of these root ideas.

15. See Craig Nakken, *The Addictive Personality: Understanding the Addictive Process and Compulsive Behavior*, 2nd ed. (Center City MN: Hazelden, 1996), pp. 2-4. Addictive people seek instant mood changes by such strategies as: drinking beer in a bar, bingeing on food (or deliberately starving themselves), betting on football games and then watching the games on television, shoplifting in a department store, browsing through a pornographic bookstore, going on a shopping spree, or (in the case of workaholics) staying late at work, driving themselves

into finishing one more job. There are three basic kinds of "highs" or mood changes which they seek: arousal, satiation, and fantasy. "Arousal causes sensations of intense, raw, unchecked power and gives feelings of being untouchable and all-powerful." "A satiation high gives the addict the feeling of being full, complete, and beyond pain…. it numbs the sensations of pain or distress." The addict sometimes enters a kind of "trance state…a state of detachment, a state of separation from one's physical surroundings…. floating back and forth between the addictive world and the real world, often without others suspecting it." Gambling, spending, and sexual addicts especially tend to seek this kind of trance state for their instant mood alteration.

16. I am paraphrasing Plato, *Apology* 28d-30a and 38a-39d. Plato described the death of Socrates at the end of the *Phaedo*, 116a-118. For both works see Plato, *Euthyphro, Apology, Crito, Phaedo, Phaedrus*, ed. and trans. Harold North Fowler, Loeb Classical Library (London: William Heinemann, 1914), pp. 61-145 and 193-403.

17. Luke 22:39-44, Matthew 26:36-44, and Mark 14:32-41 give three versions of the first-century Christian oral traditions about Jesus which differ only slightly in the way his words were remembered.

CHAPTER III. SPIRITUAL AWAKENING
AND THE POWER OF GRACE

1. *Alcoholics Anonymous*, 3rd ed. (New York: Alcoholics Anonymous World Services, 1976), pp. 569-70; William James, *The Varieties of Religious Experience*, Gifford Lectures on Natural Religion Delivered at Edinburgh in 1901–1902 (New York: Modern Library, 1994).

2. This is an interesting version of the Platonic doctrine of reminiscence. See Augustine, *Confessions*, trans. R. S. Pine-Coffin (Baltimore, MD: Penguin Books, 1961), and espec. 10.8-27, the long section on the human memory. He asks himself what he is ultimately looking for in his spiritual quest, and comes to the conclusion that "when I look for you, who are my God, I am looking for a life of blessed happiness," but that somewhere in his memory he already knows what this kind of happiness is (10.20). This must be so, because "unless we had some sure knowledge of it, we should not desire it with such certainty" (10.21). He finally realizes that "true happiness is to rejoice in the truth, for to rejoice in the truth is to rejoice in you, O God, who are the Truth." We have all experienced the encounter with real truth, the moment of insight into what was really going on, the joy of the sudden break-through. But all too often we cling instead to what are lies and falsehoods simply because *we hate to be proved wrong*—our overweening pride is our downfall (10.23). This kind of false pride destroys us because the truly crushing misery and unhappiness in our lives is invariably founded on lies, self-deception, denial, and fleeing. The Big Book echoes this Augustinian concept of Truth when it says (p. 58) that practically the only people who cannot be saved by the twelve-step program are "men and women who are constitutionally incapable of being honest with themselves."

3. See for example the Detroit Pamphlet, *Alcoholics Anonymous: An Interpretation of the Twelve Steps* (distributed by Alcoholics Anonymous of Greater Detroit, 380 Hilton Road, Ferndale MI 48220), written when A.A. was first established there. The Detroit Pamphlet is also available (reprinted with

reset type) as Northern Indiana Area 22 Archives Committee Pamphlet No. 1 (April 2000). Step 2: "As we strayed from the normal *social* side of life, our minds became confused and we strayed away from the normal *mental* side of life." Step 4: "Our trouble is a grave mental disease, confused by screwy thinking."

Compare also *The Little Red Book*, 50th anniversary ed. (Center City MN: Hazelden, 1996). This started out as a set of mimeographed sheets of paper used in the Twelve Step Study Classes conducted by Ed Webster, Barry Collins, and other members of the Nicollet Group in Minneapolis, which were finally published in booklet form in August 1946 by Coll-Webb Company in that city (pp. x-xiv). The alcoholic's uncontrolled drinking (p. 30) "perverts his power of reason, dulls his talent, limits his instinct of self preservation, makes him irresponsible, and adversely affects his behavior. How is the alcoholic to account for that insane impulse which prompts him to reach for the *First Drink* that starts him off on another 'binge'? Is it a sane act? Is he obsessed?" Some of the symptoms which indicate that it is a mental illness are (p. 32) "our inability to be self-critical...our refusal to consider the harm we have done to ourselves and others…. Childish faith we placed on excuses for our drinking and the alibis we thought we were getting away with…. The reckless abandon we displayed in drunken driving…. The financial risks taken…. The asinine resentments that clogged our minds— our decided loss of responsiblity—our retreats to childish levels of hilarity…. Contemplated or attempted suicide."

4. See St. Gregory of Nyssa, *From Glory to Glory: Texts from Gregory of Nyssa's Mystical Writings*, ed. Herbert Musurillo (New York: Scribner, 1961). The introduction (pp. 1–78), by Jean Daniélou, is an excellent summary of some of the major themes in Gregory's teaching. See also for example St. Bonaventure's *The Soul's Journey into God* 7.4-5 in Bonaventure, *The Soul's Journey into God – The Tree of Life – The Life of St. Francis*, trans. Ewert Cousins (New York: Paulist Press, 1978) and St. John of the Cross, *Ascent of Mount Carmel*, trans. and ed. E. Allison Peers (Liguori, Missouri: Triumph Books, 1991).

Two general works on the history and concepts of mysticism and other allied forms of the spiritual life are Evelyn Underhill, *Mysticism: A Study in the Nature and Development of Man's Spiritual Consciousness* (London: Methuen & Co., 1930) and Louis Bouyer, *Introduction to Spirituality*, trans. Mary Perkins Ryan (Collegeville MN: Liturgical Press, 1961).

5. See note 4 above, and also chapt. 1, nn. 2 and 10.

6. In Mahayana Buddhism for example, see the *Heart of Transcendent Wisdom Sutra*: there is a good English translation in James Fieser and John Powers, eds., *Scriptures of the World's Religions* (Boston: McGraw-Hill, 1998), pp. 98-100. "Form is emptiness; emptiness is form.... In the same way, feelings, discriminations, compositional factors, and consciousness are empty.... there is no suffering, no source [of suffering], no cessation [of suffering], no path, no exalted wisdom, no attainment, and also no non-attainment.... because bodhisattvas have no attainment, they depend on and abide in the perfection of wisdom. Because their minds are unobstructed, they are without fear. Having completely passed beyond all error, they go to the fulfillment of nirvana." Coming to the realization of the radical incomprehensibility of the ground of being is also the ultimate goal of all the puzzling little Zen Buddhist paradoxes.

7. Sue C. (South Bend IN). Her talk on "Sex in Sobriety: the Last Taboo," given at the A.A. Mini-Conference in Anderson IN on April 28, 2001 is available from Blueprint Tapes, 950 Morgan St., Clinton IN 47842 (phone 765 832-9901).

8. See chapt. 2, n. 7.

9. See for example the Sanskrit proverb set at the beginning of *Twenty-Four Hours a Day*, Compiled by a member of the Group at Daytona Beach, Fla. [this was Richmond Walker, in 1948], rev. ed. (Center City MN: Hazelden, 1975): "Look to this day, / For it is life, / The very life of life. / In its brief course lie all / The realities and verities of existence."

10. *What Is the Oxford Group?* by the Layman with a Notebook, foreword by L. W. Grenstead (who was at that time Oriel Professor of the Philosophy of the Christian Religion at Oxford University), orig. pub. in 1933, reprinted as the second half of *Practice These Principles* and *What Is the Oxford Group?* ed. Bill P. (Center City MN: Hazelden, 1997). The first half of the 1997 ed. is an alteration of the original with the words changed to fit A.A. terminology. See ch. 6 (pp. 57-63) of *What Is the Oxford Group?* on "Guidance."

There are a number of passages on guidance in *Twenty-Four Hours a Day*: Dec. 10—the basic techniques for seeking guidance. Dec. 13—it means choosing the good, knowing that "the whole power of the universe is behind us." Dec. 18—if the universe "was once…only a thought in the mind of God," then "we must try to think God's thoughts after Him." Dec. 21—"yield to the gentle pressure of your conscience." Dec. 26—"leave the outcome of the things we do to the Higher Power." Nov. 7—"your own pride and selfishness are the greatest blocks." Nov. 27—"to truly desire to do God's will, therein lies happiness for a human being."

Richmond Walker drew some of the material for the fine-print sections of the *Twenty-Four Hour* book from an Oxford Group work, *God Calling*, by Two Listeners, ed. by A. J. Russell (whose *For Sinners Only*, which came out in 1932, was one of the most important Oxford Group books). As is explained in the introduction to *God Calling*, it was produced by two women who began praying together in December 1932, seeking the kind of guidance which A. J. Russell had talked about in *For Sinners Only*. It was discovered that one of the women had what scholars of comparative religion call the gift of ecstatic prophecy (compare the way Mohammed received the verses of the Koran): caught up in a trance, she would deliver the meditations verbatim, while the other woman wrote down the words with a pencil on a piece of paper. Now this goes *far beyond* what twelve-step people normally call guidance, where most people simply receive a sense within their minds of what God wants—it is a positive feeling and conviction, but not put into words at all, or at least not in the form of long speeches. But see *God Calling*, by Two Listeners, re-edited by Bernard Koerselman (Uhrichsville OH: Barbour and Company, 1993).

11. See chapt. 1, n. 7.

12. See the pamphlet "The Four Absolutes" (Cleveland OH: Cleveland District Office of Alcoholics Anonymous, 1701 E. 12th St., Cleveland OH 44114, n. d.), pp. 8-9. The Second Absolute is Unselfishness, and the Second Question is "How will this affect the other fellow?" Using these guidelines is part of the old Oxford Group tradition that still lives on in Cleveland area A.A.

13. *Alcoholics Anonymous*, 3rd ed. (New York: Alcoholics Anonymous World Services, 1976), pp. 64-68. Our *resentments* (the number one killer of alcoholics) and our *fears* (which run like an evil and corroding thread throughout our resentments and even beyond) set the basic agenda for doing the fourth step.

14. This was James' basic working hypothesis throughout *The Varieties of Religious Experience*, as he studied "once-born" and "twice-born" characters, the religion of healthy-mindedness, the sick soul, the divided self, and so on. He cites for example (pp. 264-5) the work of the American psychologist George A. Coe (*The Spiritual Life*, New York, 1900), who showed that sudden religious conversion experiences of the revivalistic kind were closely linked with a personality type marked by emotional sensitivity, a tendency towards automatisms, and an especially strong hypnotic suggestibility of the passive type. William James, *The Varieties of Religious Experience*, Gifford Lectures on Natural Religion Delivered at Edinburgh in 1901–1902 (New York: Modern Library, 1994).

For a view of the basic disputes, and shifts in attitude, which were affecting the professional Christian theologians (both Protestant and Catholic) at the time when James was writing these lectures (1901-02), see Glenn F. Chesnut, "A Century of Patristics Studies 1888–1988," in Henry Warner Bowden (ed.), *A Century of Church History* (Carbondale: Southern Illinois University Press, 1988), pp. 36–73. This article is focused primarily on the different ways these theologians interpreted the Christianity of the first few centuries A.D., but it gives a good introduction to the fundamental disputes going on among Roman Catholic thinkers in the ninety years or so between Vatican I and Vatican II, and the ideas of the classical Protestant liberals like Albrecht Ritschl (1822-98), and especially Adolf Harnack (1851-1930), whose *Das Wesen des Christentums* came out in 1900, only a year before James began his Edinburgh lectures. Harnack's style of liberalism had a strong influence on the way Bill W. and many early A.A. people came to terms with their childhood Christian training, and deeply permeates the way the twelve-step movement regards particular religious institutions and their rules and doctrines as non-essential to real spirituality.

15. One of the best books I have ever read on ordinary, low-level chronic depression and the way it can be produced by excessive judgmentalism, pathological self-criticism, refusal to forgive, falling prey to the tyranny of should's and ought's, global labeling, over-generalization, and so on, is Matthew McKay, Ph.D., and Patrick Fanning, *Self-Esteem: A Proven Program of Cognitive Techniques for Assessing, Improving, and Maintaining Your Self-Esteem*, ed. Kirk Johnson (Oakland CA: New Harbinger Publications, 1987). See also the account of the discovery of the role played in a number of psychological problems by continual toxic self-talk in Aaron T. Beck, M.D., *Cognitive Therapy and the Emotional Disorders* (New York: Penguin Books/Meridian, 1976).

16. See for example John Bradshaw, *Healing the Shame that Binds You* (Deerfield Beach FL: Health Communications, 1988).

17. St. Teresa of Ávila, *Interior Castle*, trans. E. Allison Peers (Garden City NY: Image Books/Doubleday & Company, 1961), Third Mansions (ch. 2) and Sixth Mansions (ch. 1).

18. John Calvin, *Institutes of the Christian Religion*, 2 vols., ed. John T. McNeill, trans. Ford Lewis Battles (Philadelphia: Westminster, 1960), the sections on justifying faith: 3.2.14 and 3.2.19-20. Even "a small drop of faith" enables us to behold God's glory with such effect that we are transformed into his very likeness. Nevertheless, since "our heart especially inclines by its own natural instinct toward unbelief," the genuine faith we have will be mixed with "the

greatest doubts and fear." We should be very careful, because the forces of evil direct their strongest attack toward making us feel like we are so evil that not even God could love us. These forces have one central lie which they are continually trying to dupe us into believing: "that, thinking God to be against us and hostile to us, we should not hope for any help from him, and should fear him as if he were our deadly enemy."

19. The Detroit Pamphlet, *Alcoholics Anonymous: An Interpretation of the Twelve Steps*, see n. 3 above. Emmet Fox, *The Sermon on the Mount: The Key to Success in Life* and *The Lord's Prayer: An Interpretation* (San Francisco: HarperSan Francisco, 1938).

20. My copy was obtained from Unity Church of Peace, 905 E. Colfax Ave., South Bend IN 46617.

21. On Augustine, see Frederick Copleston, *A History of Philosophy*, Vol. 2. *Mediaeval Philosophy: Augustine to Scotus* (Westminster MD: Newman Press, 1950) pp. 62-67; see s. v. "Illumination, Divine" in the index for the treatment of this Augustinian concept in the writings of later medieval theologians and philosophers. Jonathan Edwards, "A Divine and Supernatural Light," in Jonathan Edwards, *Basic Writings*, ed. Ola Elizabeth Winslow (New York: New American Library, 1966), pp. 123-134.

22. John Wesley, *Journal* for May 24, 1738, in Albert C. Outler, ed., *John Wesley*, Library of Protestant Thought (New York: Oxford University Press, 1964), pp. 66-7. "I felt my heart strangely warmed…. I began to pray with all my might for those who had in a more especial manner despitefully used me and persecuted me." In the aftermath, he discovered that whenever he was tempted to fall back into his old resentment, self-pity, and personal despair, he could now simply cry out to God for help and these feelings would flee away. Before that point, he said, he was sometimes conquered by these feelings, but now (having learned to ask for and draw upon the power of God's grace), "I was always conqueror."

CHAPTER IV. THE PRESENCE OF GOD

1. *Oxford Dictionary of the Christian Church*, 2nd ed., ed. F. L. Cross and E. A. Livingstone (London: Oxford University Press, 1974), s. v. "Meditation" and "Contemplation." Meditation is *discursive* mental prayer, that is, I take a text or theme and reflect on it thoughtfully in a spiritual way. I do this to gain greater understanding and insight in spiritual matters, to become more deeply involved at the emotional and feeling level, to sharpen my commitment and strengthen my will, and to help push the images and phrases down into my unconscious mind (so they will begin to automatically affect the way I think and act at all times). I try to understand the original context better (e.g., "what was the person who wrote this text thinking and feeling, and what was probably going on in his or her heart?"), but I also try to get a better grasp of how the topic of meditation applies concretely to specific parts of my own life and behavior. The *Spiritual Exercises* of St. Ignatius Loyola (the founder of the Jesuits) were used as a model for this kind of meditation by many Roman Catholic priests and religious in the United States in the first half of the twentieth century. A.A. members who had gone to Roman Catholic parochial schools prior to the Second Vatican Council (1962-5) had often absorbed many of the basic principles of the *Spiritual Exercises* subconsciously.

Contemplation on the other hand is *non-discursive* mental prayer, that is, I regard the object of contemplation in a manner which is intuitive and non-ana-lytical, by just attending to it in my mind without distraction. There may not even be an object in the normal sense, but total non-reflective immersion in a par-ticular feeling, or I may simply let myself float in the void or abyss of primordial no-thing-ness: One well-known kind of contemplation for example is the vision of the ineffable primordial oneness which is described in St. John of the Cross, St. Bonaventure, St. Gregory of Nyssa, the fifth-century spiritual master who wrote under the name of Dionysius the Areopagite, and so on. But St. Teresa of Ávila writes in great detail about other forms of contemplation, and a variety of other, different kinds of powerful spiritual experiences; her writings moved the whole discussion of spiritual experience to a new level of detail.

2. It was St. Augustine above all who emphasized that God was *verum ipsum* (Truth Itself)—see chapt. 3, n. 2 and also the reference at the end of chapt. 1, n. 5. On the idea of the *scintilla* see chapt. 1, n. 7

3. Rudolf Otto, *The Idea of the Holy: An Inquiry into the Non-Rational Factor in the Idea of the Divine and Its Relation to the Rational*, 2nd ed., trans. John W. Harvey (Oxford: Oxford University Press, 1950); *Das Heilige: Über das Irrationale in der Idee des göttlichen und sein Verhältnis zum Rationalen*, 11th ed. (Stuttgart: Friedrich Andreas Perthes, 1923). Otto had been pointed this direction by the work which he earlier carried out on the Kantian commentator Jakob Friedrich Fries: Rudolf Otto, *The Philosophy of Religion Based on Kant and Fries*, trans. E. B. Dicker (London: Williams & Norgate, 1931). At the end of that volume, Otto said that Fries' ideas about the way we could sometimes sense the hint (an *Ahnung*) of the infinite shining through when we viewed the world around us, clearly showed how valuable it would be to carry out a systematic phenomenological study of the idea of the holy (and what people actually felt in its presence) among the various religions of the world. Otto's most famous work (*The Idea of the Holy*) was the result: all the religions of the world (even those which have no real concept of a central God-figure) have a profound sense of the holy or sacred. The basic work in which Fries first set out his major ideas— *Wissen, Glaube, und Ahndung*—has now been translated into English: Jakob Friedrich Fries, *Knowledge, Belief, and Aesthetic Sense*, ed. Frederick Gregory, trans. Kent Richter (Köln: Jürgen Dinter Verlag für Philosophie, 1989). In modern German, the last word in the title is spelled *Ahnung*, and the word basically means a kind of hint or intuition or non-rational feeling or premonition: to translate it as "aesthetic sense" is perhaps overinterpreting, although Fries did link his idea of an *Ahnung* of the infinite to the concept of the sublime in Kant's aesthetics.

4. The Word of God being spoken to us (in and through another person) may be a quiet reminder of responsibility or a gentle word of reassurance, or it may be a single pointed sentence that is a real blockbuster. On the one hand we hear (and often somehow *know* that we are hearing) the Word of God, but at another level

we cannot fully analyze and "explain" what is going on when this happens. Whenever God sends his grace from outside the created realm to alter the course of an individual human life at some point, it introduces a mysterious x-factor into the story of the person's life at that point: if the person hears and responds to God's Word, his life changes (often suddenly and dramatically) for the better, and we can never totally "explain it all" in terms of a this-worldly account of what had been happening in that person's life up to that point, and what (in the normal this-worldly scheme of things) should by rights have happened next. The chain of normal cause and effect is suddenly broken by this outside force, and a new and different kind of chain of events begins to occur: a person who was plunging inexorably to his doom, for example, suddenly turns his life around and begins growing in a positive direction instead. See Jonathan Edwards, "A Divine and Supernatural Light," in Jonathan Edwards, *Basic Writings*, ed. Ola Elizabeth Winslow (New York: New American Library, 1966), pp. 123-134, and his other writings on the way God's grace intervenes from outside the laws of normal physics and psychology. Edwards (1703-58) was the only native-born American philosophical theologian we have had so far, who could rank with the truly great philosophers and theologians of European history. He was very much a man of the modern scientific age, who had learned his physics from Newton and his psychology from John Locke (the Father of Modern Psychology), but he was also (along with John Wesley) one of the two great theoreticians who founded the modern Protestant evangelical movement.

See also the writings of the Swiss theologian Karl Barth, one of the most formative Christian thinkers of the first half of the twentieth century. Barth was the great theologian of the Word of God. In his commentary on the Apostle Paul's epistle to the Romans, he likened the act of God's grace (the "speaking of the Word of God," as he called it) to a bomb explosion. The historical analysis of the act, after the event, could provide no more than a description of the houses and buildings and landscape as it was before the bomb went off, and of the bomb crater and the totally changed landscape after the explosion. But the living experience of having seen the bomb go off could not be genuinely comprehended by anyone who was not there as a participant. Karl Barth, *The Epistle to the Romans,* trans. E. C. Hoskyns (London: Oxford University Press, 1933), pp. 29 and 37.

As a final comment, we should note that the Bible never talks about people immersing themselves in the vision of God (or the vision of the ultimate ground) simply for enjoyment's sake. When God reveals himself to people in the Bible, he always ends the conversation *by giving them a job to do.* See e.g., Exodus 3:10 (Moses' mission), 1 Kings 19:15-17 (the frightening task Elijah was given), Isaiah 6:8-13 (Isaiah's chore), and Ezekiel 2:3-7 (that prophet's grim assignment), plus the jobs given to people like Joshua, Deborah, and David. Likewise at the end of each of the New Testament gospels, the immortal, deathless Christ-principle personified in Jesus gives us his tasks to carry out: e.g., Matthew 28:19-20 and Luke 24:47 (spread the message, pass it on), and John 21:15-17 (if you love me, *feed my sheep*).

5. *Twenty-Four Hours a Day,* Compiled by a member of the Group at Daytona Beach, Fla. [Richmond Walker, in 1948], rev. ed. (Center City MN: Hazelden, 1975), June 5.

> Very quietly God speaks through your thoughts and feelings. Heed the Divine voice of your conscience. Listen for this and you will never be disappointed in the results in your life. Listen for this small, still voice and your tired nerves will become rested. The Divine voice comes to you as strength.

The "still small voice" was a reference to a story about the prophet Elijah (1 Kings 19:8-18). He had had to flee in fear and despair from the soldiers of wicked Queen Jezebel, who were pursuing him with orders to kill him on the spot, and had finally travelled forty days and forty nights into the southern desert to Mt. Sinai (where Moses had received the Ten Commandments). There was an enormous rushing wind, strong enough to tumble the rocks down and break them, and an earthquake, and then a great fire—but (for Elijah at least) the God of the Ten Commandments was not in any of these awe-inspiring and cataclysmic events. Then in the silence afterwards he heard "a still small voice"—in Hebrew the *bath qol,* literally the "daughter of a voice," the faint echo of something like a voice speaking in our hearts, and yet it was not actually hearing a voice—and he realized that he had to stop running away. He had to return and start a counterattack on the wicked queen, for the Heavenly Voice assured him, "I have left for me seven thousand in Israel who have not bowed their knees to Baal." (Baal was the god whom Jezebel served, the god of material success, worshipped in obscene, bloody rituals involving sexual intercourse with prostitutes and slashing oneself with a sword or spear).

This story of the *bath qol* became a central image in later western spirituality for what we mean by the "voice" of conscience "speaking" in my heart: not a real voice speaking inside my head (or at least not usually, but who can tell what a great man of the spirit like Elijah would have been able to hear?). But if I take the time to listen in the silence, I can in fact know what God wants me to do.

6. Matthew McKay, Ph.D., and Patrick Fanning, *Self-Esteem: A Proven Program of Cognitive Techniques for Assessing, Improving, and Maintaining Your Self-Esteem*, ed. Kirk Johnson (Oakland CA: New Harbinger Publications, 1987), see for example chapt. 7 (pp. 99-121) on the should's, and pp. 60-61 on either-or "polarized thinking."

7. John Bradshaw, *Healing the Shame that Binds You* (Deerfield Beach FL: Health Communications, 1988) has been read by many people in the twelve-step program.

8. *Alcoholics Anonymous*, 3rd ed. (New York: Alcoholics Anonymous World Services, 1976), p. 60.

9. *Having Had a Spiritual Awakening* (Virginia Beach VA: Al-Anon Family Group Headquarters, 1998), p. 21.

10. *Ibid.*, p. 25.

11. *Ibid.*, pp. 16-17.

12. My translation, but based on the 1927 Swan Press translation, repr. in St. Francis of Assisi, *The Hymn of the Sun*, designed and illus. Tony Wright (Rhinebeck NY: Broken Glass, 1990).

13. *Having Had a Spiritual Awakening*, p. 14.

14. See n. 3 above.

15. This was the annual Michiana (i.e. Michigan-Indiana) A.A. conference held in the Scottish Rite building in downtown South Bend IN. The Northern Indiana Area 22 A.A. Archives Committee has a full tape recording of these old-timers speaking.

16. On Eusebius' concept of the demonic, see Glenn F. Chesnut, *The First Christian Histories: Eusebius, Socrates, Sozomen, Theodoret, and Evagrius*, 2nd rev. ed. (Macon, GA: Mercer University Press, 1986), p. 106; also Glenn F. Chesnut, "The Pattern of the Past: Augustine's Debate with Eusebius and Sallust," in John Deschner, Leroy T. Howe, and Klaus Penzel, eds., *Our Common History as Christians* (New York: Oxford University Press, 1975), pp. 69–95, espec. pp. 72-3 and 77.

Shortly after the Great Persecution, at the beginning of the fourth century, Eusebius (the bishop of Caesarea in Palestine) wrote the first lengthy history of early Christianity: if one wants to see what is really meant by the demonic, one should read some of his detailed accounts of the unbelievably sadistic tortures imposed on the Christian martyrs of that time. Early Christians knew that there were forces of real evil in the world.

What made St. Macarius the Homilist important was that his "prayer of the heart" was the ancient alternative to the more intellectualistic spirituality of St. Gregory of Nyssa and the Dionysian writings (which dominated so much western medieval intellectual theory). Macarius' ideas were at the heart of the spirituality of the monks of Mt. Athos and the later Greek Orthodox spiritual tradition which arose from that source (including the Hesychastic idea of the vision of the

Uncreated Light). In the west, he was also read and admired by many of the Lutheran pietists (e.g. Johann Arndt, Johann Gerhard, and especially Gottfried Arnold), and (above all) over in England by John Wesley (the founder of the Methodists and teacher of the religion of the heart) who combined Macarius' spiritual warfare motif with Mohammed's emphasis on the necessary battle between good and evil to inspire his travelling preachers and frontier circuit riders. It was Macarius above all who taught Wesley to break away from a blind following of St. Augustine's more intellectualistic and hence mechanically deterministic ideas (such as the Augustinian concept of a fatalistic universal predestination), along with Wesley's reading of Ephraem Syrus, another Syrian spiritual writer who was Macarius' rough contemporary, and Clement of Alexandria's concept of serenity (*apatheia*) as the goal of the spiritual life. (Wesley was fluent not only in classical Latin and Greek, but also in Arabic and Syriac.)

The best English translation of the sermons of St. Macarius the Homilist is still the *Fifty Spiritual Homilies of St. Macarius the Egyptian*, trans. A. J. Mason (London: S.P.C.K., 1921). This work is one of the handful of great seminal western spiritual classics. The author of these sermons was not in fact the Egyptian desert monk known as Macarius the Great, who lived c. 300-c. 390 (that was a later medieval misidentification) but the head of a monastery somewhere in eastern Syria or western Mesopotamia. Macarius (the author's name as given in the earliest dependable textual traditions) meant "Blessed," and was a common religious name among pious monks and bishops of that period. He probably wrote in the second half of the fourth century or perhaps even early fifth century—at any rate, after most theologians in his part of the world had come to understand that Arianism would not work, but before the fifth-century christological controversy began truly heating up in that area. He is regarded to this day as one of the great formative orthodox theologians in the Greek Orthodox and Russian Orthodox churches, and a writer who can lead one into the heart of the deepest kind of spiritual life.

CHAPTER V. TWO CLASSICAL AUTHORS
OF A.A. SPIRITUALITY

1. Any number of good old-timers in the A.A. program have told me personally that they got sober on two books: the Big Book and this one. *Twenty-Four Hours a Day*, Compiled by a member of the Group at Daytona Beach, Fla. [i.e., Richmond Walker in 1948], rev. ed. (Center City MN: Hazelden, 1975). Rich was born on August 2, 1892 and died on March 25, 1965 with around twenty-three years of sobriety. See also his little book *For Drunks Only*, and his last work, which he wrote in 1956: Richmond Walker, *The 7 Points of Alcoholics Anonymous*, rev. ed. (Center City MN: Hazelden/Glen Abbey Books, 1989). Telephone orders for books from Hazelden Publishing and Educational Services may be placed at (800) 328–9000.

2. Cf. Aldous Huxley, *The Perennial Philosophy* (New York: Harper & Row, 1945), chapt. 1, "That Art Thou" (pp. 1-21).

3. *Ibid.* chapt. 2, "The Nature of the Ground" (pp. 21-35). What is the great transcendent power which lies above and beyond all other things? "To this the fully developed Perennial Philosophy has at all times and in all places given fundamentally the same answer. The divine Ground of all existence is a spiritual Absolute, ineffable in terms of discursive thought, but (in certain circumstances) susceptible of being directly experienced and realized by a human being."

4. One excellent general introduction to the philosophy of Kant is S. Körner, *Kant* (Baltimore MD: Penguin Books, 1955). For the philosopher himself (whose prose is exceptionally difficult reading), see Immanuel Kant, *Critique of Pure Reason*, trans. Norman Kemp Smith (London: Macmillan & Co., 1933). One of the earliest German commentators on Kant's *Critique* was Jakob Friedrich Fries, whose interpretation was summarized in especially clear language in Rudolf Otto, *The Philosophy of Religion Based on Kant and Fries*, trans. E. B. Dicker (London: Williams & Norgate, 1931). Given my own training as an

ancient philosopher, I myself tend to follow Fries in part by seeing Kant as a sort of pathologically sceptical Neo-Platonist: Kant's technical term *noumenon* was clearly etymologically just a variant Greek form of the Middle and Neo-Platonic words *Nous* and *noêta*, which referred to the realm of the Platonic ideas, but influenced by Locke's concept of the unknowable "real essence" of sense objects, so that Kant argued that the constraints of having to think within a box of space and time prevented us from ever directly knowing the noumenal reality which lay behind all the phenomena of the sense-world. If we take Kant as he reads, he fairly much blocks us from having any real knowledge of God at all, which has thrown western philosophy and theology into considerable chaos for over two centuries now. Fries and Otto suggested one route past the Kantian blockage which I think has merit if it is further developed. But as both these thinkers knew well, such a route had to be based on a thorough knowledge of what real spirituality actually perceived and experienced at the practical, everyday level. That is where works like Richmond Walker's *Twenty-Four Hour* book are so especially important, in setting down so clearly what is actually needed to draw closer to God, in ways that can be directly felt and experienced.

5. For *Gefühl* (feeling) see the classic work by Friedrich Schleiermacher, *On Religion: Speeches to Its Cultured Despisers*, trans. J. Oman (New York: Harper & Brothers, 1958). The original German edition appeared in 1799. Spirituality was based on intuition and feeling, not doctrines and dogma. It was an attack by the Romantic era on seventeenth and eighteenth-century Protestant orthodoxy and eighteenth-century rationalism. Jakob Friedrich Fries used the concept of the *Ahnung* or hint of the infinite instead of the word *Gefühl*, and Rudolf Otto used both terms, though in *The Idea of the Holy* he preferred the word *Gefühl*—see chapt. 4, n. 3. See also Hoxie Neale Fairchild, *Religious Trends in English Poetry*, Vol. III. *1780-1830, Romantic Faith* (New York: Columbia University Press, 1949), for the use of the concept of feeling in the spirituality of the poets of the English Romantic period. In a more modern vein, see also William P. Alston, "Religious Experience and Religious Belief," *Nous* 16 (1982) 3-12, who defends the idea of immediate personal religious experience of God within the criteria of

modern British linguistic philosophy: norms, reliability, justification, and comparison with the epistemological limitations of sense experience.

6. Exodus 33:11, James 2:23. Eusebius of Caesarea (c. 260-c. 340 A.D.), the Palestinian bishop who wrote the first full-length history of early Christianity, used this idea of the *theophileis* or Friends of God as a major motif in his writings, and included Noah, Abraham, Isaac, Jacob, Job, and Joseph in his list, as well as some of the minor figures from the early part of the book of Genesis (such as Enosh, Enoch, Seth, and Japheth). Glenn F. Chesnut, "The Pattern of the Past: Augustine's Debate with Eusebius and Sallust," in John Deschner, Leroy T. Howe, and Klaus Penzel, eds., *Our Common History as Christians* (New York: Oxford University Press, 1975), pp. 69–95, see espec. pp. 71-2.

Eusebius and Augustine (354-430 A.D.) between them set the basic guidelines for the way Europeans wrote history, and thought about history and individual human responsibility, for the next thousand years. Glenn F. Chesnut, "Eusebius, Augustine, Orosius, and the Later Patristic and Medieval Christian Historians," in Harold W. Attridge and Gohei Hata, eds., *Eusebius, Christianity, and Judaism* (Detroit: Wayne State University Press, 1992; published simultaneously in Japanese by Yamamoto Shoten Publishing House, Tokyo), pp. 687-713.

7. See chapt. 3, n. 10.

8. A distinctive idea found in the gospel of John in the New Testament in passages like John 17:3: "This is (*estin*) eternal (*aiônion*) life, that they should know (*ginôskôsin*) you the only true God." The first verb "is" (*estin* in Greek) is present tense, not future tense: it refers to something accessible to us here and now. In the gospel of John the verb that means to know (the noun form is *gnôsis*) does not mean intellectual or analytical knowledge, or having book-knowledge or grand theories about something, but means the personal apprehension or awareness of something that is immediately present. By having a direct *Gefühl* or *Ahnung* or consciousness of God, we are able to live in the light of the Eternal Now. The *aiôn* (the Eternal Now) is not a static thing that goes on forever

because it simply does not change with the passage of time, but is pure immediate process itself, reality in itself before our minds force it into the framework of *chronos* (chronological time, Kantian time) with its division into past and future, and its sequences of over-simplied versions of phenomena formed into neat over-analyzed chains linked by cause and consequence.

For a fuller account of the ancient Christian Greek understanding of time and eternity, see Glenn F. Chesnut, *The First Christian Histories: Eusebius, Socrates, Sozomen, Theodoret, and Evagrius*, 2nd rev. ed. (Macon, GA: Mercer University Press, 1986), pp. 91–3. In this understanding of the relationship between God and the world, the act of creation is not something that took place once upon a time, thousands or millions of years ago, after which God removed himself from the universe and dwelt in some far-off heavenly realm, like the kind of Absentee Landlord who buys a tenement house in the slums and then lives in one of the nicer suburbs himself. One of the most important names of the real God is *Immanu-el*, God-who-is-with-us. In each new Now in which I live, for every moment of my life, the miracle of creation is worked for me before my eyes. Each moment is a brand-new miraculous gift from God to me, unfolding the next installment in the story in which God wants me to play a part. When I learn to live the spiritual life properly, I will begin to see throughout every day a countless string of marvellous presents and gifts given to me by a generous God who loves above all to give, and to have his beloved children enjoy and delight in his gifts: the first spring flowers, a magnificent sunset, the pristine whiteness of a new blanket of snow, the smell of rain on a sidewalk, the taste of hot buttered toast with strawberry jam, the joy of exercising my muscles, an unexpected compliment from an acquaintance, the touch of a friendly hand, the chance to hear an inspiring speaker, an opportunity to be of genuine help to another person.

9. Richmond Walker talked about death in a lead he gave at an A.A. meeting in Rutland, Vermont, in 1958. The text is given in the *Northern Indiana Archival Bulletin* (published by the A.A. Area 22 Archives Committee) 4.1 (2001): 1–4. See the foreword by Mel B., Toledo, Ohio, to Hazelden's 40th Anniversary

Edition of *Twenty-Four Hours a Day* (special 1994 edition) for the date and location where Rich gave his talk.

> Above all, my faith in the Great Intelligence behind the universe, which can give me all the strength I need to face whatever life has to offer, is the foundation of my present life. When I die, my body will return to dust. Heaven is not any particular place in the sky, but my intelligence or soul, if it is in the proper condition, will return to the Great Intelligence behind the universe and will blend with that Great Intelligence and be at home again whence it came. My problem, in what is left of my life, is to keep my mind or intelligence in the proper condition—by living with honesty, purity, unselfishness, love, and service—so that when my time comes to go, my passing to a greater sphere of mind will be gentle and easy.

10. Ralph Pfau ("Father John Doe"), born Nov. 10, 1904, came into A.A. on his thirty-ninth birthday, on Nov. 10, 1943. During his lifetime his works were published in that city by his own private printing operation, called SMT Guild, but at some point after his death (which was on Feb. 19, 1967), the Hazelden Foundation took over the printing and distribution to keep his works available. The fourteen Golden Books were *The Spiritual Side* (1947), *Tolerance* [orig. entitled *Charity*, which in the older English of the King James era simply meant "Love"] (1948), *Attitudes* (1949), *Action* (1950), *Happiness* (1951), *Excuses* (1952), *Sponsorship* (1953), *Principles* (1954), *Resentments* (1955), *Decisions* (1957), *Passion* (1960), *Sanity* (1963), *Living* (1964), and *Sanctity* (1964). He published three large books: two of them, *Sobriety and Beyond* (Center City MN: Hazelden, 1955) and *Sobriety Without End* (Center City MN: Hazelden, 1957), dealt with the same sort of topics as the Golden Books, and reprinted some of the same material. The third was an autobiography, Ralph Pfau and Al Hirshberg, *Prodigal Shepherd* (Indianapolis IN: SMT Guild, 1958).

Telephone orders for books from Hazelden Publishing and Educational Services may be placed at (800) 328–9000. We should all be grateful that they have kept Ralph's books in print as an act of support for the A.A. way of life.

One issue of the *Northern Indiana Archival Bulletin* (published by A.A.'s Northern Indiana Area 22 Archives Committee) 2.2 (1999) 9-20, was devoted completely to Ralph Pfau and his sponsor, Doherty "Dohr" Sheerin, who had founded the first A.A. group in Indianapolis on October 28, 1940, only three years before Ralph came into the program. It also reprinted Ralph's obituary, from the *Chicago Tribune* for Feb. 20, 1967. See also the issue of that *Bulletin* containing "How A.A. Came to Indiana," by Glenn F. Chesnut, which puts Ralph and Dohr's contributions in a larger context: 3.1 (2000) 1-14. Dohr's work in Indiana was singled out for praise in *Dr. Bob and the Good Oldtimers* (New York: Alcoholics Anonymous World Services, 1980), p. 258. Dohr worked closely with J. D. Holmes, who had been the tenth person to get sober in A.A. (up in Akron in September 1936, see "J. D. H." in the index to *Dr. Bob and the Good Oldtimers*). J. D. had been forced by job circumstances to move to Evansville, Indiana, and had started the first A.A. group in Indiana in that city in April or May of 1940. By the fall of that year, J. D. (in Evansville, down on the Ohio river) and Dohr (up in Indianapolis, in the center of the state) were working together as a team to spread A.A. to other parts of Indiana. Ralph was therefore closely associated with two of the most influential and formative A.A. good old-timers in Indiana.

In the 1940's, 50's, and 60's in my part of the midwest, A.A. groups would read from the Big Book and the *Twenty-Four Hours a Day* book during their meetings, but members would also often gather in little groups after the regular meetings to study and discuss the *Golden Books*. Ralph also travelled all over the rest of the country (750,000 miles in the first ten years of his activities), giving talks and leading weekend spiritual retreats: California, Arizona, New Mexico, Texas, Louisiana, Kentucky, Tennessee, Mississippi, Alabama, Georgia, Florida, and North and South Carolina, to list some of the states where he was known and loved.

11. Ralph Pfau (Father John Doe), *The Golden Book of Resentments* (Indianapolis IN: SMT Guild, 1955), pp. 41–55, "The Myth of Perfection." Hazelden Publishing and Educational Services (telephone orders at 800 328–9000) are now keeping his works in print.

12. The classic work on the life of St. Augustine (354-430 A.D.) is Peter Brown, *Augustine of Hippo: A Biography* (London: Faber & Faber, 1967). See pp. 146-161. In 391 A.D., Augustine still believed that he could learn to become a perfect man of wisdom, living in total tranquillity under the unclouded light of changeless truth. When he was finally forced to look through new eyes at Paul's epistle to the Romans, most especially by a set of questions posed to him by Simplicianus of Milan around 395, he began to see the spiritual life from a new perspective. He began to realize that we were utterly dependent on God's grace, and he finally took the position that we were dependent on grace even for the power to turn to God when we first came to believe. What delighted us and made us feel happiness lay beyond our power of control, buried deep down in the unconscious: only the power of God's grace could make us love the right things even in part. And we were never going to become perfect.

In 397, when he was around forty-three, he began writing his *Confessions*, in which he talked frankly and openly about his own life, from early childhood on, from this new perspective. There was no need to pretend to anyone any longer. He spoke freely about his egotism and vanity and public ambitions and womanizing during his early years. He talked about how his mother, St. Monica, had been a childhood alcoholic; when she finally realized in horror what she had become and faced it honestly, she had found God, and through God the power to stop drinking. Augustine himself had now likewise come to realize that all that had happened to him, even the degrading parts of his early life, had been in one way or another a necessary part of God's leading and God's grace. He had had to go through what he had gone through to get to where he was now. And where he was now was something for which he could now feel an overwhelming gratitude that came out over and over again in the pages of that work. What had he gained by finally acknowledging the reality of God's power and grace, and his own human imperfections? The ability to love God even more fully, and to live his life with a new energy and satisfaction and inner poise, and above all the spontaneous capacity now to turn to God at all times and simply say, from the bottom of his heart, "Thank you."

13. Compare 1 John 1:8, 2:4, 4:20 and Romans 3:23.

14. See also Ralph Pfau and Al Hirshberg, *Prodigal Shepherd*, pp. 26-34, where Ralph talked about how he himself had been driven into a complete nervous breakdown by his own over-perfectionism while he was still a young student at the Roman Catholic seminary at St. Meinrad's in southern Indiana. When the time approached to ordain his class as subdeacons (the ordination was held on May 28, 1928), he drove himself into a frenzy with thoughts of his own "moral imperfections" which made him in his own mind "totally unworthy" to be a priest: as a child, he had had fist fights with other children, had sometimes talked back to his mother, and had once stolen an apple from a pushcart. Once he had pestered his widowed mother (who was having to raise her children on her own) about wanting a sled which she could not afford to buy him, until she was driven to tears. He could not believe that God would let him be a normal child, and could not believe (until he came into the A.A. program) that God would let him be a normal, fallible human being. It is important to remember that Ralph was not preaching at us from some pretended position of infinite moral superiority; he was writing this section on "The Myth of Perfection" *for himself* above all, because neurotic over-perfectionism was one of the major character defects he had discovered in doing his own fourth step.

15. *Golden Book of Resentments*, p. 53. See also Ralph Pfau (Father John Doe), *Golden Book of Sanctity* (Indianapolis IN: SMT Guild, 1964), espec. pp. 12-13, which is entirely devoted to this concept of sanctification. On pp. 12-13, he says it can be useful to think of *sanctificatio* as receiving God's *sanctio* (sanction, approval) rather than being made *sanctus* (holy, a saint). We obtain his approval if we (1) admit our powerlessness and sinfulness with real humility, and then (2)

make an authentic decision to *try* to grow along spiritual lines. Then God sanctions this (approves of our *willingness*) and supplies his grace. We are "sinner saints" who have been sanctioned by God from the moment we begin to move down the road which leads to the fullness of sanctity. And then eventually (perhaps in this world, but certainly in the next) we shall become fully saints. Hazelden Publishing and Educational Services (telephone orders at 800 328–9000) is now keeping Ralph's works in print.

CHAPTER VI. RESENTMENT

1. *Alcoholics Anonymous*, 3rd ed. (New York: Alcoholics Anonymous World Services, 1976).

2. Codependents are usually in deep denial (at first) that they are filled with resentment. But *self-pity* and *continually feeling injured* are simply more passive forms of resentment. When all the codependent can talk about at meetings is the bad things the other person has done, this is proof positive that it is resentment we are dealing with. See p. 61 in the Big Book for example: the person feeling the resentment "may sometimes be quite virtuous. He may be kind, considerate, patient, generous; even modest and self-sacrificing." When the other person doesn't act right, the Big Book goes on to say, the codependent then "begins to think life doesn't treat him right" and starts falling into greater and greater self-pity.

When a codependent gives a lead in which all he or she can talk about are lurid accounts of the other person's sins (the drunken escapades, the irresponsibility, the hurtful actions, or the like), this also shows that the codependent is still locked into some unresolved resentment, because what is actually coming out is a sense of deep personal hurt at the hands of others, which is still dominating that person's sense of self. When codependents enter more deeply into recovery, they begin telling the story of their lives instead as a journey into their own uniquely personal growth and transformation, where the other figures in the story recede into the background and often totally disappear.

The existentialist psychiatrists (e.g. Fritz Perls) follow Nietzsche in seeing resentment as the natural result of trying too hard to be a Good Boy or Good Girl (that is, a person who is locked into rigid should's and ought's and guilt-driven perfectionism), and this may sometimes be an underlying cause of at least part of the resentful attitude. Ralph P. (Father John Doe of the Golden Books) saw his own two greatest spiritual problems as perfectionistic demands on himself and soul-destroying resentments—the two often go hand in hand.

3. Ralph Pfau (Father John Doe), *The Golden Book of Resentments* (Indianapolis IN: SMT Guild, 1955), p. 6.

4. *Twelve Steps and Twelve Traditions* (New York: Alcoholics Anonymous World Services, 1953), pp. 42-54.

5. It is all right to *feel* feelings like anger and hurt, and in fact we have to let ourselves consciously feel them in order to deal with them properly. See what has already become a modern classic of the twelve-step movement, Melody Beattie, *The Language of Letting Go: Daily Meditations for Codependents* (San Francisco: Harper & Row/Hazelden, 1990), January 8, March 1-2, April 2-3, and so on.

6. Father Ralph talks about the cyclic character of resentment in *The Golden Book of Resentments*, p. 5.

7. The *Twelve Steps and Twelve Traditions* (New York: Alcoholics Anonymous World Services, 1953) suggests looking at the later medieval list of the Seven Deadly Sins for possible character defects: PRIDE, GREED, LUST, ANGER, GLUTTONY, ENVY, and SLOTH. That last vice means more than simple laziness, and is better described by its actual medieval name, ACCIDIE (or Acedia), which means "no longer caring"—by the end of their drinking careers, alcoholics reach a point where they no longer *care* what happens to them or anyone else. They drive drunk and smash in someone else's car, and they don't care. Their families are going without food and clothes, and they don't care. They're going to lose their jobs, and they don't care.

Going back to earlier parts of the western spiritual tradition, St. Augustine also talked at great length about a specific list of destructive vices: *AMBITIO*: over-ambition, degenerated into plotting, scheming, back-stabbing and deceiving. *LUXURIA*: the over-powering desire for more and more sex, drink, and expensive material baubles and decorations and toys. *AVARITIA*: wanting money and wealth and houses and property above all things. *CUPIDO GLORIAE*: the thirst for glory, fame, being praised and admired by other people, being the center of attention, being a Big-Shot, or being regarded by everyone as a Good Boy or Good Girl. *LIBIDO DOMINANDI*: the desire to dominate and control others, to be the stage director who tells everyone else how to act—and especially, not only to be the one who is *right*, but *to be able to enforce it* and make the other person not only comply but *agree* that I was right. And *SUPERBIA* of course was to Augustine the root of all the other vices. *Superbia* (which is normally translated as Pride) was a Latin noun formed from the preposition *super*, and it literally meant the attempt to be above everyone else, to be the Master of the Universe, to play God. When people first come into the twelve-step program, their frequent attitude is, "No one's going to tell *me* what to do, not even God."

On Augustine's characteristic list of vices, see Glenn F. Chesnut, "The Pattern of the Past: Augustine's Debate with Eusebius and Sallust," in John Deschner, Leroy T. Howe, and Klaus Penzel, eds., *Our Common History as Christians* (New York: Oxford University Press, 1975), pp. 69–95, see espec. pp. 83-90.

8. Over in the eastern end of the Mediterranean, the early Egyptian desert fathers, along with later spiritual writers like St. Maximus the Confessor, added several more vices to Augustine's list: One was the vice of OVER-COMPLICATION (let us call it), which was the opposite of the virtue called *haplotês* (Simplicity). True simplicity was one of the greatest of all the virtues: a good person was honest, open, and sincere, as opposed to being duplicitous and manipulating; this kind of person knew how to "keep it simple" and avoid over-complicating things; he did not fritter away his time trying to pursue several different mutually incompatible goals simultaneously.

St. Maximus the Confessor talked about the dangers of letting the GNOMIC WILL dominate our decisions: he said that the "natural will" in human beings automatically desired what was truly good, and *wanted* to know what was better. Since God was the Good Itself, what was real and genuine in me would in fact never see any conflict between "doing what I myself really wanted to do" and doing the will of God, because what God always wanted was the best. The conflict occurred within my heart because part of me was motivated instead by the "gnomic will," where I let myself be swayed by all the common opinions about what was good and bad, which were expressed so loudly and so often by those around me who were *not in reality* leading truly good spiritual lives. *Gnômê* in Greek meant inclination, judgment, or opinion. I relied too much on the uncritical, opinionated judgments which I had learned from the most ignorant of the people around me, and (on this distorted basis) simply jumped into things on the impulse of the moment. Back when he was a young man in his thirties, Maximus had been the Imperial Secretary in the court of the Byzantine emperor Heraclius, until he gave it all up around 614 A.D. to enter a Greek Orthodox monastery. He knew at first hand what it meant to live in a world of constant political posturing and scheming and back-stabbing and status games, where everyone was dominated by the gnomic will, and found that he himself *could not live that way.*

The DEVIL OF THE NOON-DAY SUN: The Egyptian desert monk Evagrius Ponticus said that it was not Lust or Anger which was the most difficult deadly sin to master, but Accidie, which he called the "devil of the noon-day sun." I could begin a task going great guns, but when I had to start doing real work, I would lose interest and promptly discover something else I "needed to be doing" instead. So I never finished any of my grandiose projects, and never carried a major task through to completion.

See also the list of character defects in n. 20 below, drawn up by Sue C. (Al-Anon, South Bend), for some excellent additional advice about character defects to watch out for.

9. From a tape-recorded interview with him by Beth M. (Lafayette IN) slightly before his death, in the Northern Indiana Area 22 A.A. Archives. Transcript in the *Northern Indiana Archival Bulletin* 4.2 (2001): 5–6.

10. The idea of making *systematic, disciplined progress* in improving my moral and spiritual character came more from the Roman Catholic side than from the Protestant side, if we look at the influences on early A.A. Catholic spiritual literature gave more useful advice in the area of *sanctificatio*, while the Protestants tended to have richer insights in the area of *justificatio*. Some of the alcoholics

coming into the program had been raised as Catholics, others as Protestants, and people from each side contributed their own wisdom. In particular, St. Ignatius Loyola's *Spiritual Exercises* (and the kind of Jesuit spirituality which it taught) had almost as much influence on early A.A. as the Protestant spirituality of the Oxford Group, although the Catholic influence was sometimes more deeply buried, and often appeared more in the form of the general type of approach which was used. The *Spiritual Exercises* were used as a fundamental guideline for the conduct of the spiritual life by many Roman Catholic priests and religious in the United States in the first half of the twentieth century, and as a result, A.A. members who had gone to Roman Catholic parochial schools prior to the Second Vatican Council (1962-5) had often absorbed many of the basic principles of the *Spiritual Exercises* subconsciously.

The influence of Ignatian spirituality was sometimes more direct: Mary C. Darrah, *Sister Ignatia: Angel of Alcoholics Anonymous* (Chicago: Loyola University Press, 1992), notes that Sister Ignatia had immersed herself deeply for many years in Loyola's *Spiritual Exercises*—it was Jesuit priests who guided the spiritual lives of the Sisters of Charity of Saint Augustine—along with another great spiritual classic, Thomas à Kempis' *Imitation of Christ* (pp. 24 and 56). Sister Ignatia gave newly recovering alcoholics a copy of either the *Imitation of Christ* or a small book called *A Thought from Saint Ignatius for Each Day of the Year* when they left the ward at St. Thomas hospital in Akron (p. 36). When the Jesuit priest Father Edward Dowling first read a copy of the Big Book, he spotted the influence of St. Ignatius' *Spiritual Exercises* immediately (pp. 25-26). The *highly disciplined* and *systematic* carrying out of the fourth through seventh steps in the A.A. program, for example, with written lists of one's greatest character defects and so on, is far more reminiscent of Ignatian spirituality than of any ordinary Protestant spiritual practices of the past century or so. The tenth step in particular reminds one immediately of the section entitled "Particular Examination of Conscience to Be Made Every Day"—see Ignatius Loyola, *The Spiritual Exercises of St. Ignatius*, trans. Anthony Mottola (New York: Image Books/Doubleday, 1964), First Week (at the beginning), pp. 48-49. The point is, that it is not good enough to just say "have faith" and make a few general statements about higher moral principles, no matter how lofty these principles—I have to be willing to carry out some structured and highly focused footwork over an extended period of time, if I expect to grow in serenity and closeness to God.

11. *Twelve Steps and Twelve Traditions*, p. 99.

12. From the Sermon on the Mount, Matthew 5:43-44, "You have heard that it was said, you shall love your neighbor and hate your enemy, but I say to you, love your enemies and pray for those who persecute you." See *Alcoholics Anonymous* pp. 66-7 for one way of wording this basic kind of prayer, a very good and simple way of doing it: "When a person offended we said to ourselves, 'This is a sick man. How can I be helpful to him? God save me from being angry. Thy will be done.'"

13. Louise L. Hay, *You Can Heal Your Life* (Carlsbad CA: Hay House, 1987), p. 115.
14. See the last part of chapt. 3 in this present work for the full text.

15. *Alcoholics Anonymous*, 3rd ed., in the story "Doctor, Alcoholic, Addict," the paragraph towards the end of the story, beginning "And acceptance is the answer to all my problems today...."

16. The original Serenity Prayer (created c. 1932, written by Reinhold Niebuhr, author of a number of influential books, who became Professor of Applied Christianity at Union Theological Seminary in New York City in 1928, and was one of the most important American theologians of the first half of the twentieth century) was longer than the version usually recited at twelve-step meetings, and has some useful thoughts for people who are suffering from resentment:

> God grant me the serenity to accept the things I cannot
> change, the courage to change the things I can, and the wisdom
> to know the difference. Living one day at a time, enjoying one

moment at a time, accepting hardship as a pathway to peace. Taking this sinful world as it is, not as I would have it, as God's people have always done; trusting that He will make all things right if I surrender to His will. So that I may be reasonably happy in this world and supremely happy with Him in the world above.

See Richmond Walker, *The 7 Points of Alcoholics Anonymous* (Center City MN: Hazelden/Glen Abbey Books, 1989), p. 46, for an account of how a copy of the prayer eventually reached the early New York A.A.'s in 1939. Additional information is given in *Pass It On: The Story of Bill Wilson and How the A.A. Message Reached the World* (New York: Alcoholics Anonymous World Services, 1984), pp. 252 and 258 n. 6.

Reinhold Niebuhr said he got some of the basic ideas for his version from an eighteenth-century writer named Friedrich Oetinger. The attempt made by someone to trace the ideas back to the philosopher Boethius (c. 480–c. 524 A.D.) was, I believe, simply a crude guess, made because his *Consolation of Philosophy* had a certain Stoic flavor; at any rate I myself have been unable to find anything in that work which matches up with the specific teaching of the Serenity Prayer. If Oetinger was in fact Niebuhr's source in part, Oetinger would have certainly read ancient Roman Stoics in his Latin classes as part of the educational system of his century, but would have been very unlikely to have read Boethius. Incidentally, contrary to the note in *Pass It On*, Boethius was a Roman Christian, not a pagan, and was executed by seventy-year-old King Theodoric (i.e. Dietrich von Bern), the Dark Age Germanic warlord who had begun taking over Italy in 487, on a charge of conspiring against the throne. No one knows whether the charges had any truth to them at all, or whether it was simply senile paranoia on the part of the old German.

At any rate, the basic ideas in the prayer went back two thousand years in fact to pagan Greek Stoic philosophers, like Epictetus in particular, who used the precise technical terminology of the prayer in numerous places. Epictetus had started out as a slave in the emperor Nero's palace, and had had to learn the serenity of acceptance the hard way—see chapt. 1, n. 21.

17. Sue C. (South Bend IN).

18. On the power of making "I am now willing to release the need for…" statements, see Louise L. Hay, *You Can Heal Your Life*, p. 58. If I think of it as a kind of grief work, then this is taking the last step in Elisabeth Kubler-Ross's five stages of grief: denial, anger, bargaining, sadness, and acceptance. If I have been hurt deeply, I will have to allow myself to *feel* the hurt and sadness and sense of tragedy (as well as the anger) before I can let go of the resentment. See the reading for November 2 in Melody Beattie, *The Language of Letting Go*, a work of the third generation of the twelve-step movement which has already achieved the status of a classic.

19. Among the many recent books on this topic, two especially good ones are Melody Beattie, *Codependent No More: How to Stop Controlling Others and Start Caring for Yourself* (San Francisco: Harper San Francisco, 1987) and Pia Mellody (with Andrea Wells Miller and J. Keith Miller), *Facing Codependence: What It Is, Where It Comes From, How It Sabotages Our Lives* (San Francisco: Harper San Francisco, 1989).

The concept of codependency in its present form is a relatively new one among psychotherapists and counselors, which began to develop gradually (in my own observation) as professionals began exploring some of the ramifications of the psychiatric theory called transactional analysis. For that system, see Eric Berne, M.D., *Games People Play: The Psychology of Human Relationships* (New York: Ballantine Books, 1964) and *What Do You Say After You Say Hello? The Psychology of Human Destiny* (New York: Bantam Books, 1972), espec. the Persecutor-Victim-Rescuer "Drama Triangle" in chapt. 10, sect. D of the latter book (pp. 186-8). Alcoholics and addicts play Victim and search for another person to play Rescuer or Caretaker; once they have the other person hooked on their con game, they pull the switch which is the vital move in all con games, and start portraying him or her as the Persecutor. The would-be Rescuers then try to switch the con back the other way by portraying the alcoholic or addict as the true Persecutor, while they play helpless Victim.

20. Sue C. (Al-Anon, South Bend IN, see chapt. 3, n. 7) has a short piece on learning to love ourselves, and what she calls the self-hate syndrome, which she originally wrote up for some of the people she sponsored: Sue C., "The Self-Hate Syndrome" (South Bend IN: Hindsfoot Foundation [P.O. Box 4081, South Bend IN 46634], 1999). On her check-list for the fourth step, she includes some important character defects not listed in nn. 7 and 8 above. Pride, anger, and trying to play God are indeed moral issues, she says, but it is also true that:

> Not setting boundaries to protect ourselves from harm is a
> moral issue. Not taking care of ourselves is a moral issue.
> Accepting mistreatment and allowing other people to use us is a
> moral issue. Not allowing ourselves to have fun and enjoy life is
> a moral issue. Expecting perfection all the time is a moral issue.
> Self-neglect is a moral issue.

So if I have codependent tendencies, she says, I must add to my list of possible character defects such items as playing Rescuer (with a capital R), caretaking, playing the martyr, trying to suppress all my feelings, being dependent on others in an unhealthy way (and refusing to take emotional responsibility for myself), worrying minor things to death, constantly condemning myself and my efforts, feeling victimized, not trusting my own deepest feelings and instincts about what feels right to me, feeling unsafe and as though I am walking around on eggshells all the time, not being able to ask for what I want, holding unreasonable expectations of others, being totally rigid and inflexible, feeling guilt over events I did not create, feeling a generalized shame about myself as a person, and consistently withdrawing from relationships when they start to become too close (a sign that I am still bound into shame-based and fear-based behavior).

This is the self-loathing syndrome described in the paragraph at the top of p. 45 in the chapter on the Fourth Step in the *Twelve Steps and Twelve Traditions* (New York: Alcoholics Anonymous World Services, 1953):

> If temperamentally we are on the depressive side, we are apt
> to be swamped with guilt and self-loathing. We wallow in this
> messy bog, often getting a misshapen and painful pleasure out
> of it. As we morbidly pursue this melancholy activity, we may

sink to such a point of despair that nothing but oblivion looks possible as a solution.

As the next paragraph says, this is simply the flip side of the kind of grandiose, out-of-control egomaniac and power-driver whom we also see coming into the program. These two types have to do their fourth steps differently, that chapter of the *Twelve Steps and Twelve Traditions* goes on to say, and have to approach the problem of their lives from opposite directions. And it is not usually either-or, because most people are a mixture of those two types, and it is more a matter of which parts of their lives they are looking at.

21. See Berne, *Games People Play* for colorful descriptions of some of the psychological con games and manipulative techniques people use for taking advantage of others. Beyond the Persecutor-Victim-Rescuer game (see n. 19 above), there are also games which he calls Kick Me; Now I've Got You, You Son of a Bitch; See What You Made Me Do; Courtroom; Look How Hard I've Tried; Ain't It Awful; Yes But; Peasant; Wooden Leg; and so on. We cannot make much progress in the twelve-step program until we stop playing phony games of that sort and start getting honest with ourselves.

22. This was Ernie G. the second of Toledo, see the many references to him in the index to *Dr. Bob and the Good Oldtimers: A Biography, with Recollections of Early A.A. in the Midwest* (New York: Alcoholics Anonymous World Services, 1980). Dr. Bob was Ernie's sponsor, Ernie was Larry W.'s sponsor, and Larry was the man who first introduced me to the A.A. program.

23. *Twenty-Four Hours a Day*, Compiled by a Member of the Group at Daytona Beach, Fla. [i.e., Richmond Walker in 1948], rev. ed. (Center City MN: Hazelden, 1975). The italics are mine.

24. *Alcoholics Anonymous*, 3rd ed., the story entitled "Doctor, Alcoholic, Addict," pp. 450-52.

CHAPTER VII. GRATITUDE

1. Ralph Pfau (Father John Doe), *The Golden Book of Principles* (Indianapolis IN: SMT Guild, 1954), pp. 7-8.

2. Augustine, *Confessions*, trans. R. S. Pine-Coffin (Baltimore, MD: Penguin Books, 1961) 1.1.

CHAPTER VIII. BEING AT HOME

1. The first word was *erôs*, from which we got our English word "erotic"; the second word was *philia*, from which we got English words like "Philadelphia" (city of brotherly love), "bibliophile" (someone who admires and collects fine books), and so on. In addition to *erôs*, *philia*, and *agapê*, there was also a fourth biblical Greek word for what was in fact a kind of love: in the New Testament (and subsequently in the liturgy of the Greek Orthodox church) the Greek noun *eleos* (which meant "mercy" in classical pagan Greek) was sometimes used to represent the Hebrew term *chesed*. This was one of the Hebrew words for love, and meant a kind of unselfish, dependable, compassionate loving-kindness which could be counted on to give concrete and useful help to someone in need.

2. *Alcoholics Anonymous*, 3rd ed. (New York: Alcoholics Anonymous World Services, 1976), pp. 83–84. I italicized the sentence towards the end.

Bibliography

Big Book = *Alcoholics Anonymous*.
Twelve & Twelve = *Twelve Steps and Twelve Traditions*.

Alcoholics Anonymous. 3rd ed. New York: Alcoholics Anonymous World Services, 1976.

Alcoholics Anonymous: An Interpretation of the Twelve Steps: see Detroit Pamphlet.

Alcoholics Anonymous Comes of Age: A Brief History of A.A. New York: Alcoholics Anonymous World Services, 1957.

Alston, William P. "Religious Experience and Religious Belief," *Nous* 16 (1982) 3-12.

Aquinas, Thomas: see Thomas Aquinas.

Arterburn, Stephen, and Jack Felton. *Toxic Faith: Understanding and Overcoming Religious Addiction*. Nashville: Oliver-Nelson/Thomas Nelson, 1991.

Augustine. *Confessions*. Trans. R. S. Pine-Coffin. Baltimore, MD: Penguin Books, 1961.

Barth, Karl. *The Epistle to the Romans*. Trans. E. C. Hoskyns. London: Oxford University Press, 1933.

Beattie, Melody. *Codependent No More: How to Stop Controlling Others and Start Caring for Yourself.* San Francisco: Harper San Francisco, 1987.

_____ . *The Language of Letting Go: Daily Meditations for Codependents.* San Francisco: Harper & Row/Hazelden, 1990.

Beck, Aaron T., M.D. *Cognitive Therapy and the Emotional Disorders.* New York: Penguin Books/Meridian, 1976.

Berne, Eric, M.D. *Games People Play: The Psychology of Human Relationships.* New York: Ballantine Books, 1964.

_____ . *What Do You Say After You Say Hello? The Psychology of Human Destiny.* New York: Bantam Books, 1972.

Bonaventure. *The Soul's Journey into God – The Tree of Life – The Life of St. Francis.* Trans. Ewert Cousins. New York: Paulist Press, 1978.

Bouyer, Louis. *Introduction to Spirituality.* Trans. Mary Perkins Ryan. Collegeville MN: Liturgical Press, 1961.

Bradshaw, John. *Healing the Shame that Binds You.* Deerfield Beach FL: Health Communications, 1988.

Brown, Peter. *Augustine of Hippo: A Biography.* London: Faber & Faber, 1967.

Calvin, John. *Institutes of the Christian Religion.* 2 vols. Ed. John T. McNeill. Trans. Ford Lewis Battles. Philadelphia: Westminster, 1960.

Carnes, Patrick. *Don't Call It Love: Recovery from Sexual Addiction.* New York: Bantam Books, 1991.

_____ . *Out of the Shadows: Understanding Sexual Addiction*. Minneapolis MN: CompCare Publishers, 1992.

Chesnut, Glenn F. "A Century of Patristics Studies 1888–1988." Pp. 36–73 in Henry Warner Bowden (ed.), *A Century of Church History* (Carbondale: Southern Illinois University Press, 1988).

_____ . "Eusebius, Augustine, Orosius, and the Later Patristic and Medieval Christian Historians." Pp. 687-713 in Harold W. Attridge and Gohei Hata, eds., *Eusebius, Christianity, and Judaism*. Detroit: Wayne State University Press, 1992. Published simultaneously in Japanese by Yamamoto Shoten Publishing House, Tokyo.

_____ = Glenn C. *The Factory Owner and the Convict: My Story Is My Message—the Words of Early Pioneers in the Alcoholics Anonymous Movement in the St. Joseph River Valley*. 1st ed. South Bend IN: Hindsfoot Foundation (P.O. Box 4081, South Bend IN 46634), 1996.

_____ . *The First Christian Histories: Eusebius, Socrates, Sozomen, Theodoret, and Evagrius*. 2nd rev. ed. Macon, GA: Mercer University Press, 1986. [1st ed. Paris: Éditions Beauchesne, 1977.]

_____ . "How A.A. Came to Indiana," *Northern Indiana Archival Bulletin* (published by A.A.'s Northern Indiana Area 22 Archives Committee) 3.1 (2000): 1-14. One of the preceding year's issues, 2.2 (1999): 9-20, also put together by him, was devoted completely to Ralph Pfau (Father John Doe) and his sponsor, Doherty "Dohr" Sheerin.

_____ . *Images of Christ: An Introduction to Christology*. San Francisco: Harper & Row/Seabury, 1984.

_____ . "The Pattern of the Past: Augustine's Debate with Eusebius and Sallust." Pp. 69–95 in John Deschner, Leroy T. Howe, and Klaus Penzel, eds., *Our Common History as Christians*. New York: Oxford University Press, 1975.

_____ . "The Ruler and the Logos in Neopythagorean, Middle Platonic, and Late Stoic Political Philosophy." Pp. 1310-32 of H. Temporini and W. Haase, eds., *Aufstieg und Niedergang der Römischen Welt: Geschichte und Kultur Roms im Spiegel der neueren Forschung* 2.16.2. Berlin: Walter de Gruyter, 1978.

Copleston, Frederick. *A History of Philosophy*. Vol. 2: *Mediaeval Philosophy: Augustine to Scotus*. Westminster MD: Newman Press, 1950.

Daniélou, Jean. Introduction (pp. 1-78) to Gregory of Nyssa, *From Glory to Glory: Texts from Gregory of Nyssa's Mystical Writings*. Ed. Herbert Musurillo. New York: Scribner, 1961.

Dante Alighieri. *Inferno*. Italian and English. Ed. Terence Tiller. New York: Schocken Books, 1966.

Darrah, Mary C. *Sister Ignatia: Angel of Alcoholics Anonymous*. Chicago: Loyola University Press, 1992.

Detroit Pamphlet: *Alcoholics Anonymous: An Interpretation of the Twelve Steps*. Distributed by Alcoholics Anonymous of Greater Detroit, 380 Hilton Road, Ferndale MI 48220, written when A.A. was first established there. Also available (reprinted with reset type) as Northern Indiana Area 22 Archives Committee Pamphlet No. 1 (April 2000).

Dictionary of Latin and Greek Theological Terms: Drawn Principally from Protestant Scholastic Theology. Ed. Richard A. Muller. Grand Rapids MI: Baker Book House, 1985.

Doe, Father John: see Ralph Pfau.

Dr. Bob and the Good Oldtimers: A Biography, with Recollections of Early A.A. in the Midwest. New York: Alcoholics Anonymous World Services, 1980.

Edwards, Jonathan. "A Divine and Supernatural Light." Pp. 123-134 in Jonathan Edwards, *Basic Writings.* Ed. Ola Elizabeth Winslow. New York: New American Library, 1966.

Emotions Anonymous. Saint Paul MN: Emotions Anonymous International, 1978.

Epictetus. *Discourses and Manual.* 2 vols. Trans. W. A. Oldfather. Loeb Classical Library. Cambridge MA: Harvard University Press, 1959–61.

Fairchild, Hoxie Neale. *Religious Trends in English Poetry.* Vol. III. *1780-1830, Romantic Faith.* New York: Columbia University Press, 1949.

Fieser, James, and John Powers (eds.). *Scriptures of the World's Religions.* Boston: McGraw-Hill, 1998.

"The Four Absolutes." Cleveland OH: Cleveland District Office of Alcoholics Anonymous (1701 E. 12th St., Cleveland OH 44114), n. d.

Fox, Emmet. *The Sermon on the Mount: The Key to Success in Life* and *The Lord's Prayer: An Interpretation.* San Francisco: HarperSan Francisco, 1938.

_____ . "The Golden Key." My copy of this small leaflet, printed by Unity Church, was obtained from Unity Church of Peace, 905 E. Colfax Ave., South Bend IN 46617.

Francis of Assisi. *The Hymn of the Sun*. Repr. of the 1927 Swan Press translation, designed and illus. Tony Wright. Rhinebeck NY: Broken Glass, 1990.

Frankl, Viktor E. *Man's Search for Meaning*. Rev. ed. New York: Washington Square Press/Simon & Schuster, 1984.

Fries, Jakob Friedrich. *Knowledge, Belief, and Aesthetic Sense*. Ed. Frederick Gregory. Trans. Kent Richter. Köln: Jürgen Dinter Verlag für Philosophie, 1989.

Gilson, Etienne. *History of Christian Philosophy in the Middle Ages*. New York: Random House, 1955.

God Calling. By Two Listeners. Ed. A. J. Russell. Re-edited by Bernard Koerselman for the 1993 edition. Uhrichsville OH: Barbour and Company, 1993.

Goodenough, Erwin R. *An Introduction to Philo Judaeus*. 2nd ed. New York: Barnes and Noble, 1962.

Gregory of Nyssa. *From Glory to Glory: Texts from Gregory of Nyssa's Mystical Writings*. Ed. Herbert Musurillo. New York: Scribner, 1961. Introduction (pp. 1–78) by Jean Daniélou.

Harvey, Van A. *A Handbook of Theological Terms*. New York: Macmillan, 1964.
Having Had a Spiritual Awakening. Virginia Beach VA: Al-Anon Family Group Headquarters, 1998.

Hay, Louise L. *You Can Heal Your Life*. Carlsbad, CA: Hay House, 1987.

Hicks, R. D. *Stoic and Epicurean*. New York: Charles Scribner's Sons, 1910.

Hofstadter, Douglas R. *Gödel, Escher, Bach: an Eternal Golden Braid*. New York: Vintage/Random House, 1979.

Huxley, Aldous. *The Perennial Philosophy*. New York: Harper & Row, 1945.

Ignatius Loyola. *Spiritual Exercises of St. Ignatius*. Trans. Anthony Mottola. New York: Image Books/Doubleday, 1964.

James, William. *The Varieties of Religious Experience*. Gifford Lectures on Natural Religion Delivered at Edinburgh in 1901–1902. New York: Modern Library, 1994.

John of the Cross. *Ascent of Mount Carmel*. Trans. and ed. E. Allison Peers. Liguori, Missouri: Triumph Books, 1991.

John S. (Gary IN). Tape-recorded interview with him on August 26, 1999 in Lafayette, Indiana (shortly before his death) by Beth M. (Lafayette IN), in the A.A. Northern Indiana Area 22 Archives. Transcript in the *Northern Indiana Archival Bulletin* (published by the Area 22 Archives Committee) 4.2 (2001): 5–6.

Kant, Immanuel. *Critique of Pure Reason*. Trans. Norman Kemp Smith. London: Macmillan & Co., 1933.
Körner, S. *Kant*. Baltimore MD: Penguin Books, 1955.

Kurtz, Ernest. *Not-God: A History of Alcoholics Anonymous*. Center City MN: Hazelden Educational Services, 1979.

Little Red Book. 50th anniversary ed. Center City MN: Hazelden, 1996. Started out as a mimeographed handout used in the Twelve Step Study Classes conducted by Ed Webster, Barry Collins, and other members of the Nicollet Group in Minneapolis; first published in booklet form in August 1946 by Coll-Webb Company in that city.

Lossky, Vladimir. *In the Image and Likeness of God*. Ed. J. H. Erickson and T. E. Bird. Crestwood NY: St. Vladimir's Seminary Press, 1974.

_____ . *The Vision of God*. Trans. A. Moorhouse. Crestwood NY: St. Vladimir's Seminary Press, 1963.

Loyola, Ignatius: see Ignatius Loyola.

Macarius the Homilist. *Fifty Spiritual Homilies of St. Macarius the Egyptian*. Trans. A. J. Mason. London: S.P.C.K., 1921.

Mary Pearl T. (Al-Anon). "12 Step Study for AA's and Al-Anon's." Tape recording of talk given at the Edisto Beach Roundup on April 13, 1995. Dicobe Tapes, Box 200, Bellevue NE 68005.

McKay, Matthew, Ph.D., and Patrick Fanning. *Self-Esteem: A Proven Program of Cognitive Techniques for Assessing, Improving, and Maintaining Your Self-Esteem*. Ed. Kirk Johnson. Oakland CA: New Harbinger Publications, 1987.

Mellody, Pia (with Andrea Wells Miller and J. Keith Miller). *Facing Codependence: What It Is, Where It Comes From, How It Sabotages Our Lives*. San Francisco: Harper San Francisco, 1989.

Meyendorff, John. *Byzantine Theology*. New York: Fordham University Press, 1974.

Nakken, Craig. *The Addictive Personality: Understanding the Addictive Process and Compulsive Behavior*. 2nd ed. Center City MN: Hazelden, 1996.

Olitzky, Rabbi Kerry M. and Stuart A. Copans, M.D. *Twelve Jewish Steps to Recovery: A Personal Guide to Turning from Alcoholism and Other Addictions.* Woodstock VT: Jewish Lights Publishing, 1991.

Otto, Rudolf. *Das Heilige: Über das Irrationale in der Idee des göttlichen und sein Verhältnis zum Rationalen.* 11th ed. Stuttgart: Friedrich Andreas Perthes, 1923.

_____ . *The Idea of the Holy: An Inquiry into the Non-Rational Factor in the Idea of the Divine and Its Relation to the Rational.* 2nd ed. Trans. John W. Harvey. Oxford: Oxford University Press, 1950.

_____ . *The Philosophy of Religion Based on Kant and Fries.* Trans. E. B. Dicker. London: Williams & Norgate, 1931.

Overeaters Anonymous. Torrance CA: Overeaters Anonymous, 1980.

Oxford Dictionary of the Christian Church, 2nd ed., ed. F. L. Cross and E. A. Livingstone. London: Oxford University Press, 1974.

Pass It On: The Story of Bill Wilson and How the A.A. Message Reached the World. New York: Alcoholics Anonymous World Services, 1984.

Peck, M. Scott. *The Road Less Traveled: A New Psychology of Love, Traditional Values and Spiritual Growth.* New York: Touchstone/Simon & Schuster, 1980.

Pfau, Ralph (Father John Doe). His books are now being kept in print by Hazelden Publishing and Educational Services, telephone orders at (800) 328–9000. They were originally published by his own printing operation in Indianapolis. Works cited in this present volume:

_____ . *The Golden Book of Principles.* Indianapolis IN: SMT Guild, 1954.

_____ . *The Golden Book of Resentments*. Indianapolis IN: SMT Guild, 1955.

_____ . *The Golden Book of Sanctity*. Indianapolis IN: SMT Guild, 1964.

_____ . *The Golden Book of the Spiritual Side*. Indianapolis IN: SMT Guild, 1947.

_____ and Al Hirshberg. *Prodigal Shepherd*. Indianapolis IN: SMT Guild, 1958.

_____ . *Sobriety and Beyond*. Center City MN: Hazelden, 1955.

_____ . *Sobriety Without End*. Center City MN: Hazelden, 1957.

Pfau, Ralph (Father John Doe), obituary in the *Chicago Tribune* for Feb. 20, 1967.

Pieper, Josef. *Guide to Thomas Aquinas*. Trans. R. and C. Winston. New York: Mentor-Omega Books, New American Library, 1962.

Plato. *Euthyphro, Apology, Crito, Phaedo, Phaedrus*. Ed. and trans. Harold North Fowler. Loeb Classical Library. London: William Heinemann, 1914.

_____ . *Republic*. 2 vols. Trans. Paul Shorey. Loeb Classical Library. London: William Heinemann, 1935–7.

Randall, John Herman, Jr. *Aristotle*. New York: Columbia University Press, 1960.

Schleiermacher, Friedrich. *On Religion: Speeches to Its Cultured Despisers*. Trans. J. Oman. New York: Harper & Brothers, 1958.

Seneca. *Moral Essays*. Ed. and trans. John W. Basore. 3 vols. Loeb Classical Library. Cambridge MA: Harvard University Press, 1928–35.

Sue C. (Al-Anon, South Bend IN). "Sex in Sobriety: the Last Taboo." Talk given at the A.A. Mini-Conference in Anderson IN on April 28, 2001. Blueprint Tapes, 950 Morgan St., Clinton IN 47842 (phone 765 832-9901).

_____ . "The Self-Hate Syndrome." South Bend IN: Hindsfoot Foundation (P.O. Box 4081, South Bend IN 46634), 1999.

Teresa of Ávila. *Interior Castle*. Trans. E. Allison Peers. Garden City NY: Image Books/Doubleday & Company, 1961.
Thomas Aquinas. *The Pocket Aquinas*. Ed. Vernon J. Bourke. New York: Washington Square Press, 1960.

Tiebout, Harry M., M.D. "Conversion as a Psychological Phenomenon." Read before the New York Psychiatric Society on April 11, 1944. Available as reprint from National Council on Alcoholism, 733 Third Avenue, New York NY 10017.

_____ . "Surrender Versus Compliance in Therapy: With Special Reference to Alcoholism," *Quartery Journal of Studies on Alcohol* (Yale University) 14 (1953): 58-68. Available as reprint from National Council on Alcoholism, 733 Third Avenue, New York NY 10017.

_____ . "The Act of Surrender in the Therapeutic Process: With Special Reference to Alcoholism," *Quartery Journal of Studies on Alcohol* (Yale University) 10 (1949): 48-58. Available as reprint from National Council on Alcoholism, 733 Third Avenue, New York NY 10017.

Turing, Alan M. "Computing Machinery and Intelligence," *Mind* 59, No. 236 (1950). Repr. in Alan Ross Anderson (ed.), *Minds and Machines*. Englewood Cliffs, N.J.: Prentice-Hall, 1964.

Twelve Steps and Twelve Traditions. New York: Alcoholics Anonymous World Services, 1953.

Twelve Steps of Overeaters Anonymous. Torrance CA: Overeaters Anonymous, 1990.

Twenty-Four Hours a Day: see Richmond Walker.

Underhill, Evelyn. *Mysticism: A Study in the Nature and Development of Man's Spiritual Consciousness.* London: Methuen & Co., 1930.
Waite, A. E. *The Holy Kabbalah.* New Hyde Park NY: University Books, n.d.

Walker, Richmond. Lead given at an A.A. meeting in Rutland, Vermont, in 1958. *Northern Indiana Archival Bulletin* (published by the A.A. Area 22 Archives Committee) 4.1 (2001): 1–4.

_____ . *The 7 Points of Alcoholics Anonymous.* Rev. ed. Center City MN: Hazelden/Glen Abbey Books, 1989.

_____ . *Twenty-Four Hours a Day.* Compiled by a Member of the Group at Daytona Beach, Fla. Rev. ed. Center City MN: Hazelden, 1975.

Watson, Philip S. *Let God Be God! An Interpretation of the Theology of Martin Luther.* Philadelphia: Fortress, 1947.

Wesley, John. "Heaviness through Manifold Temptations." Sermon 47, pp. 222-35 in Vol. 2 of *The Works of John Wesley.* Ed. Albert C. Outler. Nashville: Abingdon Press, 1985.

_____ . *Journal.* The portion running from Sunday, April 2–Wednesday, June 7, 1738 is given in pp. 53-69 of Albert C. Outler (ed.), *John Wesley.* Library of Protestant Thought. New York: Oxford University Press, 1964.

_____ . "The Original, Nature, Properties, and Use of the Law." Sermon 34, pp. 1-19 in Vol. 2 of *The Works of John Wesley*. Ed. Albert C. Outler. Nashville: Abingdon Press, 1985.

_____ . "The Original, Nature, Property, and Use of the Law." Sermon 29, pp. 2.37-57 in his *Standard Sermons*. Ed. Edward H. Sugden. 4th ed. 2 vols. London: Epworth Press, 1955–6. Same as Sermon 34 in Outler's more recent and better edition of Wesley's sermons.

_____ . "The Wilderness State." Sermon 46, pp. 202-21 in Vol. 2 of *The Works of John Wesley*. Ed. Albert C. Outler. Nashville: Abingdon Press, 1985.

What Is the Oxford Group? By the Layman with a Notebook. Foreword by L. W. Grenstead. Orig. pub. in 1933, reprinted as the second half of *Practice These Principles* and *What Is the Oxford Group?* Ed. Bill P. Center City MN: Hazelden, 1997. (The first half of this Hazelden edition is simply an alteration of the original with the words changed to fit A.A. terminology.)

Wittgenstein, Ludwig. *Preliminary Studies for the "Philosophical Investigations": Generally Known as the Blue and Brown Books*. Oxford: Basil Blackwell, 1969.

About the Author

Glenn F. Chesnut, an ordained United Methodist minister, completed his bachelor of divinity degree at Perkins School of Theology at Southern Methodist University, and then went as a Fulbright scholar to Oxford University, where he earned a doctorate in theology. He has won a *Prix de Rome* in Classics as well as recognition from the American Society of Church History for his work on Christianity and paganism in the early Greco-Roman world. He has taught at the University of Virginia and Boston University, and is now Professor of History and Religious Studies at Indiana University (South Bend). In 1988 he received Indiana University's prestigious Herman Frederic Lieber Award. He is the author of several previous books, including one of the standard works on the Christian history-writers of the Roman and early medieval world, as well as numerous articles in journals, books and encyclopedias.

He has more recently turned his hand to the study of the early twelve-step movement here in the United States. His book *The Factory Owner and the Convict*, which came out five years ago, told the story of some of the colorful figures who started A.A. in northcentral Indiana back in the 1940's, and the profound spiritual message which they taught by their words and deeds. He has also developed extensive contacts with the Al-Anon movement, and talked in depth with members of other twelve-step programs while writing this volume. He is the editor of an area archival journal and is also involved in A.A. archival work at the national level.

His writings on the twelve-step program have been published under the sponsorship of the Hindsfoot Foundation, P.O. Box 4081, South Bend IN 46634. Tape recordings of two of the talks he has given on "The Higher Power of the Twelve-Step Program" are available from Blueprint Tapes, 950 Morgan St., Clinton IN 47842 (phone 765 832-9901).

Made in the USA
Middletown, DE
11 March 2018